WHAT FLOWER IS THAT?

WHAT FLOWER IS THAT?
STIRLING MACOBOY

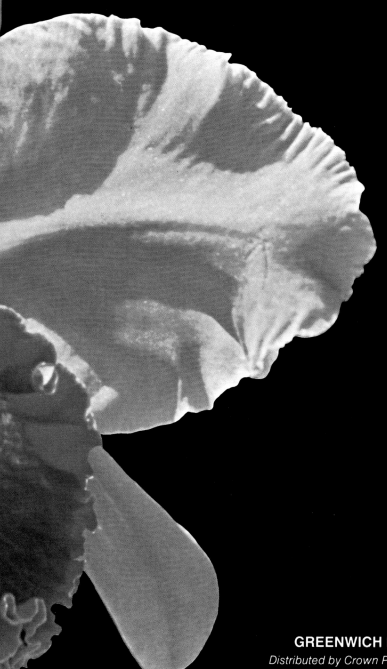

GREENWICH HOUSE
Distributed by Crown Publishers, Inc.
New York

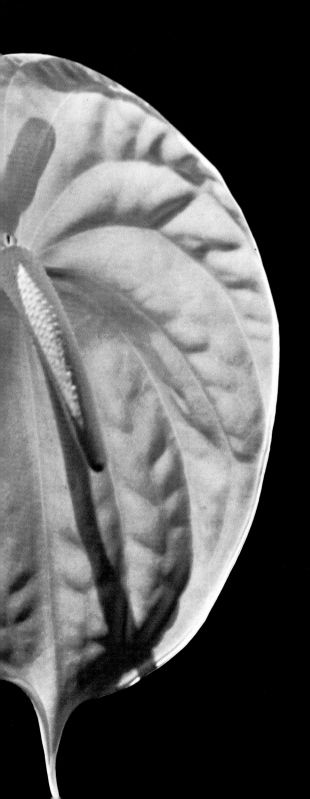

DESIGN: BARRY OWEN

Published by Lansdowne Press, Sydney
176 South Creek Road, Dee Why West. NSW. 2099
First Published 1969
Reprinted 1984

© Copyright RPLA Pty Ltd
Produced in Australia by the Publisher
Typeset in Australia
Printed in Hong Kong

This 1984 edition is published by Greenwich House,
a division of Arlington House Inc., distributed by Crown
Publishers Inc.

Macoboy, Stirling.
    What flower is that?

    Included index.
    1. Flowers – Identification. 2. Plants – Identification.
I. Title.
QK97.5.M33 1984   582.13   84-4039

ISBN 0-517-44738-X

contents

preface

The pure joy of colour! Colour and form are the bases of enjoyment of nature and art, the integral components of the theatre, dress styles, religion, architecture. And the most common and frequent source of enjoyment involving colour and form is the world of flowers. Modern technology—achieving the permanent reproduction and correct values of the spectrum—makes possible remarkable presentations that vastly multiply the opportunities to enjoy the richness of colour. That is a great part of the joy of this book.

This book accomplishes several things. Its colored photographs should help the reader to become acquainted with the world of plants. Its selections cover a large number of different kinds of flowers from the entire world.

There are trees, shrubs, vines, garden flowers and plants and greenhouse plants. They are the kinds that have been chosen by man, casually or very carefully (sometimes at great expense), from the wild plants that were worth keeping and cultivating. Some were already advancements of floral beauty, superior to wild ancestors, even before man kept records or passed on knowledge about the plants' histories. The origins of certain plants, for instance, found growing long ago in Chinese or Japanese gardens, are lost in the obscurity of prerecorded history. Other popular plants were brought, without record, to a new continent or country by slaves or immigrants, so that we cannot be sure of their origins. And so many humans have accidentally or deliberately crossed two or more differing kinds, making new forms called hybrids—for which the real parentage cannot be established with certainty. There is however, a host of plants that can be pegged.

The aim and ambition of the botanical fraternity is to have *one* Latinized name for each plant for all peoples, no matter what their mother tongue. All too frequently the same plant has been named and recorded differently in the writings of various botanists. Sometimes the same botanist has described the same plant more than once with differing names; and in some cases the recorded names for a single plant amount to dozens.

When a name has been accepted as valid, all other names for the same plant are called 'synonyms'. In putting together a book on many plants, there is a hazard of letting a synonym creep in instead of the valid name. It is difficult to avoid such mischances, but no crime, since we are talking about the same plant. In making up this book, a few synonyms were included: HEERIA for SCHIZOCENTRON; ISOLOMA for KOHLERIA; SASA for ARUNDINARIA. In this revised edition, all of these have been noted and appropriately cross-referenced in the index.

There is a good example of difference of botanical opinion in this book in connection with the general headings of AMARYLLIS and HIPPEASTRUM. Some botanists have been influenced by the theory that those plants generally known in the United States as AMARYLLIS belong to the genus HIPPEASTRUM, and that the true AMARYLLIS is something else again. Consensus may yet change this back again.

This book includes many plants found in the seed catalogues issued for gardeners all over the world; but much more than this, it includes many others—choice ones—with which our northern-temperate and warm-temperate gardeners are unfamiliar. As one goes from the colder latitudes toward the tropics, the flowers become more colorful, more exciting, more unusual. This book includes colored photos of a large number of Southern Hemisphere plants and flowers—warm-climate plants—that have never before been collectively illustrated in color in one book.

Readers of this book will find a broader understanding of the organization of plant life, some knowledge of plant geography and a grasp of plant relationships.

George Kalmbacher
Brooklyn Botanic Gardens.

introduction

Australia has been called of late 'The Lucky Country', and this at least is true: our garden lovers are far luckier than their fellows of the northern hemisphere. In addition to a striking native flora, we can see practically all of the world's great flowers growing to perfection in some part of our land—the largest island or smallest continent according to point of view.

Our latitude ranges from approximately 10° south of the equator (equivalent to Addis Ababa, Saigon or Caracas in the northern hemisphere) to 45° south (equivalent to Venice, Montreal or Vladivostok in the northern hemisphere). Our city of Townsville is on the same latitude as Tahiti; Rockhampton as Rio de Janeiro.

We have vast sand plains on one continental margin, and on the other a lush temperate zone separated by watershed mountain ranges from the arid interior. The humid jungles of our North are counter-balanced by a range of Southern Alps where there is snow all year round.

Our land mass is the focal point of three great oceans: Pacific, Indian and Antarctic. We are washed by their varying currents and temperatures; airconditioned by the prevailing winds that follow to give us an astonishing range of micro-climates.

This geographical variation presents the Australian flower lover with an embarrassment of botanical riches but makes the identification and selection of the many flowers he sees quite a problem.

For just as no other English speaking country has our range of climates and temperatures—so none of them produces books of flowers that tell us—and show us—what we need to know in Australia. South Africa and California most nearly approximate our conditions, but their garden writers show no awareness of our own dazzling range of native plants.

So that is why this book has been planned and produced—to display, in full colour, as wide a range of plants as practicable (not all, for that would need a book many times the size and cost) and to present in convenient form the important facts about each one: how and when it is propagated; what sort of soil it likes; how much cultivation and fertilization; which varieties are available. Such information is essential even to the amateur gardener when planning his home selection, for it is impossible to please all plants in any one district.

Much of our Australian soil contains either a surfeit of minerals or an almost complete absence even of the trace elements necessary for healthy growth. It ranges from the heavily alkaline in Adelaide where roses bloom superbly but Azaleas won't grow at all—to the extremely acid in Sydney, where mountain plants from China and Japan enjoy life in the shelter of tropical trees.

Most of us live within range of the sea, where salt air and humidity cause inland flowers to wilt. But at the same time, the moisture-loving plants of Europe's and America's hothouses grow splendidly in the open garden.

Only the cold-lovers are a problem. Except in mountain districts, our winters are rarely cool enough to suit many of the northern hemisphere's favourite bulbs and perennials. Without a dormant season, few survive more than a year or two. We must leave them, with regret, to their own hemisphere or to our New Zealand neighbours, particularly in the South Island.

In this book then, you will find a selection of plants to be grown for the beauty of their flowers, fruits or foliage, and all recommended for gardens in the southern hemisphere. They come from every continent except Antarctica and from many islands all over the world. The common has been balanced with the uncommon, and many an old favourite omitted in favour of its more beautiful, if unfamiliar, cousin.

The final choice in every case, has been my own; based on personal experience of seeing and photographing the plants in cultivation.

STIRLING MACOBOY

how to use this book

A

C

B

D

(A) ROSA indica
(B) ROSA minima
(C) ROSA monstrosa
(D) ROSA floribunda

Pictures tell the story best. These four lovely flowers share the Latin generic name ROSA — but have individual specific names to describe their different habits.
From top to bottom — ROSA indica (the Indian Tea Rose), a bushy plant with red flowers, one to a stem. ROSA minima (the Fairy Rose), tiny multiple flowers on a nine-inch plant. ROSA monstrosa (the Green or Monstrous Rose) has an overdeveloped calyx and distorted green petals. The popular Many-Flowered Rose (ROSA floribunda) grows smaller than a hybrid tea rose, bears more flowers in heavy clusters.

If a guide book is to be more than just a collection of pretty pictures it must help the reader identify its subjects clearly and quickly. As this volume contains over 1,000 colour pictures, a great deal of thought was given to its arrangement.

I decided finally to arrange all flowers and their photographs in strict alphabetical order of their scientific names: even though many of these names will be unfamiliar to the reader. There is more method to this systematic madness than you might think.

It would have been impossible to assemble the book in order of popular names. Some flowers have none, others have too many, and I have no way of knowing which is favoured where you live. Popular names vary from country to country and even from town to town.

On the other hand, each flower has only one accurate scientific name, recognized universally and possessed by no other.

These scientific names are a curious mixture of ancient Latin and Greek, including many made up names with Latin endings which commemorate the country in which the plant was found; the man who discovered it; the patron who sponsored his expedition and many other things.

But whatever you may believe, these old-world scientific names are not given to a flower out of sheer fancy as are popular names. They form a strict system of classification according to certain visible characteristics of the plant.

They also help identify close relatives. For instance, most members of the botanical family we call ROSACEAE or Roses (and that includes many plants you probably don't think of as Roses at all) have similarly shaped leaves, a similarly arranged group of reproductive organs, and develop similar fruits when fertilized. Check the pictures for CRATAEGUS (Hawthorn), FRAGARIA (Strawberry), MESPILUS (Medlar) and prove it for yourself. Don't they all seem to have a relationship to Roses that you can see?

The scientific system of botanical classification divides and subdivides the entire world of plants (including mosses, fungi, moulds and even water slime) into a number of orders, classes and families as a convenient means of identification.

The family is the largest division with which we shall concern ourselves, and it includes all plants which have certain features in common. All members of the Pea family (LEGUMINOSAE) for instance, bear their seeds in rows attached to one side of a pod that splits open at maturity. That is enough to classify them as LEGUMINOSAE, though beyond that the plant might be a tree or an annual or a vine. ACACIA, CASSIA, GENISTA, LABURNUM and LUPINE are all members of this family, as well as garden peas and beans. Family names usually end in -ae or -aceae.

Each plant included in every family has an individual botanical name consisting of at least two parts.

The first of these parts is the GENUS name or generic name (from the Latin *'Gens'*—a clan). It is this generic name by which the plant is scientifically listed—this book is arranged in alphabetical order of generic names. GERANIUM and PELARGONIUM for instance, are generic names. Both plants are obviously related, and both are in fact members of the family GERANIACEAE—but they do have differing characteristics.

Generic names are traditionally printed in CAPITAL LETTERS and we have followed the tradition in this book.

Each GENUS is further subdivided into species. Let us take ROSA: the generic name by which the rose smells as sweet as any other. There are many different ROSAS, and it is obvious that the generic name alone cannot do for them all. So a system of supplementary species or specific names has been evolved which further narrows down the classification; tells us exactly which ROSA it is, where it comes from or what individual qualities it possesses.

The illustrations on the opposite page demonstrate this specific division more clearly than words could do.

Specific or species names are always printed in small letters without an initial capital: but when you see the word 'hybrida' (as in ROSA hybrida), or a capital letter X between generic and specific names, you know that the plant does not occur in nature but is an artificial cross between two or more species.

Finally, there are 'Varietal' and 'Cultivar' names (though not all plants have these). Varietal names are used when it is necessary to distinguish between two varieties of the same GENUS and species. The variation might only be in the colour of a flower, leaf or fruit, but if it can be maintained by plant hybridizers it must be capable of identification. Varietal names are traditionally printed in quotes with an initial capital letter.

Again for instance:
ROSA indica 'Viridiflora'—would have green flowers.
ROSA indica 'Aureo-Marginata' —gold-edged leaves.
ROSA indica 'Fructu-Luteo'— yellow fruits.

Beyond the colour variations, all three would plainly be the same species of Rose.

Cultivar names (also set in single quotes with capitalisation) are given to varieties of horticultural importance which have been developed by breeders and which are capable of being propagated true to form. They are usually in a modern language.

Each flower or plant in this book then is listed and illustrated within the alphabetical order of its scientific names: Generic, specific and Varietal. A list of these names follows immediately after this introduction and you can find the plant you want either from that list or by leafing through the plants alphabetically.

If however, you know only a popular name for the plant, you should find that listed (also alphabetically) in an index following the colour plates. There are more popular names listed than there are plates in the book because one plant may have different popular names in different countries.

There are altogether 1,000 plants illustrated in colour in the alphabetical, numbered plates. They cover 634 genera within 130 botanical families.

Each alphabetical section is separated from the one next to it by a large ornamental capital.

Each plant GENUS is separated by a ruled vertical line from the GENUS next to it, with the name of the GENUS in capitals at the top of the column.

Each GENUS (no matter how many species and Varieties are illustrated) is accompanied by a small paragraph which gives you its popular names; the botanical family to which it belongs; its plant type (tree etc.); its usual height in cultivation; its country of origin and its flowering or peak display season.

Almost all the pictures were taken on Professional Ektachrome 120 film using a variety of Rolleiflex cameras.

If my pleasure is in bringing so many of my favourite plants to your notice—yours may be the discovery of a whole world of unfamiliar flowers for your own garden.

index
scientific
names

FLOWERS, FRUITS AND FOLIAGE included in this book are listed in alphabetical order of scientific names. (Unillustrated varieties in italics)

57 BILLBERGIA
   nutans
   pyramidalis
57 BIXA
   orellana
57 BLANDFORDIA
   nobilis 'Imperialis'
58 BLETILLA
   striata
58 BOMAREA
   shuttleworthii
59 BORAGO
   officinalis
59 BORONIA
   ledifolia
   megastigma 'Chandleri'
   purdeiana
   serrulata
60 BOUGAINVILLEA
   glabra 'Sanderiana'
   glabra 'Variegata'
   spectabilis
60 BOUVARDIA
   longiflora
   ternifolia
61 BRACHYCHITON
   acerifolium
   bidwillii
   discolor
   populneum
   rupestre
61 BRASSAIA
   actinophylla
62 BRASSICA
   oleracea 'Acephala Crispa'
62 BRASSOCATTLEYA
   X 'Enid'
62 BREYNIA
   nivosa 'Roseo Picta'
63 BROWNEA
   grandiceps
63 BRUNFELSIA
   calycina 'Floribunda'
63 BRYOPHYLLUM
   tubiflorum
64 BUDDLEIA
   davidii
   salvifolia
64 BUTEA
   frondosa
65 CAESALPINIA
   pulcherrima
65 CALADIUM
   bicolor
65 CALATHEA
   makoyana
66 CALCEOLARIA
   crenatiflora
   integrifolia
66 CALENDULA
   officinalis
67 CALLIANDRA
   eriophylla
   inaequilatera
   surinamensis
   tweedii
67 CALLISTEMON
   citrinus
   pinifolius
   rigidus
   salignus
   viminalis
68 CALLISTEPHUS
   chinensis
68 CALODENDRON
   capense

69 CALOSTEMMA
   purpurea
69 CALOTHAMNUS
   quadrifidus
   villosus
70 CAMELLIA
   hiemalis
   japonica 'The Czar'
   japonica 'Giulio Nucchio'
   japonica 'Margaret Davis'
   magnoliaeflora
   reticulata X 'Captain Rawes'
   sasanqua
   X williamsii
      'Margaret Waterhouse'
71 CAMPANULA
   carpatica
   isophylla
   medium
   muralis
   persicifolia
   poscharskyana
72 CAMPSIS
   chinensis
   radicans
72 CANNA
   indica
   indica 'Nana'
73 CAPSICUM
   annuum 'Fasciculatum'
73 CARICA
   papaya
73 CARPOBROTUS
   chilensis
74 CASSIA
   artemisiodes
   corymbosa
   fistula
   multijuga
74 CASTANOSPERMUM
   australe
75 CASUARINA
   stricta
75 CATALPA
   bignoniodes
75 CATANANCHE
   caerulea
   'Lutea'
76 CATHARANTHUS
   roseus 'Brighteyes'
   roseus 'Coquette
76 CATTLEYA
   X 'Mary Jane Proebste'
76 CEANOTHUS
   hybridus
77 CEDRUS
   atlantica 'Glauca'
   deodara
77 CELMISIA
   longifolia
77 CELOSIA
   argentea 'Pyramidalis'
   cristata
78 CENTAUREA
   cyanus
78 CERASTIUM
   tomentosum
78 CERATOPETALUM
   gummiferum
79 CERCIS
   canadensis
   siliquastrum
79 CESTRUM
   aurantiacum
   fasciculatum
   nocturnum

80 CHAENOMELES
   lagenaria 'Crimson and Gold'
   lagenaria 'Nivalis'
81 CHAMAECYPARIS
   lawsoniana 'Erecta Aurea'
81 CHAMAELAUCIUM
   uncinatum
82 CHEIRANTHUS
   cheiri
82 CHIONANTHUS
   retusa
83 CHIONODOXA
   luciliae
83 CHOISYA
   ternata
83 CHORIZEMA
   cordatum
84 CHRYSANTHEMUM
   carinatum
   coccineum
   frutescens
   maximum
   morifolium 'Bridesmaid'
   morifolium 'Green Goddess'
   morifolium ''Masquerade'
   parthenium
   ptamigarifolium
85 CISSUS
   rhombifolia
85 CISTUS
   corbariensis
   florentinus
   ladaniferus
   X purpureus
   rosmarinifolius
86 CITRUS
   aurantifolia
   aurantium
   aurantium 'Myrtifolia'
   limonia
   melitensis
   mitis
   nobilis
86 CLARKIA
   elegans
87 CLEMATIS
   lanuginosa
   montana
87 CLEOME
   spinosa
88 CLERODENDRON
   bungei
   nutans
   speciosissimum
   splendens
   thomsonae
   ugandense
88 CLIVIA
   miniata
   nobilis
89 CLYTOSTOMA
   callistegioides
89 COBEA
   scandens
89 CODIAEUM
   variegatum
      'Emperor Alexander'
90 COELOGYNE
   cristata
90 COLCHICUM
   agrippinum
   autumnale
   byzantinus
   speciosum
90 COLEONEMA
   album
   pulchrum

17

illustrations
and text

A

ABELIA

1

2

ABUTILON

3

4

ABELIA
CAPRIFOLIACEAE

Graceful arching branches hung in summer with masses of delicate bell flowers are the principal charm of the Abelias— a truly adaptable group of shrubs. Some evergreen, some deciduous, they can be admired for their natural fountain-like habit or trimmed into tidier shape. Full sun or part-shade suits them equally, and they are planted out in spring. New growth of Abelias is bronzy-red; and the summer flowers are followed by coppery sepals which keep the bush decorative most of the year. The evergreen Glossy Abelia (ABELIA grandiflora) is most usually seen, but deciduous A. schumannii has larger mauve-pink flowers. A. floribunda has deep rose pink blossom.

1   ABELIA X grandiflora
GLOSSY ABELIA
SHRUB   5 ft
HYBRID   SUMMER

2   ABELIA schumannii
SCHUMANN'S ABELIA
SHRUB   5 ft
CHINA   SUMMER

ABUTILON
MALVACEAE

Untidy, leggy shrubs for the most part, ABUTILONS are best trained up columns or against sunny walls so the beauty of their hanging lantern flowers can be enjoyed to the full all through the warm weather. They like damp soil, but flower best in full sun and should be pinched back often to increase flower yield. Most commonly grown varieties are hybrids in yellow, pink, orange and white; but several species are grown. These include ABUTILON striatum, with its large maple-like leaves and red-veined orange bells. Its cultivar A. striatum 'Thompsonii', with smaller, delightfully marbled green and gold leaves, is decorative even when not in flower.

3   ABUTILON X 'Vesuvius'
CHINESE BELLFLOWER
SHRUB   5 ft
HYBRID   SUMMER

4   ABUTILON X 'Milleri'
CHINESE LANTERN
SHRUB   12 ft
HYBRID   SUMMER

5

6

8

7

9

5　ABUTILON striatum
FLOWERING MAPLE
SHRUB　6 ft
BRAZIL　ALL YEAR
ALL TROPICAL

ACACIA
LEGUMINOSAE

Australia's floral emblem, the ACACIAS are a showy family of over 500 species, nearly all of them indigenous to Australia. Popular garden subjects world-wide, often under the incorrect name Mimosa, they are all evergreen, quick-growing and unfortunately, short-lived. Varying in habit from low mat-forming shrubs to tall trees, their leaves may be feathery, flat or needle-like. All have fragrant golden blossom consisting largely of pollen-rich stamens; but the shape varies widely. All prefer full sun, and grow satisfactorily in poor soil. The showiest species flower in midwinter, but in mild climates you can plan and plant for a succession of bloom over the entire year.

6　ACACIA baileyana
COOTAMUNDRA WATTLE
TREE　20 ft
NEW SOUTH WALES　WINTER

7　ACACIA longifolia
SYDNEY GOLDEN WATTLE
TREE　15 ft
NEW SOUTH WALES　SPRING

8　ACACIA podalyriaefolia
QUEENSLAND SILVER WATTLE
PEARL ACACIA
TREE　15 ft
NORTH AMERICA　SPRING

9　ACACIA pycnantha
GOLDEN WATTLE
TREE　20 ft
EASTERN AUSTRALIA　SPRING

ACALYPHA | ACANTHUS | ACER

10

11

12

13

ACALYPHA
EUPHORBIACEAE

ACALYPHAS are eye-catching plants for the warmer climate or glasshouse. The Red Hot Cat's Tail (ACALYPHA hispida) is noted for woolly red flower spikes which droop to a length of 18 in all over the plant, and are tremendously spectacular in a mature specimen. Warmth, high humidity and plenty of liquid fertilizer are advisable. Its cousin A. wilkesiana is a tall shrub with variegated red and pink leaves, and might be mistaken for an overgrown Coleus. It is actually related to the Poinsettia. Though o tropical origin, it grows quite satisfactorily in mild coastal areas, being used as a hedge or background plant. Many colour varieties are available.

10   ACALYPHA hispida
PHILIPPINE MEDUSA
RED HOT CAT'S TAIL
CHENILLE PLANT
SHRUB   8 ft
INDIA   SUMMER, TROPICAL

11   ACALYPHA wilkesiana
BEEFSTEAK PLANT
FIRE DRAGON PLANT
COPPER LEAF
SHRUB   10 ft
FIJI   SUMMER, TROPICAL

ACANTHUS
ACANTHACEAE

Giant, wonderfully shaped glossy leaves make ACANTHUS an attractive year-round feature plant for the shaded position or courtyard—but lay plenty of bait for slugs and snails! Tall spikes of oystery-grey and white flowers appear in early summer and are grand for cutting. Plant from divisions in autumn but be warned! ACANTHUS is a large plant and spreads rapidly.

12   ACANTHUS mollis
BEAR'S BREECH
BEAR'S BREECHES
BEARSFOOT
OYSTER PLANT
PERENNIAL   4 ft
ITALY   SUMMER

ACER
ACERACEAE

Maples are the most ornamental of deciduous trees and beautiful in cool-climate gardens. Graceful trees with leaves often incredibly shaped and tinted, Maples vary from grotesquely twisted dwarves to tall spreading background trees. Most ornamental garden varieties need a compost-rich, well-drained acid loam, with dressings of well-decayed manure in late autumn. They need partial shade and protection from hot summer winds to prevent scorching of the delicate leaves. The species ACER palmatum and A. japonicum include most of the ornamental varieties, but the best background subjects are A. platanoides (the Norway Maple), A. saccharum (the North American Sugar Maple), and several varieties of A. negundo (the Box Elder).

13   ACER negundo 'Aureo Marginatum'
VARIEGATED BOX ELDER
TREE   30 ft
UNITED STATES
SPRING

28

14

16

17

15

14   ACER palmatum
JAPANESE MAPLE
MOUNTAIN MAPLE
TREE   20 ft
JAPAN   AUTUMN

15   ACER palmatum dissectum
CUTLEAF MAPLE
LACELEAF MAPLE
DWARF TREE   5 ft
JAPAN   AUTUMN
ALL HARDY

ACHILLEA
COMPOSITAE

Most trouble free of perennials, the large ACHILLEA genus includes many attractive species and varieties—all requiring only full sun and occasional water to help them produce masses of bloom in the summer border. Leaves of all species are lacy and finely divided; and available flower colours include white, yellow, pink and red. The genus includes dainty dwarf plants that rarely exceed 3 in and tall perennials up to 5 ft.

16   ACHILLEA filipendulina
YARROW
MILFOIL
PERENNIAL   3 ft
CAUCASUS   SUMMER
HARDY

ACHIMENES
GESNERIACEAE

Related to Gloxinias and African Violets, the delicate ACHIMENES grow outdoors in a warm sheltered position. Of about 30 species, the most commonly seen is ACHIMENES longiflora, which flowers in autumn from spring-planted rhizomes. An acid soil mixture of peatmoss, sharp sand and leafmould gives the best results. The leaves are both shiny and hairy; the flower colours include purple, blue, pink, crimson and white. Spray against thrip and red spider.

17   ACHIMENES longiflora
TRUMPET ACHIMENES
HOT WATER PLANT
PERENNIAL   12 in
CENTRAL AMERICA   AUTUMN
TROPICAL

18

19

ACOKANTHERA
APOCYNACEAE

There may be more spectacular shrubs than ACOKANTHERA, but surely none more tolerant of poor soil, wind and salt air. Plant in full sun as a specimen, or trim as a hedge: all this useful shrub needs is plenty of water in summer to turn on a year-round show. Evergreen leaves are tinged with purple: fragrant palest pink flowers appear all year, and are followed by plum coloured poisonous fruits in autumn and winter.

18   ACOKANTHERA spectabilis
BUSHMAN'S POISON
AFRICAN WINTERSWEET
CARISSA
SHRUB   10 ft
SOUTH AFRICA   SPRING

ACROCLINIUM
COMPOSITAE

One of the few Australian annual plants in cultivation, ACROCLINIUMS are sown directly where they are to grow, in warm dry soil. The papery daisy flowers are in many shades of white, red and pink—yellow or brown centred. Cut the flowers on a dry day, hang upside down in bunches in a cool place till the stems dry out—use for dried arrangements.

19   ACROCLINIUM roseum
EVERLASTING DAISY
PAPER DAISY
ANNUAL   18 in
AUSTRALIA   ALL YEAR

ACTINIDIA

20

ACTINODIUM

21

ACTINOTUS

22

ACTINIDIA
ACTINIDIACEAE

A deciduous vine for trellis or arbour, the ACTINIDIA is not only handsome but produces delicious fruits as well. If possible buy a grafted bi-sexual plant otherwise at least one male and one female are needed. Set out in rich soil at the base of strong support. The thick velvet leaves give pleasant shade, and yellow flowers appear in warm weather before the furry plum-shaped fruits. Inside, these are sweet, pulpy and apple green, with tiny edible seeds.

20   ACTINIDIA chinensis
CHINESE GOOSEBERRY
YANGTAO
KIWI FRUIT
NEW ZEALAND FRUIT SALAD
VINE   30 ft
CHINA   ALL YEAR

ACTINODIUM
MYRTACEAE

Papery pink and white daisy flowers top the thin stems of the delicate Swamp Daisy, a useful Western Australian shrub for acid coastal soil. Plant ACTINODIUM where it receives full sun all year, but gets very wet feet during the winter flowering period. The flower stems can be dried for arrangements and botanically speaking, the flowers are not daisies at all, but members of the same family as Eucalypts.

21   ACTINODIUM cunninghamii
SWAMP DAISY
SHRUB   3 ft
AUSTRALIA   WINTER

ACTINOTUS
UMBELLIFERAE

Useful summer-flowering perennials for the bush garden or rockery, Flannel Flowers grow readily from seed or divisions set out in spring. An acid sandy loam with plenty of humus is the best type of soil, and like all Australian natives they demand good drainage and as little cultivation as possible. The greenish-white, flannel-textured flowers appear on tall stems all through summer.

22   ACTINOTUS helianthi
FLANNEL FLOWER
PERENNIAL   2 ft
NEW SOUTH WALES   SUMMER

ADIANTUM

23

AECHMEA

24

25

AGAPANTHUS

26

ADIANTUM
POLYPODIACEAE

A favourite fern genus for cool shady places. Maidenhairs include over 200 species from every part of the world. Differing only in leaf shape and size, they all have wiry stems and translucent fan-like leaves. Give them shade, a rich fibrous soil and plenty of protection from snails and slugs. In frosty climates they should be brought inside at the approach of winter.

23   ADIANTUM capillis-veneris
CHEVELURE
MAIDENHAIR FERN
FERN   12 in
WORLD-WIDE   ALL YEAR
SUBTROPICAL

AECHMEA
BROMELIACEAE

Bewildering in the variety of their leaves and flowers, AECHMEAS are fancy dress members of the Pineapple family from tropical America. They are epiphytes or air feeders, collecting moisture in the upturned cup of their leaves, and need soil only as support. They are often wired in the forks of trees in frost-free areas, but thrive potted up in old leafmould and fibrous loam. Typical of the 100-odd species are AECHMEA caudata 'Variegata' with yellow, orange and midnight blue flowers—and A. 'Foster's Favourite', in which chains of coral berries hang among the wine-dark leaves.

24   AECHMEA caudata 'Variegata'
VASE PLANT
BROMELIAD   3 ft
BRAZIL   SPRING

25   AECHMEA X 'Foster's Favourite'
BROMELIAD   2½ ft
HYBRID   SPRING

AGAPANTHUS
LILIACEAE

South African in origin, AGAPANTHUS are a world favourite for their striking sunbursts of blue or white flowers in summer and autumn. Extremely hardy, they enjoy full sun (except in hot dry districts) and will grow in any soil with spring watering. White-flowered AGA-PANTHUS orientalis 'Albus' bears up to 3 times as many flowers per stem than the more common blue-flowered A. africanus.

26   AGAPANTHUS africanus
LILY OF THE NILE
AFRICAN LILY
PERENNIAL   3–4 ft
SOUTH AFRICA   SUMMER
SUBTROPICAL

AGASTACHE

27

AGAVE

28

29

AGERATUM

30

AGASTACHE
LABIATAE

A useful aromatic leafed perennial for the open bed or border, AGASTACHE is grown from seed or spring divisions and takes any kind of soil. The stems are pliable, and where the going is too good the plant develops a floppy habit without staking. The long spikes of tubular flowers, in shades from crimson to rose-pink, are produced in summer over a long period.

27   AGASTACHE mexicana
CEDRONELLA
PERENNIAL   2½ ft
MEXICO   SUMMER
SUBTROPICAL

AGAVE
AMARYLLIDACEAE

The gigantic leaf-rosettes of these splendid succulents rank them among the most popular accent plants for modern gardens. They grow in poor soil, forming clumps, 5 to 6 ft across, and need plenty of water. AGAVE attenuata produces arching spikes of yellow flowers up to 14 ft long. The closely related Century Plant (A. americana) may take a good 10 years before it decides to send up a 20 ft spike of greenish flowers...after which it dies. While you cope with the suspense of waiting for the big flowering event, you will enjoy the dramatic appearance of its viciously spined leaves —blue-green or yellow-striped in the variety A. americana 'Marginata'.

28   AVE americana 'Marginated'
CENTURY PLANT
SUCCULENT   6 ft
MEXICO   SPRING

29   AGAVE attenuata
SUCCULENT   5 ft
MEXICO   WINTER
SUBTROPICAL

AGERATUM
COMPOSITAE

Widely planted for its effective contrast to the more gaudily flowered summer and autumn annuals, delicate AGERATUM can be moved even when in full flower. It enjoys rich, moist soil and retains colour best in filtered sun. Plant out any time in spring or summer. AGERATUM 'Blue Mink' is a bushy dwarf variety—others flower in tones of pure blue, pink or white.

30   AGERATUM houstonianum
'Blue Mink'
FLOSS FLOWER
ANNUAL   12 in
MEXICO   SUMMER

AGLAONEMA

31

AGONIS

32

AILANTHUS

33

AGLAONEMA
ARACEAE

Though they do bear occasional flowers like small green Arum Lilies, these very useful tropical perennials are grown principally for their ornamental leaves. Outdoors in the tropics—inside in cooler areas. They demand a rich potting mix, like plenty of water (except in winter) and do very well indeed in poor light. Variety AGLAONEMA pseudo-bracteata is mottled with white, yellow and lighter green.

31   AGLAONEMA pseudo-bracteata
CHINESE EVERGREEN
PERENNIAL   2 ft
MALAYSIA   AUTUMN
TROPICAL

AGONIS
MYRTACEAE

The weeping grace and rustling charm of a willow—all this and flowers too! Western Australia's native Willow Myrtle is a delightful tree for areas where the temperature does not drop below freezing. Not particular as to soil, it adopts an interesting contorted shape in drought-stricken positions. The leaves smell strongly of peppermint when crushed.

32   AGONIS flexuosa
WILLOW MYRTLE
PEPPERMINT TREE
TREE   20 ft
WESTERN AUSTRALIA   SPRING

AILANTHUS
SIMAROUBACEAE

AILANTHUS is that botanical rarity, an attractive tree that can be relied on where nothing else will grow. Deciduous and of a sparse habit, it grows fast and produces leaves over 2 ft long. The flowers are small and greenish, but its most decorative effect is the clusters of brownish-red winged fruits in summer. Its main fault is that it reproduces at an alarming rate.

33   AILANTHUS altissima
TREE OF HEAVEN
TREE   30 ft
CHINA   SUMMER

AJUGA

34

AKEBIA

35

ALBIZIA

36

AJUGA
LABIATAE

Useful and attractive as a ground cover in any position where the drainage is good, AJUGA spreads by runners and forms rosettes of shiny leaves; usually purple-bronze, but variegated with yellow, green and red according to variety. There are showy six-inch spikes of blue flowers during the warm weather. AJUGA needs regular water and spreads well only if the old flower spikes are removed in summer.

34   AJUGA reptans
BLUE BUGLE
CARPET BUGLE
PERENNIAL   4 in
EUROPE   SUMMER

AKEBIA
LARDIZABALACEAE

A delicate evergreen vine justly famed for its dainty five-leaf clusters, and fragrant purple and milk-coffee flowers in spring. Grow it in sun or shade, but with strong support, and cut back almost to the ground after flowering. It is a fast grower and sometimes produces edible fruits in mild climates. Propagate AKEBIA by cuttings or layers in early spring.

35   AKEBIA quinata
FIVE-LEAF AKEBIA
VINE   30 ft
CHINA   SPRING

ALBIZIA
LEGUMINOSAE

Rather like an overscaled Wattle, the ALBIZIA enjoys the light sandy soil of coastal areas, where it grows very fast. The leaves are dark green and similar to a Jacaranda; the greenish flowers appear as fluffy two-inch spikes in late spring. Like most fast growers, Albizia is short-lived and often used as a temporary screen for slower growing trees.

36   ALBIZIA lophantha
SIRUS
SILK TREE
CAPE WATTLE
PLUME ALBIZIA
TREE   20 ft
WESTERN AUSTRALIA   SPRING

ALLAMANDA

37

38

ALLIUM

39

ALOCASIA

40

41

ALLAMANDA
APOCYNACEAE

Colourful shrubby climbers for warm climates, ALLAMANDAS are important members of the Periwinkle family. Rich soil, regular feeding and water are essential; and regular pinching back does much to control a naturally untidy shape. Dark shiny leaves are an effective foil to the showy trumpet flowers which appear all through warm weather. ALLAMANDA neriifolia produces many flowers to a cluster, yellow streaked with orange: A. cathartica 'Hendersonii' makes up in size what it lacks in number—the flowers are often 5 in across. A. violacea flowers later, the trumpets a delicate rose-violet. ALLAMANDAS are used extensively in the tropics for informal fences, twining along heavy wire strands.

37   ALLAMANDA neriifolia
SHRUB   3 ft
SOUTH AMERICA   SUMMER

38   ALLAMANDA violacea
SHRUB   6 ft
BRAZIL   AUTUMN

ALLIUM
LILIACEAE

Alliums are related to the edible onions and garlic, and their hollow tubular leaves exude a typical onion smell when bruised. The flowers however are very different from the kitchen varieties: ALLIUM giganteum from the Himalayas bears a four-inch ball of mauve flowers on a four-foot stem in midsummer. All Alliums are grown from seed or autumn-planted bulbs, and most flower in summer. They like good drainage, full sun and regular water.

39   ALLIUM giganteum
GIANT ALLIUM
ORNAMENTAL ONION
BULB   4 ft
HIMALAYAS   SUMMER

ALOCASIA
ARACEAE

Grown mostly for tropical effect or leaf interest, the ALOCASIAS nevertheless have deliciously perfumed boat-shaped flowers typical of the Arum family. ALOCASIA macrorhiza is the most commonly cultivated of 60-odd species—growing best in a moist shady position in the average garden where it reaches 6 ft. A. macrorhiza 'Variegata' has dramatically blotched leaves. The greenish-yellow flowers appear in spring and summer. All ALOCASIAS can be grown from seed or from suckers which root easily. Both flowers and leaves make striking arrangements.

40   ALOCASIA macrorhiza
SPOON LILY
ELEPHANT'S EARS
CUNJEVOI
PERENNIAL   6 ft
EAST INDIES   SUMMER

41   ALOCASIA macrorhiza 'Variegata'
VARIEGATED SPOON LILY
PERENNIAL   6 ft
EAST INDIES   SUMMER

ALOE

42

43

44

ALPINIA

45

46

ALOE
LILIACEAE

Splendid ornamentals for dry, frost-free areas, the Aloes include more than 200 species, mostly with thick spiky leaves attractively blotched and banded with grey. The flowers are usually red to yellow, borne on tall stems in the form of a candelabra. ALOE arborescens throws spikes of vermilion flowers up to 15 ft and will tolerate drought or salt spray equally well. Aloes are attacked by mealy bug, best destroyed with regular applications of derris dust.

42   ALOE arborescens
TREE ALOE
CANDELABRA ALOE
SUCCULENT   15 ft
SOUTH AFRICA   SPRING

43   ALOE marlothii
SUCCULENT   12 ft
BOTSWANA   WINTER
SUBTROPICAL

44   ALOE speciosa
SUCCULENT   4 ft
AFRICA   WINTER

ALPINIA
ZINGIBERACEAE

Very showy flowers, much used in the south seas for making garlands, the ALPINIAS are likely to flower only in a warm, moist position. The Red Ginger, ALPINIA purpurata has a curious habit of sprouting new plantlets among the flower bracts. These take root as the dying flower stem collapses to the ground. The Shell Ginger (A. speciosa) is more often seen outside the tropics: its waxy pink and white buds appear in large clusters and pop open one at a time to reveal red and yellow spotted blossoms. This tall plant does well in part-shade, needs plenty of water and good soil to bloom well; which it does after several years' establishment.

45   ALPINIA purpurata
RED GINGER BLOSSOM
PERENNIAL   6 ft
SOUTH SEAS   SUMMER

46   ALPINIA speciosa
SHELL GINGER
PORCELAIN GINGER
PERENNIAL   10 ft
CHINA   SUMMER
BOTH TROPICAL

ALSTROEMERIA

47

48

ALTERNANTHERA

49

ALTHAEA

50

ALSTROEMERIA
AMARYLLIDACEAE

These wildly spreading perennials are seen at their best naturalized under trees, or on sloping banks of sandy soil. They are planted from root divisions in autumn, and enjoy plenty of water until the leaves yellow. Orange is the basic colour of ALSTROEMERIA aurantiaca; but hybrids are now available in shades of white, pink, yellow and brick red. Related A. pulchella is often known in Australia as the New Zealand Christmas Bell, though why is a mystery, since it comes from North Brazil. Less tolerant of cold than A. aurantiaca, its green and red flowers are more useful for cutting. ALSTROEMERIAS take years to recover from a move.

47   ALSTROEMERIA aurantiaca
CHILEAN LILY
PERUVIAN LILY
PERENNIAL   3 ft
CHILE   SUMMER

48 ALSTROEMERIA pulchella
NEW ZEALAND CHRISTMAS BELL
PERENNIAL   3 ft
BRAZIL   SUMMER

ALTERNANTHERA
AMARANTHACEAE

Rather an old-fashioned favourite, usually seen close-planted in a variety of colours spelling out the name of resort towns, ALTERNANTHERA should not be underestimated. It grows rapidly from divisions or autumn cuttings and is very useful for warm climate colour—either as a ground cover, in rockeries, or as a permanent bed edging. Cuttings are the only way to make sure it comes to true colour.

49   ALTERNANTHERA amoena
PERENNIAL   6 in
BRAZIL   ALL YEAR

ALTHAEA
MALVACEAE

Forever associated with English cottage gardens, the old-fashioned Hollyhock is still charming by fences or walls—anywhere there is protection from wind. Plant in autumn or winter, preferably in groups, and feed well...they will produce magnificent spires of large flowers in midsummer. Single and double varieties are available in shades of pink, red, yellow and white, and they self-sow readily.

50   ALTHAEA rosea
HOLLYHOCK
BIENNIAL   8 ft
ASIA   SUMMER

ALYSSUM

51

AMARANTHUS

52

53

AMARYLLIS

54

ALYSSUM
CRUCIFERAE

The true ALYSSUM produces carpets of golden yellow to light up the spring garden. Seedlings started indoors in late winter are planted out early summer. With a little care, cuttings can also be struck in sharp sand. Good drainage is essential, and the condition of the plants improved by shearing back after the flowers are done. A popular rock garden subject.

51 ALYSSUM saxatile
BASKET OF GOLD
GOLD DUST
GOLDEN TUFT
PERENNIAL 12 in
EASTERN EUROPE SPRING

AMARANTHUS
AMARANTHACEAE

The many vivid AMARANTHUS varieties take some beating for brilliant summer colour in warm districts. Provided regular watering can be maintained they are incredibly heat-resistant and grow like weeds. Dig in well-rotted manure before planting and feed regularly with soluble fertilizer. AMARANTHUS tricolor (Joseph's Coat) is the gayest, while A. hypochondriacus is eye-catching in shades of red. The willow-leafed species A. salicifolius is more delicate, both in habit and colouration. Also grown is a green-leafed species A. caudatus (Love Lies Bleeding) — a rather scrappy looking plant with long red tassel flowers, it is inferior in every way to the illustrated ACALYPHA hispida (the Red Hot Cat's Tail). (See: ACALYPHA)

52 AMARANTHUS hypochondriacus 'Sanguineus'
PRINCE'S FEATHER
ANNUAL 4 ft
TROPICAL AMERICA SUMMER

53 AMARANTHUS tricolor
JOSEPH'S COAT
ANNUAL 4 ft
TROPICS SUMMER

AMARYLLIS
AMARYLLIDACEAE

A heavy musky perfume clearly shows up this splendid South African flower from its look-alike cousin the Crinum. Plant out in summer with the neck of the bulb just at ground level and the naked flower stalks will pop right out of the soil towards autumn. The Belladonna needs good drainage and plenty of water during the winter months. There are varying shades from white to almost red. HIPPEASTRUMS (which see) are also commonly called AMARYLLIS.

54 AMARYLLIS belladonna
BELLADONNA LILY
NAKED LADY
MARCH LILY
BULB 2½ ft
SOUTH AFRICA AUTUMN

AMPELOPSIS

55

ANANAS

56

ANEMONE

57

58

AMPELOPSIS
VITACEAE

A delicate climber for the greenhouse or shaded border, charming AMPELOPSIS has pink stems and shoots which develop into attractively marbled miniature grape leaves of white, green and gold. It enjoys a cool root run, but the fine tendrils will scramble up towards the light over any hardy shrub. After producing brilliant blue berries and colourful autumn tints, AMPELOPSIS should be cut right back to the woody trunk.

55   AMPELOPSIS brevipedunculata
var. 'Elegans'
ORNAMENTAL GRAPE
BLUEBERRY CLIMBER
VINE   5 ft
JAPAN   SPRING-SUMMER
HARDY

ANANAS
BROMELIACEAE

The edible pineapple is ANANUS comosus, but a rare and delicate species of Pineapple, ANANAS bracteata is one of the most popular bromeliads among collectors. The five-foot, spiny-edged leaves are banded in green and yellow, often tinged with pink. The flowers are violet with bright red bracts and stems. ANANAS is a native of the Brazilian jungles and less tolerant of winter cold than its edible cousin.

56   ANANAS bracteata 'Striata'
VARIEGATED PINEAPPLE
BROMELIAD   5 ft
BRAZIL   SPRING
TROPICAL

ANEMONE
RANUNCULACEAE

Red, White and Blue is the patriotic colour range of Poppy-Flowered Anemones (ANEMONE coronaria). The small tubers are usually raised in boxes; planted out in autumn after the feathery leaves appear. The double-flowered St Brigid strain is spectacular in mass plantings for winter and spring colour. Less well-known is the Japanese Anemone (A. hupehensis) a handsomely foliaged perennial for partly shaded, sheltered positions. It is propagated from divisions planted out in spring, and the usual colour of the semi-double autumn flowers is a warm pink, though white and purple varieites exist. Japanese Anemones are best planted in clumps which will grow together for spectacular mass flowering.

57   ANEMONE coronaria
WINDFLOWER
POPPY-FLOWERED ANEMONE
BULB   10 in
EUROPE   SPRING

58   ANEMONE hupehensis
'Japonica'
JAPANESE ANEMONE
PERENNIAL   3 ft
CHINA   AUTUMN   HARDY

59

60

ANGOPHORA
MYRTACEAE

So closely related to the Eucalypts that only experts can tell them apart, the ANGOPHORAS are most usually represented in gardens by the rugged Dwarf Applegum (ANGOPHORA cordifolia). This has blunt gum-shaped, evergreen leaves, and masses of creamy-white flowers over weeks in early summer. These are most attractive to bees. ANGOPHORAS are hardy, and tolerate stony drought-stricken situations.

59   ANGOPHORA cordifolia
GUM MYRTLE
DWARF APPLEGUM
TREE   8 ft
NEW SOUTH WALES   SUMMER

ANIGOZANTHOS
AMARYLLIDACEAE

An interesting group of 8 perennials from Western Australia. Preferring sandy soil with good drainage, Kangaroo Paws do not like frosts or summer humidity and their tender young leaves and flower buds are irresistible to slugs ANIGO-ZANTHOS manglesii (the Green Kangaroo Paw) is the most popular, followed by the dwarf A. humilis (the Cat's Paw). Others are A. flavidus and A. pulcherrima.

60   ANIGOZANTHOS manglesii
KANGAROO PAW
PERENNIAL   3 ft
WESTERN AUSTRALIA   SPRING

ANNONA

61

ANTHEMIS

62

ANTHURIUM

63

64

ANNONA
ANNONACEAE

Delicious fruit is only one among many attractions of this easy-to-grow warm climate tree. Plant in rich acid soil, add water and watch it grow! The Custard Apple has large velvety leaves which drop in spring as the fragrant golden flowers appear. These develop into the enormous fruits which may weigh 1½ lb and are not eaten till the warty green skin begins to turn brown. More widely grown is the tropical Sugar Apple.

61   ANNONA cherimolia
CUSTARD APPLE
CHERIMOYA
TREE   20 ft
PERU   SUMMER
SUBTROPICAL

ANTHEMIS
COMPOSITAE

Most brilliant of the daisies for summer bedding, golden Chamomile shines blindingly right through to autumn. Easy to grow (from seed, cuttings or division) it forms thick mats of feathery aromatic leaves which are occasionally used as Chamomile Tea. ANTHEMIS needs full sun and makes a dazzling display in the summer border when allowed to sprawl in a haphazard fashion.

62   ANTHEMIS tinctoria
CHAMOMILE
GOLDEN MARGUERITE
PERENNIAL   15 in
EUROPE   SUMMER

ANTHURIUM
ARACEAE

A splendid family of 500 tropical species, widely grown in spite of their many demands. They must, have humidity and temperature of at least 60°F. all year. This generally means a heated greenhouse. The leaves come in many wonderful shapes and the brilliant flowers appear to have been lacquered. ANTHURIUM andreanum 'Rubrum' is the brightest red, with a yellow spadix; the hybrid A. X ferrierense a wonderful flesh-pink both spathe and spadix. The smaller A. scherzerianum is variable in colour with a coiled spadix. ANTHURIUMS are often grown and shown with orchids, although not in any way related. Cut flowers last for months.

63   ANTHURIUM andreanum 'Rubrum'
PERENNIAL   3 ft
COLOMBIA   SPRING

64   ANTHURIUM scherzerianum
FLAMINGO FLOWER
PERENNIAL   2 ft
COSTA RICA   ALL YEAR
BOTH TROPICAL

ANTIGONON

ANTIRRHINUM

APHELANDRA

65

66

67

ANTIGONON
POLYGONACEAE

A fast-growing vine for the warmer garden, romantically named Chain of Love bears a multitude of tiny pink heart-shaped flowers. It loves sun and heat, and climbs towards the light with small tendrils. Due to its lacy habit of growth, it is ideal for arbours or pergolas where it shades without cutting out the light. There is a less commonly seen white variety which grows easily from seed.

65   ANTIGONON leptopis
CHAIN OF LOVE
CORAL VINE
CORALLITA
ROSA DE MONTANA
QUEEN'S WREATH
BRIDE'S TEARS
VINE   20 ft
MEXICO   SUMMER

ANTIRRHINUM
SCROPHULARIACEAE

Fine for cutting, Snapdragons have been out of fashion in recent years because of their susceptibility to rust. Fortunately, the newer Tetraploid strains are almost completely rust-resistant, and the fungus can be controlled with Zineb. Snapdragons like a soil rich in fertilizer and sweet with lime. They can be planted any time and should be nipped back to encourage branching.

66   ANTIRRHINUM majus
SNAPDRAGON
PERENNIAL   2 ft
EUROPE   SPRING—AUTUMN

APHELANDRA
ACANTHACEAE

Both flowers and leaves are spectacular on this warm climate plant; an irresistible combination. Grow APHELANDRAS outdoors in sheltered positions or indoors as a houseplant, provided you can guarantee warmth, humidity and compost rich soil. After flowering, the entire stem drops off and a pair of new shoots appear on either side. The plant is propagated by cuttings.

67   APHELANDRA squarrosa
PERENNIAL   3 ft
MEXICO   SUMMER

AQUILEGIA

68

ARABIS

69

ARACHNANTHE

70

AQUILEGIA
RANUNCULACEAE

Semi-shade in a position that never dries out, and good rich soil—that is all you need to grow old-fashioned Columbines to perfection. Leaves like lacy Maidenhair Fern and long spurred flowers in a range of rich colours give a cool woodland effect all through the warm months. Cut back after flowering for further bloom—but leave some seed pods for self-sowing.

68 AQUILEGIA vulgaris
COLUMBINE
GRANNY'S BONNETS
PERENNIAL 3½ ft
EUROPE SUMMER

ARABIS
CRUCIFERAE

Charming but unspectacular plants for the rock garden or crevices in paving, perennial Rock Cresses form dense mats of grey-green leaves in rosette form and are useful for overplanting spring bulbs. In late winter and early spring the flowers appear in dainty clusters; rosy-mauve, white or pink. There are both single and double forms, with plain or variegated leaves. Propagate by division.

69 ARABIS albida 'Flore Pleno'
ROCK CRESS
PERENNIAL 6 in
EUROPE–ASIA SPRING

ARACHNANTHE
ORCHIDACEAE

Strictly a hothouse or sub-tropical subject needing a minimum winter temperature of 65°F., the wicked looking Spider Orchid is a tree-dweller and produces hanging flower spikes up to 12 ft in length. The flowers, yellow with red-brown blotches are great favourites for flower arrangers. They appear in summer and open one by one as the flower stem lengthens.

70 ARACHNANTHE flos-aeris
SPIDER ORCHID
ORCHID 12 in
MALAYSIA SUMMER
TROPICAL

ARBUTUS

71

72

ARCTOTIS

73

ARDISIA

74

ARBUTUS
ERICACEAE

Rarely without some flowers or fruit any time of year, the Irish Strawberry puts on its peak performance through autumn and winter. Then, the branches are positively laden with Lily-of-the-Valley blossom and multi-coloured edible berries. Thriving in the mountains and by the sea, ARBUTUS seems to flourish in both lime and acid soil conditions. A slow grower, it needs regular spraying against aphis.

71 ARBUTUS unedo
(fruits)
IRISH STRAWBERRY
STRAWBERRY TREE
TREE 20 ft
EUROPE–IRELAND ALL YEAR

72 ARBUTUS unedo
(flowers)

ARCTOTIS
COMPOSITAE

These colourful, profusely flowering African Daisies are unexcelled for ground cover or mass-plantings on sloping sites. They grow anywhere, but prefer sandy soil and flower continuously from winter to autumn. Colours include oranges, pinks, reds, whites and yellows, usually with contrasting centres. The flowers close in dull weather and the late afternoon and need a generous hand with water.

73 ARCTOTIS X hybrid
AURORA DAISY
AFRICAN DAISY
ANNUAL 2 ft
SOUTH AFRICA WINTER–SUMMER
NOT HARDY

ARDISIA
MYRSINACEAE

Brilliant winter colour for the semi-shaded garden, ARDISIA crenata is the best-known member of a large and decorative family. In spring it produces clusters of white or pink flowers in layers up the single stem . . . later, there are coral-red berries which last all winter long. ARDISIA grows from seed or cuttings and may reach 3 ft in the cool shrubbery.

74 ARDISIA crenata
CORAL BERRY
SHRUB 3 ft
ASIA WINTER

ARGEMONE

75

ARISTOLOCHIA

76

ARMERIA

77

ARGEMONE
PAPAVERACEAE

Often seen naturalized as a roadside weed, ARGEMONE is a showy biennial for the warm sheltered position. Sow seed in summer and transplant carefully in autumn to the mixed border at least 18 in apart. The foliage of Prickly Poppy is a most attractive grey-green, sometimes with white veinings, and is almost impossible to pick without gloves. The flowers vary from lemon-yellow to orange.

75   ARGEMONE mexicana
PRICKLY POPPY
DEVIL'S FIG
MEXICAN POPPY
BIENNIAL   2½ ft
TROPICAL AMERICA   SPRING

ARISTOLOCHIA
ARISTOLOCHIACEAE

Flowers of extraordinary shape and colour are the only common feature of all members in the large ARISTOLOCHIA group. Otherwise they are shrubs and climbers of quite varying appearance. The Dutchman's Pipe is often seen in warm climate gardens; a slim, delicate vine which twines its way among trees or around columns. It needs partial shade and high humidity.

76   ARISTOLOCHIA grandiflora
DUTCHMAN'S PIPE
PELICAN FLOWER
VINE   20 ft
GUATEMALA   SUMMER

ARMERIA
PLUMBAGINACEAE

Showy perennials for sandy soil in full sun, the ARMERIAS are hardy in the rockery or paved area, where they form compact tufts of short leaves. In spring and summer globular clusters of pink or white flowers develop on tall single stalks. Good drainage is important, and occasional light fertilization is required. Propagate from seed or division in autumn.

77   ARMERIA maritima
THRIFT
SEA PINK
PERENNIAL   12 in
EUROPE   SUMMER

ARUM

78

79

ARUNDO

80

ASCLEPIAS

81

ARUM
ARACEAE

Though giving their name to a very large group of plants indeed, the real members of the ARUM family are few. All of them enjoy rich soil, plenty of water and full-shade; and are usually recognizable by their arrow-shaped leaves and curious hooded flowers borne on short stems. ARUM italicum has a delicate, almost transparent green spathe and yellow spadix: A. palaestinum is green outside, purple-black inside, with a jet black spadix: other species bear brown violet and white flowers, but the so-called Arum Lily, of popular use, is not an ARUM at all, but a Zantedeschia. (See: ZANTEDESCHIA)

78   ARUM italicum
ITALIAN ARUM
PERENNIAL   2 ft
EUROPE   SPRING–SUMMER

79   ARUM palaestinum
BLACK CALLA
JERUSALEM LILY
PERENNIAL   15 in
ISRAEL   SPRING

ARUNDO
GRAMINEAE

Though rampant in its spreading habits, the Giant Reed is still widely planted for dramatic foliage effect. It needs rich soil and plenty of water, while the older stems should be cut out regularly to preserve the wonderful translucent quality of the striped leaves. ARUNDO bears typical grass spikes of feather flowers in autumn. Plant only where it can be controlled without difficulty.

80   ARUNDO donax Variegata
GIANT REED
PERENNIAL GRASS   12 ft
SOUTHERN EUROPE   AUTUMN

ASCLEPIAS
ASCLEPIADACEAE

A dull narrow-leafed shrub, grown more for the amusement value of its swan-shaped green seed pods than for anything else. It is easily raised from seed—a little too easily if the truth be known, ASCLEPIAS prefers a warm sunny position with plenty of moisture, and flowers all year. The Bloodflower (A. curassavica) is popular as an annual.

81   ASCLEPIAS fruticosa
MILKWEED
SWAN PLANT
SHRUB   6 ft
SOUTH AFRICA   SUMMER

ASPARAGUS

82

ASTER

83

84

AUBRIETA

85

ASPARAGUS
LILIACEAE

Apart from the popular edible variety, the Asparagus genus includes over 150 ornamental plants, many incorrectly thought of as ferns. Most useful is the Sprenger Asparagus, a curious plant with arching stems like Christmas tinsel and wonderful masses of red, green and violet berries in winter. It is great for rock gardens, hanging baskets, and can even climb a reasonable distance.

82   ASPARAGUS sprengeri
SPRENGER ASPARAGUS
ASPARAGUS FERN
TUBER   3 ft
WEST AFRICA   WINTER

ASTER
COMPOSITAE

The varieties of this popular perennial border genus are almost endless, with flowers in every shade of blue, mauve, pink, crimson, white and yellow. Great clusters of tiny half-inch flowers in ASTER ericoides; large two-and-a-half-inch flowers in the modern A. frikartii hybrids. And in between, the many types generally lumped together as Easter or Michaelmas Daisies. Perennial Asters enjoy full sun and spread rapidly in rich soil. Clumps should be divided every autumn, and only the outside young divisions replanted. With careful choice of variety, Asters can now be had in flower from midspring to winter. Some types grow to 5 ft and need stake support.

83   ASTER amellus 'Eventide'
ITALIAN ASTER
PERENNIAL   2 ft
ITALY   SUMMER

84   ASTER ericoides
HEATH ASTER
PERENNIAL   3 ft
NORTH AMERICA   AUTUMN

AUBRIETA
CRUCIFERAE

Colourful miniature perennials for paving chinks or border edges, AUBRIETAS are grown from seed sown in spring or cuttings taken immediately after flowering. AUBRIETA forms dense mats of grey-green leaves which burst into flower for long periods in spring. Colours include pink, lilac and purple, and there are many named varieties. AUBRIETAS flower best the second year after planting.

85   AUBRIETA deltoidea
ROCK CRESS
PERENNIAL   6 in
ASIA MINOR   SPRING

86

87

AUCUBA
CORNACEAE

Indispensible for the shady garden, the brilliantly marked leaves of Japanese Laurel shine and sparkle throughout the year. Rich, light soil and plenty of water are needed to promote growth and keep the leaves healthy. Many named leaf varieties are available and if bushes of both sexes are planted, AUCUBAS will bear small scarlet fruit, which persist through winter. Often grown in the greenhouse.

86   AUCUBA japonica 'Variegata'
GOLD DUST TREE
JAPANESE LAUREL
SPOTTED LAUREL
SHRUB   10 ft
ASIA   ALL YEAR

AVERRHOA
OXALIDACEAE

A fruit-bearing and highly ornamental tree for warm climates only, AVERRHOA prefers part-shade, an acid soil and regular water. The leaves are compounded of many leaflets, rather like Oxalis to which it is related. The red flowers often appear directly from the trunk; are followed by waxy, juicy five-cornered fruits, tasting rather like apricots. AVERRHOA fruit is particularly refreshing when chilled.

87   AVERRHOA carambola
FIVECORNER FRUIT
CARAMBOLA TREE
CARAMBOLE
TREE   20 ft
ASIA   ALL YEAR

88

90

92

89

91

93

AZALEA
ERICACEAE

Though botanists now class Azaleas as species of Rhododendron, we will stick to tradition and use the name everyone knows—Azalea. There is more to this decision than taste—the Azalea group thrive in a much wider climatic range than the other Rhododendrons, which are mostly mountain or cold climate plants. Azaleas, particularly the evergreen types, enjoy life anywhere the soil is light and acid—and even where it is not, they can be grown in containers. The Azaleas we grow are nearly all hybrids, cross-bred from literally dozens of species—but even so they fall into several main groups with differing habits and tastes. By far the most common are the evergreen Indica Azaleas, mostly pink, mauve or white, which grow up to 8 ft in height and width. But Indicas include two other groups: The Belgian Hybrid Indicas, mostly double, in a wider colour range and reaching only 3 ft; and the late-flowering Gumpos which rarely reach 10 in and are used as ground cover.
The second most common group are the Kurume Azaleas—dainty mountain plants most often used in rockeries.

These flower in both spring and autumn and a proportion of the leaves colour in winter.
Third are the perfumed Mollis Azaleas, with flowers including yellow and orange tones. Fourth are the deciduous Ghent hybrids, with twiggier growth and smaller pointed flowers that include cream, scarlet and flame tones. Mollis and Ghent type Azaleas prefer a cooler climate and rarely survive long in coastal gardens.
All Azaleas are shallow rooters and must be planted quite firmly to prevent wind damage. The Indica types are often disfigured by lacefly, which can be controlled by spraying *under* the leaves in warm weather with D.D.T. The other principal problem is Azalea blight, a fungus which causes the flowers to rot in humid weather. Spray regularly with Zineb and destroy all affected flowers.

88   AZALEA indica (massed)
Varieties 'Magnifica', 'Splendens', 'Alba Magna'

89   AZALEA indica 'Alphonse Anderson'
INDIAN AZALEA
SHRUB   6 ft
HYBRID   SPRING

90   AZALEA indica 'Magnifica'
SHRUB   6 ft
HYBRID   SPRING

91   AZALEA indica 'Gretel'
SHRUB   4 ft
HYBRID   SPRING

92   AZALEA kurume 'Rose Queen'
KURUME AZALEA
SHRUB   2 ft
JAPAN   SPRING

93   AZALEA mollis
MOLLIS AZALEA
SHRUB   6 ft
HYBRID   SPRING

94

95

94 AZALEA indica 'White Gumpo'
GUMPO AZALEA
SHRUB 10 in
JAPAN SPRING

BABIANA
IRIDACEAE

The fragrant Baboon Flower (because
Baboons dig and eat the bulbs in its
native Africa) adds a useful range of blue
and violet tones to the spring bulb
spectrum. The flowers resemble Freesias
but the leaves are strongly pleated and
hairy. BABIANA bulbs are planted in
autumn in sandy soil; require plenty of
water in winter and at flowering time.

95 BABIANA stricta
BABOON FLOWER
BABOON ROOT
BULB 12 in
SOUTH AFRICA SPRING

96

97

99

98

100

BACKHOUSIA
MYRTACEAE
A slim, elegant tree from Australia's coastal rain forests, BACKHOUSIA is a slow grower but extremely tough. Plant it in open sun, but with shrubby shade for the roots. The dense, glossy foliage is strongly lemon scented, and the small greenish-white flowers appear in dense clusters during early summer, lasting for weeks. A rich mulch about the roots and plenty of water are beneficial.

96   BACKHOUSIA citriodora
**SWEET VERBENA TREE
LEMON SCENTED MYRTLE
LEMON SCENTED VERBENA
TREE   30 ft
NORTHERN AUSTRALIA   SUMMER
SUBTROPICAL**

BANKSIA
PROTEACEAE

Spectacularly flowering shrubs and small trees as unique to Australia as are the Proteas to South Africa—both families being closely related. There are almost 50 Banksia species; all enjoying a warm position in sandy acid soil, enriched with leafmould. They can be planted virtually any time of year, are mostly slow-growing, and flower largely around winter. Banksia flowers dry well and are popular in arrangements. The leaves too are interesting, mostly shiny above, hairy beneath, and very deeply serrated. Colours vary from greenish-white through yellow and orange to scarlet; many with stamens in contrasting white, brown, red or purple.

97   BANKSIA coccinea
**SCARLET BANKSIA
SHRUB   8 ft
WESTERN AUSTRALIA   WINTER**

98   BANKSIA collina
**HAIRPIN HONEYSUCKLE
SHRUB   6 ft
EASTERN AUSTRALIA   SPRING**

99   BANKSIA ericifolia
**HEATH BANKSIA
SHRUB   10 ft
NEW SOUTH WALES   AUTUMN**

100   BANKSIA integrifolia
**COAST BANKSIA
TREE   20 ft
EASTERN AUSTRALIA   ALL YEAR**

101

102

BARLERIA
ACANTHACEAE

Neither a violet, nor from the Philippines, this charming evergreen shrub will not flower well more than 30° away from the equator. It enjoys summer humidity, dry winters and an acid soil rich with compost and manure. Both white and pale mauve flowered varieties are available, and in the tropics BARLERIA is often seen trimmed into a hedge. It propagates easily from cuttings under glass.

101   BARLERIA cristata
PHILIPPINE VIOLET
SHRUB   3 ft
INDIA   SUMMER
TROPICAL

BAUERA
SAXIFRAGACEAE

BAUERA hates lime in any form, and in its native state is usually found clinging to the sandy peaty soil of mountain stream banks. In cultivation, it prefers much the same conditions, but will take more sun. BAUERAS propagate easily from cuttings and flower lightly the year around. In spring they are a mass of delicate six-petalled pink flowers.

102   BAUERA rubioides
RIVER ROSE
SHOWY BAUERA
SHRUB   2 ft
NEW SOUTH WALES   SPRING

103

105

107

104

106

108

BAUHINIA
LEGUMINOSAE

Showiest members of the pea family, Bauhinias are magnificent when well grown, their bare branches covered in great flowers like tropic orchids. Warm climate trees, they will adapt to mild winter areas where the soil is sandy and acid. As Bauhinias are inclined to grow with multiple trunks, a good deal of pruning and training is required if a neat tree is your wish. Mauve BAUHINIA variegata and its white variety 'Candida' are first to flower in late winter; followed by the shrubby pink B. monandra in early spring. B. galpinii (more of a woody climber) and B. tomentosa follow in summer. The cycle comes full turn in autumn when B. blakeana bursts into spectacular red and violet blossom. All Bauhinias look raggy for awhile after flowering, decked with untidy brown pea pods, but these soon fall and the trees are clothed again with green butterfly-shaped leaves.

103 BAUHINIA punctata (syn. galpinii)
RED BAUHINIA
SHRUB 6 ft
AFRICA SUMMER

104 BAUHINIA tomentosa
YELLOW BAUHINIA
SHRUB 6 ft
CEYLON SPRING

105 BAUHINIA variegata
MOUNTAIN EBONY
PURPLE ORCHID TREE
TREE 20 ft
INDIA SPRING

106 BAUHINIA variegata 'Candida'
WHITE ORCHID TREE
TREE 30 ft
INDIA SPRING

BEGONIA
BEGONIACEAE

A particularly large genus with at least 300 species and a myriad of varieties, the Begonias are succulents which in some cases have developed a tuberous root system. Their striking leaf shapes and colours have endeared them to gardeners everywhere. The dainty Bedding Begonia is used for mass planting in shades of white, pink and red. Gorgeous BEGONIA tuberhybrida is a splendid glasshouse plant with large rose-like flowers of every colour. It is planted in spring, and there is a hanging variety 'Pendula' which cascades over the sides of hanging baskets. The tall Angel Wing type (B. coccinea) has bamboo-like canes with spotted leaves and coral flowers all year. Hybrids between the many forms are legion, mostly valued for the leaves. These include the superbly translucent maple leaves of B. X 'Cleopatra' patterned in green and chocolate.

107 BEGONIA X 'Cleopatra'
PERENNIAL 12 in
HYBRID SPRING

109

111

112

110

108　BEGONIA coccinea
ANGEL WING BEGONIA
PERENNIAL　to 15 ft
BRAZIL　ALL YEAR

109　BEGONIA semperflorens
'Tausendschoen'
BEDDING BEGONIA
PERENNIAL　10 in
BRAZIL　AUTUMN

110　BEGONIA tuberhybrida
TUBEROUS BEGONIA
PERENNIAL　2½ ft
SOUTH AMERICA　AUTUMN

111　BEGONIA tuberhybrida
'Pendula'
BASKET BEGONIA
TUBER　3 ft
SOUTH AMERICA　AUTUMN

BELLIS
COMPOSITAE

The old-fashioned English lawn daisies
have been increased in size and colour-
range through the efforts of hybridizers
and now make a worthwhile subject for
the low border or rock garden. Spring
flowering, they need the moisture and
good soil of their native meadows to
flower heavily. Plant out in early winter
for spring colour in the bulb season.

112　BELLIS perennis
LAWN DAISY
ENGLISH DAISY
ANNUAL　6 in
EUROPE　SPRING

BELOPERONE

113

BERBERIS

114

115

BERGENIA

116

BELOPERONE
ACANTHACEAE

Nature was working overtime as a mimic when she designed this flower, for a bush in full bloom really does appear to be festooned with prawns. The pinkish-brown petal forms are actually bracts and the tiny white flowers are almost hidden among them. BELOPERONE is a weak sprawling plant and needs regular cutting back. Any warm sunny position suits it.

113   BELOPERONE guttata
(syn. DREJERELLA)
SHRIMP PLANT
PRAWN PLANT
SHRUB   3 ft
MEXICO   SPRING-SUMMER

BERBERIS
BERBERIDACEAE

No less than 480 species of these colourful cool-climate shrubs have been recorded from the northern and southern hemispheres. There are both deciduous and evergreen types and as a general rule they have sharp spines, gay yellow flowers in spring and attractive berries in autumn. They are at their best in colder districts where the autumn colouring develops and will survive in extraordinary soil conditions. Most Barberries are pruned heavily in winter, otherwise they tend to die in the centre and become untidy. BERBERIS thunbergii 'Artropurpurea' has dark purple foliage, changing to scarlet in autumn. It is often used as a low hedge.

114   BERBERIS darwinii
DARWIN BARBERRY
SHRUB   6 ft
CHILE   SPRING-AUTUMN

115   BERBERIS vulgaris
COMMON BARBERRY
SHRUB   6 ft
EUROPE   SPRING—AUTUMN

BERGENIA
SAXIFRAGACEAE

Useful winter cut flowers, BERGENIAS grow easily in almost any soil, but improve wonderfully with compost-rich loam, regular watering and part-shade with morning sun. They should also be divided every year or so as they develop leggy stems and become shy of flowering. There are white, pink and rose varieties, all with large glossy foliage which makes a useful pattern all year.

116   BERGENIA cordifolia
MEGASEA
SAXIFRAGA
HEARTLEAF BERGENIA
PERENNIAL   12 in
SIBERIA   WINTER

BILLBERGIA

117

BIXA

119

BLANDFORDIA

120

118

BILLBERGIA
BROMELIACEAE

Most popular genus in the Bromeliad or Pineapple family, BILLBERGIAS are perfectly reliable in the open warm climate garden or indoors. They flourish in ordinary soil, on trees or as a spectacular ground cover in filtered shade, increasing by suckers produced after flowering. BILLBERGIA nutans (the Queen's Tears) is most popular, flowering with pendant sprays of green and navy blossom that are useful for cutting. More spectacular is B. pyramidalis which shoots up dense spikes of scarlet, violet and bright pink flowers from a three-foot, vase-shaped leaf cluster. As BILLBERGIAS are really epiphytic it is possible to keep the entire plant indoors for decoration and freshen it up merely by filling the leaf hollow with water.

117   BILLBERGIA nutans
QUEEN'S TEARS
BROMELIAD   18 in
SOUTH AMERICA   SUMMER

118   BILLBERGIA pyramidalis
PERENNIAL   3 ft
BRAZIL   AUTUMN
BOTH   TROPICAL

BIXA
BIXACEAE

The red seeds of this ornamental shrub provide a dye for colouring many food-stuffs and are used by native women as lip colouring. BIXA likes rich acid soil and plenty of water, and can be raised from cuttings. It flowers well in a semi-tropical climate where the orchid-pink flowers open in hot weather. The seed pods are used in dried arrangements.

119   BIXA orellana
ANNATTO TREE
LIPSTICK PLANT
SHRUB   20 ft
WEST INDIES   SUMMER
TROPICAL

BLANDFORDIA
LILIACEAE

This colourful Australian bulb is popular in many countries, preferring acid soil with a high sand content. Plant in autumn and increase the water supply as the wiry leaves appear. After flowering, let them dry out. BLANDFORDIAS are propagated by seeds or offsets and the colours include crimson, orange or yellow. The illustrated variety is BLAND-FORDIA nobilis 'Imperialis', most vivid of all.

120   BLANDFORDIA nobilis
CHRISTMAS BELLS
BULB   2 ft
NEW SOUTH WALES   SUMMER
SUBTROPICAL

121

122

BLETILLA
ORCHIDACEAE

Like miniature florists' Cattleyas, BLET-ILLAS are charming ground orchids for the open garden, easily grown in the shelter of large shrubs. Rampant growers for their size, spreading rapidly from snail-shaped tubers, they do best in a compost of peat and leafmould with sharp sand for drainage. Plenty of water except in winter when they are dormant. Grow BLETILLAS in large Azalea pots.

121   BLETILLA striata
CHINESE GROUND ORCHID
BULB   12 in
CHINA   SPRING

BOMAREA
AMARYLLIDACEAE

Next time you see Alstroemeria flowers hanging on a vine, don't rush for the aspirin. Odds are you just saw a BOMAREA. There are 50-odd varieties, all propagated from divisions of the underground stem or tuber, and romping in a well-drained compost of leafmould and sand. They will grow in the green-house or outdoors in partial shade.

122   BOMAREA shuttleworthii
CLIMBING ALSTROEMERIA
CLIMBING PERENNIAL   6 ft
COLOMBIA   SPRING

BORAGO

123

BORONIA

124

125

126

BORAGO
BORAGINACEAE

Really a herb, grown for the cucumberish taste of its leaves in Pimm's No. 1 Cup, Borage is also an attractive summer bedding plant, resembling giant furry Forget-me-nots. It grows in sun or shade, even with poor soil, and is sometimes used as a soil binder in sandy areas. Borage is best grown directly from seed, as it does not transplant well.

123 BORAGO officinalis
BORAGE
ANNUAL 2½ ft
MEDITERRANEAN SUMMER

BORONIA
RUTACEAE

Dainty Australian natives that are somewhat difficult to grow away from their natural bushland, Boronias must have a sandy acid soil that drains quickly; and yet is sufficiently rich in humus that it never dries out. Best-known species is the short-lived chartreuse and brown Western Australian Boronia which spreads an unforgettable perfume in early spring; but there are several dozen others worth growing, including BORONIA ledifolia which bears spicily fragrant pink star flowers in winter, and B. serrulata (the Native Rose) with fragrant deep pink flowers now heavily protected in their native habitat. All species will live longer if pruned by cutting the flowers.

124 BORONIA ledifolia
SYDNEY BORONIA
SHRUB 2½ ft
EASTERN AUSTRALIA WINTER

125 BORONIA megastigma 'Chandleri'
BROWN BORONIA
WEST AUSTRALIAN BORONIA
SHRUB 4 ft
WESTERN AUSTRALIA SPRING

126 BORONIA purdeiana
SHRUB 3 ft
WESTERN AUSTRALIA SPRING

127

128

129

130

131

BOUGAINVILLEA
NYCTAGINACEAE

Hardy evergreen vines for warm climates (within 30° of the equator). Bougain-villeas are decked with dazzling flower bracts throughout the warm weather. Rampant growers, they do best on walls facing the sun with strong support; but can be pruned heavily and trained to any shape—even as standard trees. Propagate from cuttings but transplant with care, as they resent root disturbance. BOUGAINVILLEA sanderiana is the common magenta type, but the many hybrids of B. spectabilis have the show-iest bracts. There are named varieties in white, yellow, orange, scarlet, deep red and rose. Cut back long shoots to avoid damage from the vicious thorns.

127 BOUGAINVILLEA glabra
'Sanderiana'
SANDERS BOUGAINVILLEA
SHRUBBY VINE 30 ft
BRAZIL SUMMER

128 BOUGAINVILLEA glabra
'Variegata'
VARIEGATED BOUGAINVILLEA
SHRUBBY CLIMBER 20 ft
BRAZIL SUMMER

129 BOUGAINVILLEA spectabilis
REMARKABLE BOUGAINVILLEA
ROSE BOUGAINVILLEA
SHRUBBY CLIMBER 20 ft
BRAZIL SUMMER
ALL SUBTROPICAL

BOUVARDIA
RUBIACEAE

Often misunderstood, and with a difficult reputation, Bouvardias are really easy to grow in sheltered places with good soil. As they are from Central America, they cannot stand frosts—also they will always be untidy unless you cut them back almost to the ground after flowering and pinch back regularly. Whatever you do, only the white species BOUVARDIA longiflora will ever develop that sweet Bouvardia perfume. The coloured types are scentless hybrids of quite a different species, B. ternifolia. These coloured hybrids (of which there are at least 20 named varieties) are easier to grow than the white type.

130 BOUVARDIA ternifolia
BOUVARDIA
SHRUB 2 ft
CENTRAL AMERICA SPRING

131 BOUVARDIA longiflora
SCENTED BOUVARDIA
WHITE BOUVARDIA
SHRUB 3 ft
MEXICO SPRING

BRACHYCHITON

132

134

BRASSAIA

135

133

BRACHYCHITON
STERCULIACEAE

Most noble and spectacular of Australian flowering trees, the BRACHYCHITONS are native to the lush rain forests of the eastern coast. They grow well in the average garden, though only to a fraction of full jungle height, and are extremely erratic in flowering. But the season after a hot wet summer—an unbelievably beautiful sight! The pyramid-shaped Illawarra Flame (BRACHYCHITON acerifolium) is the most brilliant, dropping its large maple-like leaves in late spring as it becomes decked with vivid scarlet bell-flowers. B. bidwillii is smaller (to 20 ft), almost completely evergreen with larger deep rose bells. Deciduous B. discolor is a giant of more spreading habit, its dull pink flowers covered with brownish fur on the outside. B. populneum has small leaves which vary widely in shape and becomes a mass of greenish-white spotted bells. It is at home in quite desert conditions—even in alkaline soil—and the leaves are sometimes used for cattle fodder. The Bottle Tree (B. rupestre) develops an enormous trunk girth of up to 30 ft.

132   BRACHYCHITON acerifolium
ILLAWARRA FLAME
TREE   40–100 ft
NEW SOUTH WALES–QUEENSLAND
SPRING

133   BRACHYCHITON discolor
WHITE KURRAJONG
QUEENSLAND LACEBARK
PINK FLAME TREE
TREE   20–80 ft
NORTHERN AUSTRALIA   SUMMER

134   BRACHYCHITON populneum
KURRAJONG
TREE   30 ft
EASTERN AUSTRALIA
LATE SPRING

BRASSAIA
ARALIACEAE

From Queensland's rain forest comes this striking summer-blooming tree, much favoured in tropical gardens everywhere. The heavily divided leaves unfold exactly like green umbrellas, and red-flowered spikes appear in radiating groups like octopus tentacles, the individual flowers having the appearance of suckers. BRASSAIA will grow in any frost-free district, in deep rich soil, and strikes easily from large cuttings.

135   BRASSAIA actinophylla
QUEENSLAND UMBRELLA TREE
OCTOPUS TREE
TREE   30 ft
QUEENSLAND   SUMMER

BRASSICA

136

BRASSOCATTLEYA

137

BREYNIA

138

BRASSICA
CRUCIFERAE

Only a cabbage in fancy dress really, and no better smelling than the edible variety, the Ornamental Kale brings wonderfully subtle colour combinations to the winter garden, and helps inspire unusual floral arrangements. Raise the seed in boxes in late summer and plant out in the autumn, 12 in apart. Give them plenty of water and spray regularly against caterpillars.

136   BRASSICA oleracea
'Acephala Crispa'
ORNAMENTAL KALE
ANNUAL   2 ft
EUROPE   WINTER

BRASSOCATTLEYA
ORCHIDACEAE

BRASSOCATTLEYAS are possibly the most beautiful of all orchids — hybrids between the two species of Brassavola and Cattleya. They are strictly glasshouse plants except in the sub-tropics; though are often displayed indoors when they bloom. Light humidity and a minimum night temperature of 55°F are essential. Epiphytic by nature they are usually grown in heavy pots filled with coarse chips of fir bark and other organic matter.

137   BRASSOCATTLEYA X 'Enid'
ORCHID   15 in
HYBRID   SUMMER

BREYNIA
EUPHORBIACEAE

Useful for bedding or the warm-climate shrubbery, the delicate Leaf Flower of the Pacific Islands is charming at any time of year, given protection from cold and drying winds. As with many island plants, the leaves and stems are more colourful than the flowers and berries. BREYNIA likes a sandy loam with plenty of old fertilizer and is easily increased by root cuttings.

138   BREYNIA nivosa 'Roseo-Picta'
SNOW BUSH
LEAF FLOWER
SHRUB   3 ft
PACIFIC ISLANDS   ALL YEAR

BROWNEA

139

BRUNFELSIA

140

BRYOPHYLLUM

141

BROWNEA
LEGUMINOSAE

A small group of trees and shrubs from tropical America with a deserved popularity in warm climate gardens. The flamboyant Rose of Venezuela (BROWNEA grandiceps) is a bushy tree with drooping leaves that hide enormous clusters of orange flowers resembling Rhododendrons. These can be seen properly only from below. BROWNEAS like deep rich acid soil, semi-shade and resent watering in winter.

139   BROWNEA grandiceps
ROSE OF VENEZUELA
GLORY FLAMBEAU
TREE   30 ft
VENEZUELA   SPRING
TROPICAL

BRUNFELSIA
SOLANACEAE

Handsome evergreen shrubs for the frost-free garden, BRUNFELSIAS take on a multi-coloured appearance in spring and summer. The fragrant flowers, which open violet, fade to pale blue and finally white on successive days. Soil should be rich, acid and with good drainage, while both flowers and foliage are seen at their best in a semi-shaded location.

140   BRUNFELSIA calycina 'Floribunda'
BRAZIL RAINTREE
YESTERDAY, TODAY AND TOMORROW
SHRUB   6 ft
BRAZIL   SPRING
SUBTROPICAL

BRYOPHYLLUM
CRASSULACEAE

The name BRYOPHYLLUM means simply 'sprouting leaves', and that is just what this succulent plant does. Drop a waxy leaf in a damp place and bingo! You have a new plant in no time. In warm climates they could almost be considered a pest if it were not for the beautiful waxy red flowers which shoot up on tall stems in winter—just when cut flowers are most scarce. The Bryophyllums are also called KALANCHOE (which see).

141   BRYOPHYLLUM tubiflorum
FRIENDLY NEIGHBOUR
SUCCULENT   2½ ft
MADAGASCAR   WINTER

BUDDLEIA

142

143

BUTEA

144

BUDDLEIA
LOGANIACEAE

Evergreen in warm climates, deciduous in cold, the vigorous Buddleias or Butterfly Bushes need only water and good drainage to grow like weeds. The fragrant spikes of tiny golden-throated flowers (white, purple, crimson or orange according to variety) appear at various times from winter to autumn. Silvery, sage-like BUDDLEIA salvifolia becomes almost tree-like, its branches weighed down by flowers in winter and spring. B. davidii has a more upright habit, blooms in summer and autumn and should be cut back to at least half height after flowering. The Buddleias really do attract butterflies from far and wide— but where there are butterflies, there are caterpillars; so a regular spraying is advisable.

142   BUDDLEIA davidii
BUTTERFLY BUSH
SUMMER LILAC
SHRUB   10 ft
CHINA   SUMMER

143   BUDDLEIA salvifolia
SAGE LEAF BUDDLEIA
SHRUB   15 ft
SOUTH AFRICA   WINTER

BUTEA
LEGUMINOSAE

A gorgeous flowering tree for warm districts, BUTEA is extremely hardy, especially in coastal areas, where it is often mistaken for an Erythrina (See: ERYTHRINA). BUTEA grows slowly however, and develops an exotic contorted shape. The flowers vary from crimson to a pale orange scarlet and appear on the bare branches in spring. They are a useful source of orange dye.

144   BUTEA frondosa
DHAK TREE
PULAS TREE
FLAME OF THE FOREST
TREE   50 ft
EAST INDIES   SUMMER

CAESALPINIA

145

CALADIUM

146

CALATHEA

147

CAESALPINIA
LEGUMINOSAE

Long spikes of flaming scarlet and yellow blossom hovering above a mass of pale fern-like foliage—and anywhere in the warmer parts you know brilliant Barbadoes Pride. So universally is it cultivated the original home is unknown. Long red stamens and the flat green pods of the pea family are other points that identify this graceful spiky plant. Grow it from seed and give shelter in subtropical climates.

145 CAESALPINIA pulcherrima
BARBADOES PRIDE
BARBADOES FLOWER FENCE
DWARF POINCIANA
SHRUB 12 ft
TROPICS SUMMER

CALADIUM
ARACEAE

The leaf shape clearly identifies Caladiums as members of the Arum family. Tuberous-rooted perennials from tropical America, they die down in winter and are grown purely for the spectacular summer leaf colours which include silver, white, pink, red, bronze and green in psychedelic combination. Caladiums like warm shade and light humidity and do well indoors or in a sheltered courtyard. Regular fertilization improves both leaf colour and size.

146 CALADIUM bicolor
FANCYLEAF CALADIUM
TUBEROUS PERENNIAL 2½ ft
SOUTH AMERICA SUMMER
TROPICAL

CALATHEA
MARANTACEAE

A spectacularly beautiful plant grown solely for its leaf colourings—outdoors as ground cover in the semi-tropics—indoors elsewhere. There are over 100 species, each worth knowing. CALATHEA makoyana has iridescent leaves, patterned in cream and olive coloured ovals, with the reverse in matching patterns of mauve, pink and grey. CALATHEAS need a warm moist atmosphere and repotting every summer.

147 CALATHEA makoyana
ZEBRA PLANT
PEACOCK PLANT
PERENNIAL 2 ft
BRAZIL SUMMER

CALCEOLARIA

CALENDULA

148

149

150

CALCEOLARIA
SCROPHULARIACEAE

An interesting genus of 200 species, CALCEOLARIAS do not like frost; do best in the cool greenhouse or garden shade, preferably in a pot. CALCEOLARIA crenatiflora is the popular conservatory variety, with one-inch flowers borne in groups and startlingly coloured in red, orange, yellow and buff. The soft felty leaves grow to 8 in. Related C. integrifolia is a more versatile plant, with brilliant yellow half-inch, puff-ball flowers crowded all over during the warmer weather. It enjoys heat, but will stand a mild frost too. Grow it in a hanging basket, a pot, or the open garden: indoors or out it flowers best when the going is a little crowded. Originally from Chile, it is widely grown for the attractive leaves, wrinkled above, rusty-felty below.

148   CALCEOLARIA crenatiflora
PERENNIAL   18 in
CHILE   SUMMER

149   CALCEOLARIA integrifolia
LADIES' PURSES
SUB-SHRUB   4 ft
CHILOE   SPRING-AUTUMN

CALENDULA
COMPOSITAE

Native to Southern Europe, the Pot Marigold is one of the most reliable of annuals; and when established will seed and reappear for years. It varies considerably both in the size and 'doubling' of the flowers, and also in their colours, which include orange and yellow, and softer variations in cream, lemon and apricot. Most effective planted in a single colour, CALENDULAS are happy in any position, provided the drainage is good.

150   CALENDULA officinalis
POT MARIGOLD
SCOTCH MARIGOLD
ANNUAL   2 ft
MEDITERRANEAN   SUMMER

CALLIANDRA

151

152

CALLISTEMON

153

154

155

156

CALLIANDRA
LEGUMINOSAE

From South America, really spectacular members of the pea family—aptly named from the Greek 'Kallos' (beauty) and 'Andros' (stamens)—for the three-inch flowers are quite without petals. CALLIANDRA inaequilatera has red powder-puff flowers and metallic green leaves borne in pairs, each consisting of many leaflets. Like all peas, it needs much water and good drainage, and is too delicate for frosty areas. Similar CALLIANDRAS with smaller flowers and finer foliage are C. tweedii and C. eriophylla, while C. surinamensis has pink and white blossoms.

151   CALLIANDRA inaequilatera
FAIRY DUSTER
TASSEL FLOWER
SHRUB   10 ft
BOLIVIA   WINTER

152   CALLIANDRA surinamensis
PINK POWDER PUFF
SHRUB   6 ft
SURINAM   SPRING

CALLISTEMON
MYRTACEAE

An Australian family of evergreen shrubs and trees which have become popular in frost-free areas throughout the world. Generally somewhat weeping in habit, the branches are tipped in season with exciting brush-like flowers of red, pink, white, green or purple. From the ends of these, new leaves grow, by-passing a patch of woody seed capsules which remain for years. CALLISTEMON salignus is valued additionally for coppery-pink new leaves in spring—C. pinifolius for curious green or green-tipped red brushes. C. rigidus is spectacular and drought-resistant. C. citrinus is the best all-rounder, flowering heavily in dry or damp conditions—its close relative C. viminalis presents a fully weeping habit.

153   CALLISTEMON citrinus
CRIMSON BOTTLEBRUSH
LEMON BOTTLEBRUSH
SHRUB   15 ft
EASTERN AUSTRALIA   SPRING

154   CALLISTEMON pinifolius
GREEN BOTTLEBRUSH
SHRUB   8 ft
NEW SOUTH WALES   SPRING

155   CALLISTEMON salignus
PINK TIPS
WHITE BOTTLEBRUSH
WILLOWLEAF BOTTLEBRUSH
TREE   30 ft
EASTERN AUSTRALIA   SPRING

156   CALLISTEMON viminalis
WEEPING BOTTLEBRUSH
SHRUB   12 ft
EASTERN AUSTRALIA   SPRING

157

158

CALLISTEPHUS
COMPOSITAE

Favourite annuals for midsummer colour, the China Asters are easy to grow in any soil in full sun. Three-inch flowers vary all through the purples and mauves to white and up through the pinks to crimson. The flowers come in many types, single, double, crested and curled. Set out plants in early summer, do not overwater and do not plant in the same place 2 years in a row. They make splendid cut flowers.

157   CALLISTEPHUS chinensis
CHINA ASTER
ANNUAL ASTER
ANNUAL   2 ft
CHINA   SUMMER

CALODENDRON
RUTACEAE

One of the showiest warm climate trees, native to South Africa, the CALODENDRON is inclined to vary widely both in its flowering and leaf dropping times. The flower panicles, borne high in early summer, consist of many one-and-a-half-inch spotted blossoms varying from pink through white to a rosy lilac shade. Slow to grow, its shiny green leaves are always attractive in a sheltered position, but watch out for white wax scale.

158   CALODENDRON capense
CAPE CHESTNUT
TREE   50 ft
SOUTH AFRICA   SUMMER

159

160

CALOSTEMMA
AMARYLLIDACEAE

An uncommon Australian native bulb, easily grown in a compost of sand and leafmould, the **CALOSTEMMA** is perfectly hardy outdoors. The wiry leaves resemble those of the Kangaroo Paw, and tall stems bear clusters of red-violet flowers something like the Agapanthus. These open gradually over a period of weeks. Water, while the flowers are developing, is its only vice.

159   CALOSTEMMA purpurea
BULB   2½ ft
AUSTRALIA   SUMMER

CALOTHAMNUS
MYRTACEAE

Untidy in growth, never truly spectacular, the hardy CALOTHAMNUS genus is useful wherever climatic conditions simulate their home deserts of Western Australia. Highly drought-resistant, they can be relied on in poor soil, or wherever sun, wind and salt are a problem. Of many species, CALOTHAMNUS villosus and C. quadrifidus are best, but should be pruned hard after flowering.

160   CALOTHAMNUS quadrifidus
NET BUSH
ONE SIDED BOTTLEBRUSH
SHRUB   6 ft
WESTERN AUSTRALIA   ALL YEAR

161

163

165

162

164

166

CAMELLIA
THEACEAE

Interest in the CAMELLIA genus can become tantamount to flower worship, as the existence of many CAMELLIA Societies will testify. Small wonder, for the genus includes upwards of 2,500 exquisite named varieties in a number of species. Flowering begins in autumn, with the delicate, fast-growing CAMEL-LIA sasanqua; continues into winter with C. hiemalis. Then the main flush of C. japonica begins, lasting well into late spring with a staggering variety of shape and colour. To many, the climax is reached when the enormous C. reticulata opens flowers up to 9 in across. CAMELLIAS are not hard to grow provided the soil is acid, well-drained and rich in organic material. Where there is any doubt about these conditions, grow them in tubs of prepared compost. Keep the roots cool and moist in hot weather, and protect the delicate blooms with semi-shade. Many experts suggest you do not plant CAMELLIAS where the morning sun can evaporate the dew, thus scorching the flowers. As they mostly originate from the mountains of China, Korea and Japan, CAMELLIAS are quite tolerant of frost, but they also like mildly humid conditions and appreciate a light leaf-spray with lukewarm water. Finally, do not hesitate to cut CAMELLIAS and enjoy their beauty indoors—this light pruning improves branching and growth.

161   CAMELLIA japonica 'The Czar'
SHRUB   12 ft
JAPAN   WINTER

162   CAMELLIA japonica 'Giulio Nucchio'
SHRUB   8 ft
JAPAN   SPRING

163   CAMELLIA japonica 'Margaret Davis'
SHRUB   8 ft
HYBRID   SPRING

164   CAMELLIA magnoliaeflora
SHRUB   10 ft
KOREA   SPRING

165   CAMELLIA reticulata X 'Captain Rawes'
TREE   35 ft
CHINA   SPRING

166   CAMELLIA sasanqua
SHRUB   12 ft
JAPAN   AUTUMN

167

168

170

169

167 CAMELLIA X williamsii 'Margaret Waterhouse'
SHRUB 12 ft
CHINA SPRING

CAMPANULA
CAMPANULACEAE

CAMPANULAS (or Bellflowers) belong to a group of almost 250 species, mostly differing widely in size and shape, but all providing a welcome range of blue tones for every part of the garden. All the popular species except one (See CAM-PANULA medium) are perennials, and almost all of them are found wild in Northern Europe. Species include the trailing C. isophylla (Star of Bethlehem), valued for its pale blue star flowers in rockeries or hanging baskets; tiny C. muralis (the Dalmatian Bellflower), splendid in shady spots around walls and paths; C. persicifolia, (the Peachleafed Bluebell) with three-foot flower spikes, useful for groups in the border.

168 CAMPANULA carpatica
TUSSOCK BELLFLOWER
PERENNIAL 9 in
CARPATHIA SPRING

169 CAMPANULA medium
CANTERBURY BELLS
BIENNIAL 3 ft
SOUTHERN EUROPE SUMMER

170 CAMPANULA poscharskyana
SERBIAN BELLFLOWER
PERENNIAL 6 in
DALMATIA SPRING

171

172

174

173

CAMPSIS
BIGNONIACEAE

Sometimes known (incorrectly) as either Tecoma or Bignonia, this handsome creeper will cling to almost any surface and is useful for fast cover. Brick, wood and other plants all give generous support. The dark shining pinnate leaves are attractive in themselves, and the flowers appear in a cluster at the end of new shoots, persisting almost to winter in warmer areas. It is quite frost-resistant

171 CAMPSIS chinensis
CHINESE TRUMPET CREEPER
TRUMPET VINE
CLIMBER 40 ft
CHINA SUMMER

CANNA
CANNACEAE

Popularly named for its hard round seeds which are very difficult to germinate unless soaked or filed through; this useful perennial brings a touch of the tropics to any garden with brilliant green or bronze leaves and dazzling range of flower colours—scarlet, orange, yellow, white, pink and cream in single tones or mottled and spotted variations. In temperate climates Cannas can be planted out any time from divisions of the rhizomes; and this is the best way, for seed rarely comes true to type. Stems should in any case be cut right back to the ground when they have flowered. The Latin name, by the way, refers not to India, but to the West Indies, where the plants originate.

172 CANNA indica
(Massed display in Brisbane)

173 CANNA indica
INDIAN SHOT
RHIZOMATOUS PERENNIAL 6 ft
WEST INDIES SUMMER

174 CANNA indica 'Nana'
DWARF CANNA
RHIZOMATOUS PERENNIAL 2 ft
SOUTH AMERICA SUMMER

CAPSICUM

175

CARICA

176

CARPOBROTUS

177

CAPSICUM
SOLANACEAE

Valued more for their pungent fruits than the insignificant white flowers, many varieties of the CAPSICUM family are grown in warmer climate gardens or as greenhouse specimens in cooler districts. As a general rule, the varieties with the smallest pods have the hottest taste and are valued for home pickling or eating with curries. Sow seeds indoors in winter, under heat and gradually harden before planting outdoors in spring.

175   CAPSICUM annuum var. Fasciculatum
CHILLI
CAYENNE PEPPER
RED PEPPER
PERENNIAL   2 ft
AUTUMN

CARICA
CARICACEAE

Though botanically an exotic tropical plant (from South America), the Paw Paw can be grown (and fruited) surprisingly well if positioned by a sun-drenched wall. And in this position they are often used as specimen plants because of their tall straight trunks and large leaves. Though easy to raise from seed or cuttings, trees of both sexes are needed for fruiting. The easy way out is to buy a grafted bi-sexual variety.

176   CARICA papaya
PAPAYA
PAW PAW
TREE   20 ft
SOUTH AMERICA   SUMMER

CARPOBROTUS
AIZOACEAE

CARPOBROTUS is a curious genus of coarse trailing perennials, particularly useful for binding sandy soil, or as ground cover in seaside holiday homes. Plant from cuttings 2 ft apart for quick cover and water while growing. The magenta flowers are spectacular and quite fragrant, the three-sided succulent leaves are green and decorative at all times of the year.

177   CARPOBROTUS chilensis
SEA FIG
SUCCULENT   12 in
AMERICAN WEST COAST   SUMMER

178

180

182

179

181

CASSIA
LEGUMINOSAE

Fast-growing shrubs and trees from the old and new world, Cassias glow golden in warm gardens everywhere. CASSIA corymbosa, (the Buttercup Tree) is most widely cultivated for its butter-yellow clusters of one-and-a-half-inch flowers. These have a curious musty smell which is objectionable to some. C. fistula is one of the loveliest tropical trees, though hardy in any frost-free district. Its great beauty is in the long chains of purest yellow flowers, borne in hot weather and attractive to butterflies. These are followed by remarkable two-foot seed pods which are used in many medicines. C. multijuga is another tree; this time from Brazil, and valued for its fast growth and flowering in the second year from seed. C. artemisioides is one of several native Australian Cassias, particularly suited to dry districts.

178   CASSIA artemisioides
FEATHERY CASSIA
SILVERY CASSIA
OLD MAN SENNA BUSH
SHRUB   6 ft
AUSTRALIA   WINTER

179   CASSIA corymbosa
BUTTERCUP TREE
SCRAMBLED EGGS
SHRUB   10 ft
TROPICAL AMERICA   SPRING

180   CASSIA fistula
GOLDEN SHOWER
INDIAN LABURNUM
PUDDING PIPE TREE
TREE   25 ft
INDIA–CEYLON   SUMMER

181   CASSIA multijuga
CALCEOLARIA SHOWER
TREE   20 ft
BRAZIL   AUTUMN

CASTANOSPERMUM
LEGUMINOSAE

This splendid evergreen Australian tree is named because of the likeness of its fruits to the European chestnut. The Aboriginals were reputed to eat them, but few modern Australians are prepared to follow their example. The dark trunk and leaves are impressive and in mid-summer clusters of orange and yellow flowers appear all over, even from the main trunk. CASTANOSPERMUM will flourish in all but the coldest areas.

182   CASTANOSPERMUM australe
SPANISH CHESTNUT
MORETON BAY CHESTNUT
TREE   60 ft
NEW SOUTH WALES   SUMMER

CASUARINA

183

CATALPA

184

CATANANCHE

185

CASUARINA
CASUARINACEAE

A family of trees from tropical Australia and the South Pacific, CASUARINAS are now seen all over the world, where-ever the going is tough. They tolerate almost every soil condition; salt air, freezing and even desert heat. At a distance they resemble spidery pine trees, but close examination reveals that the 'needles' are really finely-jointed stems with the leaves reduced to pointed scales. The seed pods however are similar to a small cone.

183   CASUARINA stricta
SHEOKE
BEEFWOOD
IRONWOOD
HORSETAIL TREE
TREE   60 ft
AUSTRALIA   ALL YEAR

CATALPA
BIGNONIACEAE

America's Mississippi Valley is home to this fine spring-flowering tree; deci-duous, completely hardy in heat or cold. The downy leaves are large and evil-smelling when crushed; the flowers quite lovely frilly bells of whitish-pink with purple and yellow markings. The trees are inclined to branch heavily and young specimens are pruned to a single leader until 10 ft high.

184   CATALPA bignonioides
INDIAN BEAN
CIGAR TREE
TREE   60 ft
UNITED STATES OF AMERICA
SPRING

CATANANCHE
COMPOSITAE

From Southern Europe comes this useful 'everlasting' type of daisy; useful for drying and somewhat resembling the cornflower. CATANANCHES will grow in all climatic and soil conditions and are particularly successful in dry areas. Faded blooms should be removed promptly to prolong flowering. Propagation is by division or by seed in the case of yellow-flowered species CATANANCHE lutea (an annual).

185   CATANANCHE caerulea
CUPID'S DART
BLUE CUPIDONE
PERENNIAL   2 ft
SOUTHERN EUROPE   SUMMER

CATHARANTHUS

186

CATTLEYA

187

CEANOTHUS

188

CATHARANTHUS
APOCYNACEAE

Invaluable for summer-autumn colour in hot climates, the Madagascar Periwinkle bursts with bloom all through the warm season, whether the climate is dry or humid. It grows from seed or cuttings planted in late winter in warm climates and self-sows yearly when conditions are right. It looks very sad in winter away from the tropics. Popular varieties include the red-centred white 'Brighteyes' and rosy 'Coquette'.

186   CATHARANTHUS roseus
MADAGASCAR PERIWINKLE
VINCA ROSEA
PERENNIAL   2 ft
TROPICS   SUMMER

CATTLEYA
ORCHIDACEAE

Showiest of the orchids, CATTLEYAS include myriad varieties of size, shape and colour among their 40-odd species. Though native to South and Central America, they can be grown in quite moderate climates provided temperature can be kept up in winter. The key is the control of light (filtered), heat (60° or over) and humidity (50% or better). Grow them in porous pots filled with special compost or fir bark.

187   CATTLEYA X 'Mary Jane
Proebste'
ORCHID   2½ ft
ALL YEAR

CEANOTHUS
RHAMNACEAE

Every imaginable shade of blue, violet and purple can be found among the 40-odd species of Californian Lilac, glossy-leafed evergreen shrubs for a sheltered position. Regular feeding and plenty of water is appreciated, but CEANOTHUS is not averse to a dry summer, preferring it to humidity. Annual pruning is helpful in preventing top-heaviness, and the flowers are seen more effectively when placed against a background of greenery.

188   CEANOTHUS X hybrid
BLUE BLOSSOM
CALIFORNIA LILAC
WILD LILAC
SHRUB   4-10 ft
CALIFORNIA   SPRING

CEDRUS

189

190

CELMISIA

191

CELOSIA

192

193

CEDRUS
PINACEAE

Among the noblest of cone-bearing trees, the tall Cedars with broad weeping branches are successful where the soil is rich, and the sub-soil deep—but choose the position carefully, for they grow large indeed and pruning is not advisable. Many colour varieties are available of the two most popularly grown types, with the needles in many shades of silver, gold, blue, grey and bright green. CEDRUS atlantica (the Mount Atlas Cedar) has a stiff angular appearance. C. deodara (the Indian Cedar) develops a more graceful weeping habit. Both are very long-living trees and do not develop their mature flat-topped appearance for 40 years or more.

189   CEDRUS atlantica 'Glauca'
MOUNT ATLAS CEDAR
ATLANTIC CEDAR
TREE   80 ft
NORTH AFRICA   ALL YEAR

190   CEDRUS deodara
INDIAN CEDAR
DEODAR
TREE   60 ft
HIMALAYAS   ALL YEAR

CELMISIA
COMPOSITAE

A genus of 55-odd daisy species from Australia and New Zealand. Useful for the scree garden or sunny bank with well-drained acid soil in colder districts, CELMISIAS grow easily from cuttings. Set out in late winter or autumn. The silver-downy leaves are attractive at all times, the yellow-centred daisy flowers are white or purple according to variety.

191   CELMISIA longifolia
SNOW DAISY
PERENNIAL   18 in
AUSTRALIA—NEW ZEALAND
SUMMER

CELOSIA
AMARANTHACEAE

Fast-growing tropical annuals with showy flowers for hot summer climates. Raise them from spring-sown seeds and plant out in well-drained soil. Fertilize and water regularly until flower buds appear, and then cut down watering to stimulate flower development. CELOSIA argentea 'Pyramidalis' is the showy Prince of Wales Feathers in gold or glowing crimson. C. cristata (the lower-growing contorted Cockscomb) has a variety of pink, red and gold tones.

192   CELOSIA argentea 'Pyramidalis'
CHINESE WOOL FLOWER
PRINCE OF WALES FEATHERS
ANNUAL   18 in
TROPICAL ASIA   SUMMER

193   CELOSIA cristata
COCKSCOMB
ANNUAL   12 in
TROPICAL ASIA   SUMMER

CENTAUREA

194

CERASTIUM

195

CERATOPETALUM

196

CENTAUREA
COMPOSITAE

Best in cool districts, Cornflowers will do well in almost any climate provided the soil is on the alkaline side. (Use lime in acid soils.) Blue varieties are traditionally grown for use in arrangements or boutonnieres; but less attractive pink, white and crimson types are available. Plant in autumn or spring, and keep watch for both mildew and aphis, to which Cornflowers are particularly prone.

194   CENTAUREA cyanus
BACHELOR'S BUTTON
CORNFLOWER
BLUEBOTTLE
ANNUAL   2½ ft
EUROPE   SPRING-SUMMER

CERASTIUM
CARYOPHYLLACEAE

A fast-growing blanket of silver for ground cover or rockery, CERASTIUM is planted from divisions in autumn, and may spread to 3 ft in a single year. Cold climate or hot, it enjoys them both; any soil will do so long as the position is well-drained. Water regularly and scatter packaged fertilizer twice a year. The snowy-white flowers appear in early summer, so densely they sometimes hide the plant itself.

195   CERASTIUM tomentosum
SNOW IN SUMMER
PERENNIAL   6 in
SOUTHERN EUROPE   SUMMER

CERATOPETALUM
SAXIFRAGACEAE

Of great sentimental interest in New South Wales, where its colouring signals the approach of the holiday season, CERATOPETALUM is a beautiful garden tree for any well-drained position, particularly in sandy coastal soil. Evergreen, with fine foliage, it produces tiny white flowers in summer. These soon drop, but the calyxes remain, growing larger and changing colour through pink to a bright red. Deep, regular watering is needed in the hot weather to hold these on the tree until mid-summer.

196   CERATOPETALUM gummiferum
CHRISTMAS BUSH
REDBUSH
TREE   20 ft
NEW SOUTH WALES   SUMMER
SUBTROPICAL

CERCIS

197

CESTRUM

198

200

199

CERCIS
LEGUMINOSAE

A small group of large shrubs or trees from the northern hemisphere, suitable for cold-winter areas only. Deciduous, and demanding full sunlight, they are valued for the brilliant pink pea flowers produced in late winter when colour is scarce. CERCIS canadensis, an American species, flowers in soft rose-pink; while the large C. siliquastrum produces blossom of a more purplish tone. Both flower from trunk and branches as heavily as from tips.

197   CERCIS siliquastrum
JUDAS TREE
TREE   25 ft
EUROPE   SPRING

CESTRUM
SOLANACEAE

Easy to strike from cuttings, any of the 200 species of Cestrum makes a really showy display—and with careful selection you can have one or another in flower all the time, either in the open garden or in large tubs. Cestrums grow quickly, but need regular cutting back to avoid top-heaviness. Try them in a warm sheltered position, water generously and feed at flowering time. CESTRUM aurantiacum is the showiest; the spring flowers being followed by white berries. The rampant C. nocturnum is less spectacular but produces strongly perfumed greenish flowers all through the warm weather. At night the fragrance becomes almost overpowering and unless you enjoy it, beware not to plant it too close to the windows of your home.

198   CESTRUM aurantiacum
ORANGE CESTRUM
SHRUB   8 ft
MEXICO   SUMMER

199   CESTRUM fasciculatum
SHRUB   8 ft
MEXICO   SPRING

200   CESTRUM nocturnum
NIGHT JESSAMINE
NIGHT FLOWERING CESTRUM
SHRUB   10 ft
WEST INDIES   SUMMER-AUTUMN

201

202

CHAENOMELES
ROSACEAE

Invaluable for flower arrangers, particularly in cold climates, the Japonicas commence to bloom in midwinter and continue for months. Bare, budded stems will open in water indoors. Many named varieties are available in shades of white, pink, orange and red; single and double. The shrubs themselves spread rapidly from the roots and are not fussy as to soil or situation, though they need an occasional application of iron chelates where too much lime is present. Do not hesitate to pick the twigs for decoration, as next year's flowers will appear on new wood anyway.

201   CHAENOMELES lagenaria
'Crimson and Gold'
JAPONICA
FLOWERING QUINCE
SHRUB   6 ft
JAPAN   WINTER

202   CHAENOMELES lagenaria
'Nivalis'
WHITE FLOWERING QUINCE
WHITE JAPONICA
SHRUB   6 ft
JAPAN   WINTER

203

204

CHAMAECYPARIS
CUPRESSACEAE

Most variable of all conifers, the many forms of Lawson Cypress have achieved great popularity as specimen shrubs. Tall, short, spreading, weeping or vertical— there is a variety for your purpose. The illustrated CHAMAECYPARIS lawsoniana 'Erecta Aurea' bears its golden-jointed branchlets in flat book-leaf style, but others have leaves in blue or green tones. CHAMAECYPARIS prefers an open sunny position, but colours best in cool winter districts. A slow grower.

203   CHAMAECYPARIS lawsoniana
'Erecta Aurea'
LAWSON CYPRESS
PORT ORFORD CEDAR
SHRUB   8 ft
WESTERN U.S.   ALL YEAR

CHAMAELAUCIUM
MYRTACEAE

Widley cultivated in Australia, the Geralton Wax Plant deserves world-wide popularity in spite of its hard-to-grow reputation which is completely undeserved. It simply requires warm sandy soil of a rather alkaline balance. Acid soil and too much water cause it to give up the ghost prematurely. Delicate needle leaves and waxy pink myrtle flowers make it particularly charming in the spring.

204   CHAMAELAUCIUM uncinatum
GERALDTON WAX PLANT
GERALDTON WAXFLOWER
SHRUB   8 ft
WESTERN AUSTRALIA   SPRING

205

206

CHEIRANTHUS
CRUCIFERAE

Wonderful early-blooming Wallflowers are now available in shades of pink, red, mauve and burgundy as well as the older shades of yellow, orange and brown. They are fragrant as ever and flower more heavily. In cold areas, Wallflowers must be treated as annuals and set out in spring. In milder latitudes plant them in full winter sun (by a sun-drenched wall would be ideal) and make sure the soil is thoroughly dug over with lime and old manure. Sow or plant out in early autumn.

205   CHEIRANTHUS cheiri
WALLFLOWER
PERENNIAL   2 ft
EUROPE   SPRING—SUMMER

CHIONANTHUS
CHINESE FRINGE TREE

Billows of tiny white flowers with strap-like petals appear in late spring among the new leaves of CHIONANTHUS, followed by deep blue berries. It is a hardy plant, provided the soil is good and the position open to plenty of sun. At the back of a west-facing shrubbery is ideal, for it will develop a slim trunk and branches, letting through plenty of light to the bed beneath.

206   CHIONANTHUS retusa
CHINESE FRINGE TREE
TREE   12 ft
CHINA   SPRING

CHIONODOXA

207

CHOISYA

208

CHORIZEMA

209

CHIONODOXA
LILIACEAE

A charming bulb from the mountains of Asia Minor, and growing only in cooler districts, where its blue and white starry flowers have been known to appear out of snowdrifts. Plant the bulbs 3 in deep in autumn, and leave undisturbed for years—they will multiply from offsets and even from seed if the conditions are right. These include open sun and good drainage. CHIONODOXA luciliae is the common blue and white variety.

207   CHIONODOXA luciliae
GLORY OF THE SNOWS
BULB   6 in
ASIA MINOR   WINTER

CHOISYA
RUTACEAE

A certain care is needed to flower this fragrant beauty to perfection. Acid soil, rich in humus, with the root junction above soil level. Deep but not too frequent watering is best, and a constant vigilance against thrip, aphis and red spider will require regular spraying. But the result will be healthy shiny leaves and masses of white orange blossom all through spring.

208   CHOISYA ternata
MEXICAN ORANGE
SHRUB   8 ft
MEXICO   SPRING

CHORIZEMA
LEGUMINOSAE

The gaudiest pea-flowers imaginable have brought world-wide popularity to this small group of Australian shrubs. Grow in sun (or part-shade for brighter colours): improve drainage and continue to water during dry winters. CHORIZEMA cordatum is the brightest, flowering in vivid red-violet and orange. It is attractive either spilling naturally over banks or pruned back to a neater shape.

209   CHORIZEMA cordatum
FLAME PEA
HEARTLEAF FLAME PEA
SHRUB   4 ft
WESTERN AUSTRALIA   WINTER

210

212

214

211

213

215

CHRYSANTHEMUM
COMPOSITAE

This extremely large genus of annuals and perennials is the backbone of the summer garden, under many popular names—although only the giant oriental varieties are commonly referred to as 'mums. Annual types include the brightly coloured **CHRYSANTHEMUM** carinatum (Tricolor Chrysanthemum) and C. parthenium (the Feverfew or Exhibition Border). Perennials are C. coccineum (the Pyrethrum or Painted Daisy); C. maximum (the Shasta Daisy) and the shrubby C. frutescens (Marguerite) in its many colour varieties. All of the above are planted out in autumn. The enormous range of Florists Chrysanthemums, the autumn-flowering types, are Japanese or Chinese hybrids of the original C. morifolium, yet so much do they vary from one another, it is often difficult to believe they are even related. From twelve-inch miniatures with half-inch pom-pom flowers; they range through brilliantly coloured single garden types to giant exhibition varieties in softest pastel tones. Some of these last have flowers 6 in and more across, which are achieved with a great deal of fertilization and disbudding.

210   CHRYSANTHEMUM frutescens
MARGUERITE DAISY
PARIS DAISY
PERENNIAL 3 ft
CANARY ISLANDS   SUMMER

211   CHRYSANTHEMUM maximum
SHASTA DAISY
PERENNIAL   4 ft
PYRENEES   SUMMER

212   CHRYSANTHEMUM X hybridum
'Bridesmaid'
(FANTASY QUILLED TYPE)
PERENNIAL   3 ft
JAPAN   AUTUMN

213   CHRYSANTHEMUM X 'Green Goddess'
(INCURVED EXHIBITION TYPE)
PERENNIAL   4 ft
JAPAN–CHINA   AUTUMN

214   CHRYSANTHEMUM X
'Masquerade'
(MINIATURE POM-POM TYPE)
PERENNIAL   12 in
HYBRID   AUTUMN

215   CHRYSANTHEMUM parthenium
EXHIBITION BORDER
FEVERFEW
PERENNIAL—ANNUAL   2 ft
EUROPE   SUMMER

CLEMATIS

CLEOME

225

226

227

CLEMATIS
RANUNCULACEAE

Beautiful and popular deciduous climbers for cool-winter climates, the Clematis are available in a staggering variety of form and colour. Failure to grow is almost invariably due to wrong positioning. Although they love sun, roots must be cool, which means planting on the shady side of a wall or support. Soil must be rich in humus, but neutral. Plant out in autumn; water and fertilize regularly when growth starts in spring. Prune out dead or sickly wood in spring. Peak flowering time is early summer.

225   CLEMATIS lanuginosa 'Nelly Moser'
CLIMBER   8 ft
CHINA   SUMMER

226   CLEMATIS montana
VIRGIN'S BOWER
TRAVELLER'S JOY
ANEMONE CLEMATIS
CLIMBER   20 ft
HIMALAYAS   SPRING

CLEOME
CAPPARIDACEAE

Spidery pink flowers borne high on tall green bushes make CLEOME an attractive choice for background colour in late summer or autumn. Sow where they are to grow in late spring—the seeds sprout rapidly and grow vigorously—but hold back the water or they may turn out all leaf and few flowers. CLEOME leaves are also attractive, rather like giant maples.

227   CLEOME spinosa
SPIDER FLOWER
ANNUAL   4 ft
WEST INDIES   SUMMER

228

230

231

229

232

CLERODENDRON
VERBENACEAE

Suited only to warm climates, or sunny sheltered positions, the CLERODEN-DRONS are a variable group of shrubs and woody climbers with spectacular flowering habits. Ordinary soil suits them well, but the necessary conditions of summer rain and winter warmth must be kept up for successful blooming. The Bleeding Heart (CLERODENDRON thomsonae) flowers winter and spring. The small shrubby C. nutans comes to life in autumn. Brilliant climber C. speciosissima is decked in crimson and scarlet each spring, while the shrubby C. splendens of felty leaves and large scarlet spikes is strictly a summer subject. Blue-flowering shrub C. ugandense is occasionally seen in cooler gardens. Shrubby C. bungei (the Cashmere Bouquet) is the only particularly fragrant species, spreading from suckers.

228   CLERODENDRON nutans
SHRUB   4 ft
AFRICA   AUTUMN

229   CLERODENDRON
speciosissimum
GLORY BOWER
CLIMBING SHRUB   6 ft
JAVA   WINTER–SPRING

230   CLERODENDRON thomsonae
BLEEDING HEARTS
BROKEN HEARTS
BAG FLOWER
CLIMBER   12 ft
WEST AFRICA   SPRING
ALL TROPICAL

CLIVIA
AMARYLLIDACEAE

Three species only are known of this small genus, all from South Africa—and the good news is that they all flower best and most brilliantly in shade, which they must have. Suitable for outdoors in all except the frostiest districts. Plant under trees in well-drained positions where they can collect plenty of leaf-mould, and leave undisturbed. They will reward you with their brilliant orange flowers winter after winter. CLIVIA miniata is most commonly seen, with dark leaves and open orange and yellow trumpet flowers. Its cousin C. nobilis (the Cape Clivia) has longer, more pendulous flowers, apricot tipped with green, and flowers later in spring. C. miniata, a popular houseplant, should never be dried off completely.

231   CLIVIA miniata
CAFFRE LILY
KAFFIR LILY
BULB   18 in
NATAL   WINTER

232   CLIVIA nobilis
CAPE CLIVIA
BULB   2 ft
SOUTH AFRICA   SPRING
BOTH SUBTROPICAL

CLYTOSTOMA

233

COBEA

234

CODIAEUM

235

CLYTOSTOMA
BIGNONIACEAE

A fast-growing climber, needing little support but its own tendrils except on smooth walls: CLYTOSTOMA demands sunshine, good drainage and plenty of acid compost in the soil. The delicate lilac and yellow flowers appear in both spring and summer on long terminal shoots which hang in a curtain effect over fences and branches. CLYTO-STOMA needs a little pruning in autumn, to tidy up summer growth.

233   CLYTOSTOMA callistegioides
VIOLET TRUMPET VINE
CLIMBER   10 ft
ARGENTINA   SPRING–SUMMER

COBEA
POLEMONIACEAE

Bell-shaped flowers in a large green calyx—turn them upside down and you have—Cups and Saucers! Sometimes green, sometimes lilac, sometimes white, these scentless flowers appear on a rampant vine that climbs with a system of tendrils. They are valued more for arrangements than their garden display. Seeds should be notched before planting in early spring, and the vines are usually pulled down and burned before winter renders them unsightly.

234   COBEA scandens
CUP AND SAUCER VINE
CATHEDRAL BELLS
ANNUAL VINE   25 ft
MEXICO   AUTUMN

CODIAEUM
EUPHORBIACEAE

In the tropics, brilliantly coloured foliage is almost as common as green leaves in other climates. But the most varied and vivid display is given by the many varieties of Croton. Yellow, green, red, pink and purple are among the shades represented on leaves so brightly toned that the white spring flowers go quite unnoticed. Grow them outdoors in the sub-tropics—inside with heat further away from the equator.

235   CODIAEUM variegatum
'Emperor Alexander'
CROTON
SHRUB   6 ft
PACIFIC ISLANDS   ALL YEAR

COELOGYNE

236

COLCHICUM

237

COLEONEMA

238

COELOGYNE
ORCHIDACEAE

Purest white orchid flowers with golden-haloed throats that hang lightly from their stems like a flight of angels—or so the botanist who named them COELO-GYNE (Heavenly Woman) must have thought! COELOGYNES may be grown in containers in the open even where temperatures drop as low as 38°F. Do not overwater through autumn and winter when the flowers appear, and remember they only flower well when over-crowded.

236 COELOGYNE cristata
ANGEL ORCHID
ORCHID 12 in
HIMALAYAS WINTER

COLCHICUM
LILIACEAE

Curious autumn-flowering bulbs that bloom as readily sitting on a saucer as they do planted in rich garden soil. Set out in summer, the flowers appear almost immediately the weather cools down—often more than one to a bulb. COLCHI-CUM autumnale, C. speciosum and C. byzantinus are similar species with white to mauve flowers. The more exotic C. agrippinum has a distinctly checkered appearance on its pink and mauve petals.

237 COLCHICUM autumnale
AUTUMN CROCUS
NAKED BOYS
MEADOW SAFFRON
BULB 6 in
EUROPE AUTUMN

COLEONEMA
RUTACEAE

Neat evergreen shrubs from South Africa, COLEONEMAS have aromatic heath-like leaves and miniature starry flowers in late winter and spring. Both pink and the smaller white species (COLEONEMA album) are extremely hardy and can be clipped to shape as dwarf hedges. They will grow anywhere the drainage is good. Occasional flowers can be expected any time of the year.

238 COLEONEMA pulchrum
PINK DIOSMA
BREATH OF HEAVEN
SHRUB 5 ft
SOUTH AFRICA SPRING

239

241

243

240

242

COLEUS
LABIATAE

Most popular of the many tropical plants with vivid leaf colour, Painted Nettles come in infinite variety. Superb outdoors in a warm climate, they are killed right back by winter temperatures much below 50°. A few cuttings, however, can always be kept indoors and will root in water to sprout outdoors at the first sign of summer. Coleus should be pinched back to force branching and fed regularly with a high-nitrogen fertilizer. Their vivid leaves are prey to caterpillars, and should be sprayed with a stomach poison regularly. Remove flowers as they develop to ensure continual growth. COLEUS blumei includes the brilliant bedding varieties—C. rehneltianus the trailing types. Some of the other 150-odd species are grown only by specialists.

239   COLEUS blumei
PAINTED NETTLE
PERENNIAL   18 in
EAST INDIES   SUMMER

240   COLEUS blumei 'Verschaffeltii'
FLAME NETTLE
PERENNIAL   18 in
JAVA   SUMMER

241   COLEUS rehneltianus 'Trailing Queen'
CREEPING COLEUS
PERENNIAL   9 in
MEXICO   SUMMER

242   COLEUS thyrsoideus
BUSH COLEUS
PERENNIAL   3 ft
CENTRAL AFRICA   SUMMER
ALL SUBTROPICAL

COLUMNEA
GESNERIACEAE

Remarkable hanging perennials for the hothouse or sheltered tropical garden, COLUMNEAS need a minimum winter temperature of 50°. Epiphytic in nature, they are grown in hanging baskets filled with sphagnum moss, fibrous peat and charcoal. Plenty of summer water is reduced as the weather cools down. The showy scarlet and yellow flowers appear at intervals on the weeping stems.

243   COLUMNEA gloriosa
SHOWY COLUMN FLOWER
EPIPHYTIC PERENNIAL   4 ft
COSTA RICA   SPRING
SUBTROPICAL

COMBRETUM

244

CONVALLARIA

245

CONVOLVULUS

246

COMBRETUM
COMBRETACEAE

An extremely varied genus of pan tropical evergreen climbers and shrubs, many of them suitable for frost-free gardens in temperate areas. None is native to Australia, though they are often mistaken for indigenous shrubs because of the curious flower form. Orange-flowered COMBRETUM loeflingi is best planted at the bottom of a wall and allowed to scramble upwards.

244   COMBRETUM loeflingi
LOEFLING'S COMBRETUM
PAINT BRUSH
SHRUB   5 ft
TROPICAL AMERICA   SUMMER

CONVALLARIA
LILIACEAE

To the French, this deliciously perfumed flower is the very symbol of spring, but you will find it hard to grow unless you have cold winters. In the right woodland conditions of semi-shade and soil rich in humus it can become downright invasive. Plant out the 'pips' in early winter and top-dress yearly with acid leafmould or peat. There are pink and beige varieties.

245   CONVALLARIA majalis
LILY OF THE VALLEY
MUGUET DE L'ISLE
BULB   8 in
EUROPE–ASIA   SPRING

CONVOLVULUS
CONVOLVULACEAE

In warmer climates, a popular trailing perennial for rockeries, dry banks or even hanging baskets, this delicate Morning Glory bears soft lavender-blue flowers in summer and autumn. Plant in light well-drained soil, choosing a position where the three foot stems can hang downwards. CONVOLVULUS mauretanicus prefers full sun and should be trimmed back in winter.

246   CONVOLVULUS mauretanicus
GROUND MORNING GLORY
TRAILER   3 ft
NORTH AFRICA   SUMMER

COPROSMA

247

CORDYLINE

248

249

COREOPSIS

250

COPROSMA
RUBIACEAE

New Zealand's gift to seaside gardens everywhere has the shiniest leaves in the world when well cared for. Plant in any type of soil, even sand, and protect it from full sun except in humid areas. White flowers and orange berries come and go, almost invisible under the striking leaves. Dwarf coloured-leaf varieties are available. Prune back yearly to preserve density.

247   COPROSMA baueri 'Picturata'
LOOKINGGLASS PLANT
MIRROR PLANT
SHRUB   10 ft
NEW ZEALAND   ALL YEAR

CORDYLINE
LILIACEAE

A tropical plant grown principally for leaf interest, the Ti (CORDYLINE terminalis) does bear sprays of small greenish-white flowers in summer. The leaves come in every imaginable combination of green, white, red and purple—the darker colours being most highly valued. To raise plants colour-true, they are propagated from sections of stalk, lain in a damp mixture of sand and peatmoss. Grow them indoors in frosty areas—outside in warm districts in semi-shade. C. australis is a taller palm-like shrub with sharp leaves in starburst form. The sweetly-scented spikes of tiny white flowers appear in late spring.

248   CORDYLINE australis
CABBAGE TREE
PALM LILY
GRASS PALM
SHRUB   20 ft
NEW ZEALAND   LATE SPRING

249   CORDYLINE terminalis
TI
SHRUB   10 ft
TROPICAL ASIA   SUMMER

COREOPSIS
COMPOSITAE

The problem here is not so much how to grow but how to stop once you have started them, for these lovely daisy-flowers scatter seed far and wide. Just throw some around in autumn, add water and you will have them anywhere you choose; dry soil or damp; sandy or heavy. COREOPSIS are completely heat-resistant and great for neglected garden corners. Flowers in spring and summer.

250   COREOPSIS lanceolata
CALLIOPSIS
TICK SEED
ANNUAL—PERENNIAL   2½ ft
UNITED STATES OF AMERICA
SPRING

CORNUS

251

252

CORTADERIA

253

COSMOS

254

255

CORNUS
CORNACEAE

The Dogwoods or Cornels have great decorative value for cold-climate gardens. CORNUS alba, C. sanguinea and C. stolonifera are suckering shrubs noted for vivid scarlet and yellow bare twigs in winter. C. florida, (the Flowering Dogwood of the eastern states of America) gives a brilliant spring display—tiny white flowers surrounded by 4 pink or white-notched bracts. C. mas (the Cornelian Cherry) shows bright yellow flowers on bare winter twigs, and bright red cherry-fruits later. The Evergreen Dogwood (C. capitatas) produces reddish-purple strawberry-fruits in autumn, when many of its leaves colour though it is basically evergreen.

251   CORNUS capitata
EVERGREEN DOGWOOD
STRAWBERRY TREE
TREE   30 ft
HIMALAYAS   SUMMER—AUTUMN

252   CORNUS florida
CORNEL
FLOWERING DOGWOOD
EASTERN DOGWOOD
TREE   20 ft
EASTERN UNITED STATES OF
AMERICA   SPRING

CORTADERIA
GRAMINEAE

The tall silvery plumes of giant Pampas Grass gathered dust in many a Victorian parlour—now they are right back in fashion as garden accent pieces. Plant out or divide in spring; the plumes unfold in late summer and continue to shine right through winter. Pampas Grass is best grown in deep soil away from other plants as it is kept in shape by burning off the razor-sharp dead leaves in early spring.

253   CORTADERIA argentea
PAMPAS GRASS
PERENNIAL   12 ft
SOUTH AMERICA   AUTUMN

COSMOS
COMPOSITAE

Very tall annuals for autumn cutting, Cosmos are usually grown behind shrubs or fences which disguise them till they reach full flowering height and provide summer shade. Cosmos really are easy to grow in any good soil and need no special care. The common species, COSMOS bipinnatus, provides plenty of flowers for cutting in shades of pink, lavender, crimson and white, all with yellow centres. The orange C. sulphureus is a less attractive plant, but its flowers persist into winter in warm climates. Plant Cosmos in groups for support, and stake if necessary.

254   COSMOS bipinnatus
MEXICAN ASTER
COSMOS
ANNUAL   8 ft
MEXICO   AUTUMN

255   COSMOS sulphureus
YELLOW COSMOS
ANNUAL   6 ft
MEXICO   AUTUMN

COTINUS

COTONEASTER

256

257

259

258

COTINUS
ANACARDIACEAE

A tall-growing shrub generally kept to about 8 ft with annual pruning, the COTINUS is valued both for its dazzling display of autumn tones and for its fuzzy clouds of flower stems which persist for months and really do look like puffs of low-lying smoke. The tree is completely deciduous and pruned heavily each winter. Varieties with coloured leaves are available including COTINUS coggyria 'Purpurea' and C. c. 'Royal Purple'.

256   COTINUS coggyria
RHUS
WIG TREE
SMOKE BUSH
VENETIAN SUMACH
SHRUB   8 ft
CAUCASUS   AUTUMN
HARDY

COTONEASTER
ROSACEAE

Evergreen and deciduous shrubs with many garden uses from ground cover to windbreak, the Cotoneasters are extremely hardy and produce berries prolifically in quite warm districts. All grow rapidly, but look better in a dryish position. Heavy autumn rains are a problem, because new leaves tend to hide the ripening berries. When this happens severe pruning is necessary. COTONEASTER purpusilla is an attractive ground or rock cover with purple berries and good autumn colour. C. horizontalis (the Fishbone or Rockspray Cotoneaster) has brilliant lacquer-red berries which remain right through winter. There are upwards of 50 species available with berries; red, purple, black and yellow. All bear small white rose-flowers in spring.

257   COTONEASTER frigida
CLUSTERBERRY
TREE   30 ft
HIMALAYAS   AUTUMN

258   COTONEASTER horizontalis
FISHBONE COTONEASTER
ROCKSPRAY
CREEPING COTONEASTER
SHRUB   WEEPING
CHINA   AUTUMN

259   COTONEASTER purpusilla
ROCKSPUR
ROCK COTONEASTER
GROUND COVER   6 in
CHINA   AUTUMN

95

260

262

261

263

264

CRATAEGUS
ROSACEAE

Popularly called Hawthorns, this marvellous group of deciduous shrubs and
small trees is classed in the Rose family.
The resemblances to their larger-
flowered cousins are many. Wicked
thorns, attractive shiny leaves, perfumed
rose-like flowers—but there is also a
tremendous plus—brilliantly coloured
fruits up to one-and-a-half inches in
diameter that will attract all the birds for
miles. Though very sturdy, they fruit
best in cold areas, and on no account
should they be planted where fruit fly
is prevalent.

260   CRATAEGUS ellwangeriana
GIANT HAWTHORN
TREE   20 ft
NORTH AMERICA   AUTUMN

261   CRATAEGUS mexicana
'Stipulacea'
MEXICAN THORN
TREE   30 ft
MEXICO   AUTUMN

262   CRATAEGUS oxyacantha 'Pauli'
PAUL'S SCARLET HAWTHORN
TREE   20 ft
EUROPE   SPRING

263   CRATAEGUS X Smithiana
TREE   20 ft
HYBRID   AUTUMN

CRINUM
AMARYLLIDACEAE

Similar in appearance to Amaryllis, the
CRINUM flowers while the bulb is in
full leaf—it is in fact, evergreen. Plant
6 in below surface in rich soil, spring or
autumn, and give plenty of water. Grow
only in frost-free areas, preferably near
the coast. Among the 100 or so CRINUM
species, those most commonly seen are
CRINUM asiaticus (the Poison Bulb),
C. moorei, C. powellii.

264   CRINUM moorei
VELDT LILY
BULB   3 ft
NATAL   SUMMER

CROCUS

CROSSANDRA

CROTALARIA

265

266

267

CROCUS
IRIDACEAE

Gay little flowers that pop right out of the ground in earliest spring, followed later by silver-striped leaves, CROCUS are suited only to areas with a cold winter and a hot dry summer to coincide with their dormant season. All thrive in sun or light shade, where drainage is good. There are about 80 species in shades of white, yellow, violet, blue and pink.

265   CROCUS tomasinianus
SAFFRON
BULB   6 in
YUGOSLAVIA   SPRING

CROSSANDRA
ACANTHACEAE

Useful shrubs for the tropical garden, but often used as houseplants in more temperate climates, CROSSANDRAS like an acid sandy soil, rich with decayed compost. CROSSANDRA infundibuli-formis is the most widely seen, its glossy drooping leaves attractive at any time of year. The tubular salmon-orange flowers appear from a long bracted spike over weeks.

266   CROSSANDRA infundibuliformis
SHRUB   3 ft
INDIA   SUMMER
TROPICAL

CROTALARIA
LEGUMINOSAE

Useful tropical shrubs for the warmer area, CROTALARIAS are easily propa-gated from cuttings of young wood. The pea-type flowers are almost exclusively yellow or yellow-green, and in some species resemble birds hanging on to the stems by their beaks. Low-growing CROTALARIA semperflorens has silver-grey felty leaves; flowers in spikes during summer.

267   CROTALARIA semperflorens
BIRD FLOWER
CANARY BIRD BUSH
SHRUB   4 ft
INDIA   SUMMER
SUBTROPICAL

CTENANTHE

268

CUCURBITA

269

CUPHEA

270

CTENANTHE
MARANTACEAE

Another splendid foliage plant for the glasshouse or warm garden. Like Calatheas, they are admired for the leaf patterns, though here these are borne on slim, bamboo-like stems. Again like Calatheas, they require well-drained, rich soil and plenty of humidity. The popular species CTENANTHE lubbersiana is patterned in vivid green and yellow, occasionally bears small white flowers.

268   CTENANTHE lubbersiana
BAMBURANTA
PERENNIAL   2 ft
BRAZIL   SUMMER

CUCURBITA
CUCURBITACEAE

Related to pumpkins, vegetable marrows and squashes; the ornamental Gourds are varieties and hybrids of CUCURBITA pepo; and are used for autumn arrangements. Plant seeds in enriched soil by a trellis or shed support in early spring. The chosen site should be in full sun. Water and fertilize regularly and pick the Gourds when stems have dried up in late summer. Dry in an airy place and lacquer to preserve.

269   CUCURBITA pepo ovifera
GOURDS
ANNUAL VINE   10 ft
TROPICAL AMERICA   AUTUMN

CUPHEA
LYTHRACEAE

A hardy miniature shrub for any type of soil. Plant in full sun in the rockery or mixed border and forget it. Rarely growing higher than 15 in CUPHEA produces masses of tiny red and black tubular flowers almost all year. Easily struck from cuttings, CUPHEA rarely needs pruning except in shady positions when it may grow a bit leggy.

270   CUPHEA ignea
CIGAR PLANT
SHRUB   12 in
MEXICO   SUMMER

CUPRESSUS

271

CUSSONIA

272

CYATHEA

273

CUPRESSUS
CUPRESSACEAE

Best loved of all conifers for a classic vertical accent, the Italian Cypress or Pencil Pine is tall, dark and handsome. Rather slow-growing, but trouble free once established in a well-drained deep soil, the Cypress does best in a position open to sun and wind, which are the best natural deterrents to the pesky red spider mite. Malathion spray is the alternative.

271   CUPRESSUS sempervirens 'Stricta'
COLUMN CYPRESS
ITALIAN CYPRESS
PENCIL PINE
TREE   40 ft
SOUTHERN EUROPE   ALL YEAR

CUSSONIA
ARALIACEAE

Small evergreen shrubs grown principally as accent plants, or for leaf contrast in the mixed border. Any good soil will suit them with regular water. CUSSONIA paniculata is typical of the family's extraordinary leaf shapes. It bears 7 to 12 leaflets on each long leaf stalk, and the leaflets themselves are further lobed and spine-tipped. The yellow-green summer flowers are not particularly showy.

272   CUSSONIA paniculata
SPIKED CABBAGE TREE
SHRUB   10 ft
SOUTH AFRICA   SUMMER

CYATHEA
CYATHEACEAE

Handsomest of the tree ferns, CYATHEAS encompass over 350 species, mostly native to the sub-tropics; but some from Australia and New Zealand. They demand semi-shade to protect the delicate fronds, and plenty of water about the roots with regular spraying of the trunk. A soil mixture which is largely fibrous peat and sand suits them to perfection. Remove all fronds as they fade.

273   CYATHEA cooperi
NEW ZEALAND TREE FERN
TREE FERN
NEW ZEALAND   ALL YEAR

CYCAS

274

CYCLAMEN

275

CYMBIDIUM

277

276

278

CYCAS
CYCADACEAE

Not ferns, not palms, the Cycads are a primitive form of plant related to conifers, and bear a great cone of colourful fruits. Hardy in the coldest areas, they are useful in helping to plan a tropical look. Very slow-growing, they produce one or more trunks topped with rosettes of palm-like leaves. Popular in Japan as a Bonsai plant.

274   CYCAS revoluta
CYCAD
SAGO PALM
TREE   7 ft
CHINA   ALL YEAR

CYCLAMEN
PRIMULACEAE

Among the most popular bulbs for cold weather colour, the hardy Cyclamens bloom indoors or out from late autumn to early spring. The large Florist's Cyclamens, sold in pots by the million every winter, are varieties and hybrids of the species CYCLAMEN persicum. Their colour range is white, pink, red and mauve and they come ruffled or plain in single and double varieties. There are also several species of smaller Cyclamen suitable for naturalizing outdoors. These include the dainty C. neapolitanum 'Album' which has flowers the size of white violets.

275   CYCLAMEN neapolitanum
'Album'
NEAPOLITAN CYCLAMEN
BULB   4 in
ITALY   AUTUMN

276   CYCLAMEN persicum 'Hybridum'
FLORIST'S CYCLAMEN
BULB   12 in
ASIA MINOR   WINTER

CYMBIDIUM
ORCHIDACEAE

Most improved of all the Orchid genera, modern CYMBIDIUMS are the result of extensive hybridization in the last 50 years, particularly of the two Indo-Chinese species CYMBIDIUM insigne and C. erythrostylum. They are hardy in coastal regions 35° from the equator. In areas where the winter temperature does not drop below 40°F. they can be grown in the open garden, preferably in large pots or tubs which can be moved to a favourable position at flowering time. CYMBIDIUM hybrids need all the light they can get—full sun suits them in the cooler months; light shade-cloth or broken sunlight in summer. They are grown in a special compost available at any nursery; moisture retaining yet fast draining; and should be kept particularly moist during the spring and summer when new growth develops. Flower spikes up to 5 ft long appear at varying times from midwinter to summer, according to variety. The colour range includes white, pink, gold, red, green and brown; many attractively shaded and spotted. Some of the original species make attractive garden plants also: the Australian Arrowroot Orchid (C. canaligulatum)

279

280

thrives in the warm open garden in hollow rotten tree trunks.

277   CYMBIDIUM X Hybridum
ORCHID   3 ft
HYBRID   WINTER

278   CYMBIDIUM suave
ORCHID   18 in
NORTHERN AUSTRALIA   SUMMER

279   CYMBIDIUM X hybridum
ORCHID   3 ft
HYBRID   SPRING

CYNARA
COMPOSITAE

Tall thistle-like Cardoons are spectacular foliage plants for the mixed border, producing rosettes of enormous silver-grey leaves from spring-planted suckers. The tall flower stems appear in summer, producing first the large buds which are eaten as Globe Artichokes. These later burst open into a mass of mauve-blue stamens, very decorative for cutting.

280   CYNARA scolymus
CARDOON
GLOBE ARTICHOKE
PERENNIAL   6 ft
SOUTHERN EUROPE   SUMMER

CYPERUS

281

CYPHOMANDRA

282

CYRTANTHUS

283

CYPERUS
CYPERACEAE

This graceful Egyptian plant is by nature a bog-dweller, and given plenty of water sends up tall three-sided stems bearing airy masses of green thread-like flower stems. These are valued by garden designers for their shadows and delicate reed-like effect. They can be grown in pools or damp water-logged parts of the garden. Papyrus will grow from 6 to 10 ft in height, and dead flower stems should be cut back regularly.

281   CYPERUS papyrus
EGYPTIAN PAPER PLANT
PAPYRUS
EGYPTIAN PAPER REED
PERENNIAL   6-10 ft
EGYPT   SUMMER
SUBTROPICAL

CYPHOMANDRA
SOLANACEAE

The curiously sweet Tree Tomato fruit, so intriguing to southern hemisphere newcomers, can be grown outdoors anywhere in a warm frost-free position. Soil on the rich side suits best and the new plant, more like a large perennial than a shrub, will fruit in the second year from seed. CYPHOMANDRA sends up a single frost-tender trunk with large felty leaves. The flowers are greenish-pink, in long racemes.

282   CYPHOMANDRA betacea
TREE TOMATO
TAMARILLO
SHRUB   12 ft
SOUTHERN BRAZIL   SUMMER

CYRTANTHUS
AMARYLLIDACEAE

Uncommon outside their native South Africa, the Ifafa Lilies are an interesting and attractive group of 50-odd bulb species. CYRTANTHUS mackenii flourishes in well-drained acid soil, preferably in a warm sheltered position. The bulbs grow throughout the year, reproducing rapidly from offsets. The white, yellow or pastel-toned tubular flowers appear in late winter or spring.

283   CYRTANTHUS mackenii
IFAFA LILY
AFRICAN BRIDE LILY
BULB   12 in
SOUTH AFRICA   WINTER–SPRING
SUBTROPICAL

CYTISUS

284

DABOECIA

285

CYTISUS
LEGUMINOSAE

Rangy, free-flowering shrubs often seen
naturalized in river beds or damp places
in many lands. The pea-flowers are in
gay variations of tan, yellow, crimsón
and white. Attractive garden subjects,
the plants can be kept within bounds
by cutting back at least by half after the
main spring-flowering flush. CYTISUS
scoparius is the usual variety seen, with
taller white flowering C. prolifer.

284   CYTISUS scoparius
SCOTS BROOM
SHRUB   8 ft
WESTERN EUROPE   SPRING

DABOECIA
ERICACEAE

Like all Heaths, DABOECIA needs a
lime-free soil, preferably including sand
and peat. The flowers, much larger than
on other heaths; appear in spring and
early summer towards the end of the
slender twigs. There are several varieties
in shades of white or rosy-purple. Dwarf-
growing and wide-spreading DABOE-
CIAS are suited to the semi-shaded rock
pocket or in the foreground of larger
shrubs.

285   DABOECIA cantabrica
IRISH HEATH
ST DABEOC'S HEATH
CONNEMARA HEATH
SHRUB   15 in
EUROPE—IRELAND   SUMMER
HARDY

286

287

DAHLIA
COMPOSITAE

With Dahlias, there is no half measure—
you either love them or loathe them; but
in all fairness the bulk of the gardening
public seems on the former side. They
are brilliantly coloured, scentless members of the daisy family, in a wide range
of sizes and styles. Preparation for
Dahlias involves digging the soil deeply
and conditioning it with peat moss
and fertilizer...or sand if it is too heavy.
Drive in stakes where the plants are to be
(they will need support later) and place
complete fertilizer in the bottom of a
twelve-inch hole. Cover with 4 in of soil,
then place the tuber in position. Top
with more soil, tamp into place and
water thoroughly. Tubers are normally
lifted after flowering and stored for the
winter in a cool dry place.

286 DAHLIAS
(Massed in a country garden)

287 DAHLIA X DECORATIVE TYPE
PERENNIAL   3 ft
HYBRID   AUTUMN

288

289

290

288   DAHLIA X 'Savannah'
(EXHIBITION DAHLIA)
PERENNIAL   6 ft
HYBRID   SUMMER

289   DAHLIA X 'Symphonia'
(CHARM DAHLIA)
PERENNIAL   3 ft
HYBRID   SUMMER

290   DAHLIA X
(WATERLILY DAHLIA)
PERENNIAL   4 ft
HYBRID   SUMMER

DAPHNE

291

292

DARWINIA

293

DATURA

294

295

DAPHNE
THYMELAEACEAE

Treasured and heartbreaking shrubs for a cool, well-drained position with morning sun. Treasured because of the gorgeously perfumed waxy flowers that open in winter—heartbreaking because they so often give up the ghost and die suddenly in spite of every care. The losses are mostly due to collar rot; a virus which rots the sap-conducting layer at soil level. Only way to combat it is to plant in a raised position with the root junction above soil level. Let the surface soil dry out thoroughly between summer waterings. Variety 'Marginata' with gold-edged leaves seems hardier. Do not be afraid to cut lavish sprays for decoration.

291   DAPHNE odora
SWEET DAPHNE
SHRUB   8 ft
CHINA–JAPAN   WINTER

292   DAPHNE odora 'Marginata'
VARIEGATED DAPHNE
SHRUB   8 ft
CHINA–JAPAN   WINTER

DARWINIA
MYRTACEAE

Useful Australian dwarf shrubs for sandy acid soil. Easily propagated from cuttings, they are suitable for the bush garden or large rockery, enjoying the same conditions as Erica. DARWINIA fascicularis is a decorative variety with fine needle leaves in clusters and scarlet flowers with protruding stamens. It grows wild around the Sydney sandstone area.

293   DARWINIA fascicularis
SHRUB   2 ft
NEW SOUTH WALES   SPRING

DATURA
SOLANACEAE

Enormous eight-inch flowers dangle freely from the branches of DATURAS. So unbelievably fragrant are they in the evenings that there can be no argument with the popular name, Angels' Trumpets. Any soil will do, though plenty of water is essential as well as shelter from the wind, for they are brittle and top-heavy. A certain amount of die-back can be expected in cold weather, but an early spring pruning will get them back in shape. DATURA suaveolens is the popular single species, the trumpets sometimes shaded pink, green or yellow. D. cornigera is similar with semi-double flowers; the petals exaggeratedly pointed. D. sanguinea has smaller orange-red trumpets. D. meteloides is mauve; D. chlorantha, yellow. Flowers and seeds of all species are poisonous.

294   DATURA cornigera
BRUGGMANSIA
SHRUB   10 ft
MEXICO   SUMMER

295   DATURA suaveolens
ANGELS' TRUMPETS
TRUMPET TREE
SHRUB   15 ft
NOT HARDY
MEXICO   SPRING–AUTUMN

106

DELONIX

296

DELPHINIUM

297

298

299

DELONIX
LEGUMINOSAE

In semi-tropical areas, all around the world, this is *the* tree. Fast-growing, delicately-leafed, generous with its shade—and in early summer gorgeous masses of orange-scarlet flowers appear almost overnight. Poincianas develop a most graceful spreading shape and the outer branches tend to weep—so do not plant one between you and the view. Poincianas do best in a well-drained sandy soil with plenty of water —they are quite bare in winter.

296   DELONIX regia
POINCIANA
ROYAL POINCIANA
FLAMBOYANT
FLAME OF THE FOREST
TREE   30 ft high—80 ft wide
MADAGASCAR   SUMMER
SUBTROPICAL

DELPHINIUM
RANUNCULACEAE

Although modern hybrids include shades of red, pink, yellow and white; graceful Delphiniums will always be associated with the colour blue. Most species are easy to grow, though they do best in cooler areas. The perennial Pacific hybrids of DELPHINIUM elatum are most admired; sending up five-foot flower spikes from crowns planted out in winter in warm climates or spring elsewhere. They bloom from late spring right through to autumn in shades of blue, white and mauve with eye-catching, bee-like centres. The Belladonna hybrids are less spectacular but have a longer flowering season. D. grandiflorum (the Butterfly Delphinium) is usually grown as an annual; as is D. ajacis (the Larkspur) which comes in many charming pastel shades. Delphiniums must have good drainage, revel in lime, and are very prone to attack by slugs. Chemical fertilizer during the flowering season will prolong bloom and the tall spikes must be staked against wind damage.

297   DELPHINIUM ajacis
LARKSPUR
SWEET ROCKET
ANNUAL   3 ft
SOUTHERN EUROPE   SPRING
HARDY

298   DELPHINIUM elatum
(Pacific Hybrid)
DELPHINIUM
CANDLE LARKSPUR
PERENNIAL   6 ft
HYBRID   SPRING—AUTUMN

299   DELPHINIUM grandiflorum
BUTTERFLY DELPHINIUM
CHINESE DELPHINIUM
ANNUAL   1½ ft
CHINA   SPRING

DENDROBIUM

300

302

304

301

303

305

**DENDROBIUM
ORCHIDACEAE**

Most widespread family of epiphytic or tree-dwelling orchids, the DENDRO-BIUMS include almost 1,000 species found in every part of the Far East and Australia. Unlike most of the exotic South American orchids, many DENDRO-BIUMS can be grown outdoors in pots or on trees in the sheltered frost-free garden. There are two principal types— the evergreen (including most of the Australian natives) which should never be allowed to dry out completely; and the deciduous which need a definite rest from water corresponding to the dry tropical winter. Their individual likings, habits and soil requirements are too complicated for the scope of this book. Suffice it to say that of the illustrated species: DENDROBIUM lin-guiforme and D. speciosum are hardy in the open garden removed from frost. D. nobile, D. pierardii and D. thyrsi-florum require only a sheltered bush-house and can be brought indoors or outside at flowering time. D. bigibbum, the state flower of Queensland, is not really hardy outside the tropics due to its winter-flowering habit.

300 DENDROBIUM bigibbum
COOKTOWN ORCHID
EPIPHYTE 2 ft
QUEENSLAND WINTER

301 DENDROBIUM linguiforme
TONGUE ORCHID
EPIPHYTE 4 in
AUSTRALIA SPRING

302 DENDROBIUM nobile
EPIPHYTE 3 ft
NORTH INDIA WINTER–SPRING

303 DENDROBIUM phalaenopsis
EPIPHYTE 3 ft
QUEENSLAND WINTER

304 DENDROBIUM pierardii
EPIPHYTE Hangs 8 ft
INDIA SPRING

305 DENDROBIUM speciosum
ROCKLILY
EPIPHYTE 4 ft
AUSTRALIA SPRING

306

307

308

309

306   DENDROBIUM thyrsiflorum
GOLDEN DENDROBIUM
EPIPHYTE   2½ ft
BURMA   SPRING
TROPICAL

DENDROMECON
PAPAVERACEAE

A curious flowering shrub for the dry
well-drained position in warm climates
—ideal in company with Australian and
South African natives. California's own
DENDROMECON is easily struck from
cuttings raised in sharp sand and develops into an untidy grey-leafed shrub of
up to 10 ft. Given a warm sheltered spot
it will flower in spring—rich golden-
yellow poppy blossoms with a pleasant
fragrance.

307   DENDROMECON rigidum
CALIFORNIAN TREE POPPY
POPPY BUSH
SHRUB   10 ft
CALIFORNIA   SPRING

DEUTZIA
SAXIFRAGACEAE

Splendid oriental shrubs that flower with
late spring bulbs and continue to early
summer, Deutzias are notable for their
particular grace and delicacy. Plant in a
semi-shaded position with plenty of
moisture and they will send up long
arching canes which bend under the
weight of hanging flowers in season.
Hardy but not frost-resistant; they must
be cut back after flowering.

308   DEUTZIA   gracilis
SLENDER DEUTZIA
SHRUB   4 ft
JAPAN   SUMMER
HARDY

309   DEUTZIA scabra 'Plena'
WEDDING BELLS
SHRUB   8 ft
JAPAN–CHINA   SUMMER
HARDY

310

312

314

311

313

DIANTHUS
CARYOPHYLLACEAE

Dianthus, Carnations, Pinks—all the one genus really; and so much crossed, hybridized and improved that it is difficult to make any clear distinction. Botanically they are all DIANTHUS. But in a popular sense, Dianthus are usually the annual bedding types, Carnations the tall cutting types and Pinks the wild cottage garden species. All have the delicious clove scent. All love full sun, all must have really perfect drainage (preferably in raised beds) and added lime if the soil is acid. The old-fashioned Cottage Pinks prefer a grittier soil than the others. As Border and Florist's Carnations need support, they are often planted in special wire frames. They and the old-fashioned Pinks are raised from tip cuttings. The annual and biennial types DIANTHUS barbatus and D. chinensis are raised from seed.

310   DIANTHUS arenarius
PERENNIAL   12 in
EUROPE   SPRING

311   DIANTHUS barbatus
SWEET WILLIAM
BIENNIAL   15 in
SOUTH-EASTERN EUROPE
SUMMER

312   DIANTHUS caryophyllus
CARNATION (SIM HYBRID)
CLOVE PINK
PERENNIAL   3 ft
FRANCE   SUMMER

313   DIANTHUS chinensis
CHINESE PINK
INDIAN PINK
RAINBOW PINK
ANNUAL   12 in
EAST ASIA   SUMMER

314   DIANTHUS plumarius
COTTAGE PINKS
CHELSEA PINKS
PERENNIAL   15 in
SOUTH-EASTERN EUROPE
SUMMER

DICENTRA

315

DICHORISANDRA

316

DICENTRA
PAPAVERACEAE

Successful only in cold-winter areas,
DICENTRA is a delicate old-fashioned
type of plant for the semi-shaded
shrubbery or border. Rich, well-drained
soil is necessary together with plenty of
moisture. A tangle of fleshy roots when
planted in autumn, DICENTRA sends up
ferny green foliage in spring and then
arching stems hung with heart-shaped
pink flowers. Most attractive in profuse
arrangements.

315   DICENTRA spectabilis
BLEEDING HEART
LYRE PLANT
SEAL FLOWER
LADY'S LOCKET
DUTCHMAN'S BREECHES
PERENNIAL   24 in
JAPAN   SPRING

DICHORISANDRA
COMMELINACEAE

A striking warm climate perennial for
semi-shaded positions, DICHORISAN-
DRA is usually grown in bush-houses
or under the shade of trees. It needs a
well-drained soil with plenty of peat and
leafmould and enjoys as much humidity
as possible during summer. Propagation
is by divisions or cuttings: the tall spikes
of violet-blue flowers appear in summer
and autumn.

316   DICHORISANDRA thyrsiflora
PERENNIAL   4 ft
BRAZIL   SUMMER–AUTUMN

317

318

DICKSONIA
CYATHEACEAE

Unlike the majority of tree ferns, which are sub-tropical; the DICKSONIAS will survive temperatures as low as 20°F. and are therefore suitable for outdoor planting in cold-winter areas. A typical fern compost of loam, peat and silver sand suits them and trunk spraying should be practised in summer. The fronds are altogether darker and coarser than Cyatheas.

317   DICKSONIA antarctica
TASMANIAN TREE FERN
TREE FERN   15 ft
TASMANIA   ALL YEAR

DICLIPTERA
ACANTHACEAE

Useful shrubby perennials for the warm climate rockery or bank, DICLIPTERAS are propagated from spring cuttings and enjoy a sun-drenched position with sandy soil. The leaves are velvety and compact; the tubular flowers appear in spikes: the colours blue, red or violet according to species. Cut back well after flowering and spray regularly against red spider. Also called JACOBINIA sub-erecta.

318   DICLIPTERA suberecta
PERENNIAL   9 in
URUGUAY   SUMMER

DIEFFENBACHIA

319

DIERAMA

320

DIETES

321

322

DIEFFENBACHIA
ARACEAE

A genus of about 20 species valued as indoor foliage plants—though grown outdoors in semi-tropical climates. DIEF-FENBACHIAS have earned their popular name from the extreme bitterness of the sap which is said to cause the tongue and throat to swell so much that speech is impossible. DIEFFENBACHIAS need ample light (but not sun) and water only when the container seems dry. Mature plants grow tall and leggy and should then be cut back.

319   DIEFFENBACHIA leoniae
DUMB CANE
PERENNIAL   8 ft
COLOMBIA   ALL YEAR

DIERAMA
IRIDACEAE

The many popular names of this South African bulb show how widely it has exercised gardeners' imagination. A late summer bloomer, it is best planted against a background of dark shrubbery where the incredibly delicate stems and flowers will be seen in relief. It likes sunshine, but moist soil, and when well situated will produce stems up to 7 ft in length.

320   DIERAMA pulcherrima
WAND FLOWER
FAIRY BELLS
FAIRY WAND
FAIRY FISHING FLOWER
ANGELS FISHING ROD
BULB   7 ft
SOUTH AFRICA   SUMMER

DIETES
IRIDACEAE

The evergreen sword-like foliage of DIETES makes an attractive garden feature at any time of the year—but warm weather is when they come into their own, sending up many long flower stems to produce blooms for several weeks at a time. The species DIETES bicolor has two-inch yellow and brown flowers: D. grandiflora blooms are larger: white-marked with mauve and orange-yellow. DIETES are extraordinarily drought-resistant and so tough and hardy they can be planted as hedges. They self-seed freely.

321   DIETES bicolor
FORTNIGHT LILY
PERENNIAL   3 ft
SOUTH AFRICA   SUMMER

322   DIETES grandiflora
WILD IRIS
PERENNIAL   2½ ft
SOUTH AFRICA   SUMMER

323

324

DIGITALIS
SCROPHULARIACEAE

Marvellous biennial plants for cooler climates, Foxgloves send up four-foot spikes of velvety bell-shaped flowers of mauve, pink, cream and white; beautifully marked and spotted. Planted out in autumn, they will produce great rosettes of woolly grey-green leaves before flowering in spring and summer. Fertilize and compost the soil before planting (they are gross feeders) and give plenty of water. Foxgloves will self-seed regularly.

323   DIGITALIS purpurea
FOXGLOVE
BIENNIAL   4 ft
EUROPE   SPRING–SUMMER

DIMORPHOTHECA
COMPOSITAE

Gay, free-flowering daisy plants from South Africa, but naturalized in many temperate parts of the world. DIMOR-PHOTHECA aurantiaca is a perennial, though usually raised as an annual for summer displays, growing very quickly from winter seed. D. ecklonis, a sprawling short-lived shrub is popular in mixed beds or on small banks. It grows from seed or cuttings and the normal form is white with a blue reverse and centre. There are named varieties in shades of pink and mauve. All DIMORPHOTHE-CAS enjoy full sun and good drainage and are remarkably drought-resistant.

324   DIMORPHOTHECA aurantiaca
NAMAQUALAND DAISY
AFRICAN DAISY
CAPE MARIGOLD
PERENNIAL   12 in
NAMAQUALAND   SUMMER

325

327

328

326

325 DIMORPHOTHECA ecklonis
STAR OF THE VELDT
SAILOR BOY DAISY
SHRUB   2 ft
SOUTH AFRICA   ALL YEAR

326   DIMORPHOTHECA ecklonis
'African Beauty'
SHRUB   2 ft
SOUTH AFRICA   ALL YEAR

DIOSPYROS
EBENACEAE

An easy deciduous fruit tree to grow in any mild climate, and wonderful value. The tree itself has a most pleasing shape, bears glossy leaves through spring and summer, climaxing in a wonderful display of autumn colour. The fruits light up the bare branches in winter like so many lanterns, but are eaten only when soft-ripe. 'Dai Dai Maru' is the most popular variety in Australia.

327   DIOSPYROS kaki
PERSIMMON
JAPANESE PERSIMMON
TREE   20 ft
CHINA   JAPAN   WINTER

DOLICHOS
LEGUMINOSAE

Easiest to grow of all vines, requiring only a scattering of seed in winter, DOLICHOS will rapidly climb any support or hide unsightly fences, tanks, etc. It is evergreen in mild areas and can be either cut back, or torn out and replaced each year. Recommended only for quick emergency cover as the flowers are a rather unpleasant shade of rosy purple and the many pods become quite unsightly.

328   DOLICHOS lignosus
HYACINTH BEAN
AUSTRALIAN PEA
ANNUAL VINE   15 ft
AUSTRALIA   SUMMER

329

330

331

DOMBEYA
STERCULIACEAE

Tall evergreen shrubs, mostly from tropical Africa, the DOMBEYAS flower autumn and winter and make striking specimen plants. Easily struck from cuttings and quick to grow; they really sparkle in a sandy soil that is heavy with compost. DOMBEYA natalensis has downy poplar-shaped leaves and loose clusters of fragrant white flowers which unfortunately turn brown with age.

329   DOMBEYA natalensis
CAPE WEDDING FLOWER
SHRUB   15 ft
NATAL   AUTUMN

DORONICUM
COMPOSITAE

Showy winter and spring-flowering perennials with the brightest yellow flowers imaginable, DORONICUMS like rich acid soil and prefer filtered sunlight. They develop rapidly into dense clumps which should be divided every few years. DORONICUMS have an unpleasant milky sap and bear occasional greyish-green leaves up the length of the flower stem. They are particularly long-lasting cut flowers.

330   DORONICUM X hybridum
LEOPARD'S BANE
PERENNIAL   12 in
CANADA   WINTER

DOROTHEANTHUS
AIZOACEAE

Rare among succulents; the Livingstone Daisy is an annual and can be sown from seed in early spring. It sprouts quickly, even in poor soil, and provided the water is kept up will flower in a few months. It has the typical daisy flowers of the Pigface family, in shades of pink, red and orange; centred with white.

331   DOROTHEANTHUS bellidiformis
LIVINGSTONE DAISY
ICE PLANT
MESEMBRYANTHEMUM
ANNUAL   4 in
CAPE PROVINCE   SPRING

DORYANTHES

332

333

DORYANTHES
AMARYLLIDACEAE

This gigantic Australian bulbous plant makes a huge cluster of up to 100 eight-foot leaves and then tops it all off with a tree-like flower stem 20 ft in height. It prefers semi-shade and plenty of water, and makes a striking feature plant; particularly when it multiplies. The flowers (usually seen at a distance) are scarlet and crimson lily blossoms literally dripping with honey—for this reason they are usually damaged by birds.

332   DORYANTHES excelsa
GIANT LILY
GYMEA LILY
SPEAR LILY
BULB   20 ft
EASTERN AUSTRALIA   SPRING

333   DORYANTHES excelsa
(close-up of flowers)
GYMEA LILY

DOXANTHUS

334

DOXANTHUS
BIGNONIACEAE

DOXANTHUS flowers briefly and brilliantly in early spring, when its golden blossoms are seen blanketing walls and tree trunks; even hanging in sheets from high branches. The fine tendrils cling to anything in reach by means of a series of cat-like claws. It likes full sun and can be cut back hard after flowering.

334   DOXANTHUS unguis-cati
CAT'S CLAW
YELLOW TRUMPET VINE
HUG ME TIGHT
VINE   RAMPANT
TROPICAL AMERICA   SPRING

DRACAENA

335

336

DRACAENA
LILIACEAE

This series of evergreen plants is grown specifically for tropical foliage effect indoors or out, and they prefer a standard tropical soil mixture of peat, leafmould and sand. The species DRACAENA sanderiana grows into a tall fountain of green and white-banded leaves. The smaller D. godseffiana is a spreading ground cover; glossy green with white and yellow spots. It occasionally bears small red flowers. The giant of the family is D. draco (the Canary Island Dragon Tree)—this is grown outdoors for its massed spiky leaves and interesting silhouette.

335   DRACAENA godseffiana
PERENNIAL   9 in
CONGO   SUMMER

336   DRACAENA sanderiana
PERENNIAL   10 ft
CONGO   SUMMER

DROSANTHEMUM

337

DRYANDRA

338

339

DURANTA

340

DROSANTHEMUM
AIZOACEAE

Smallest flowered of the Pigface group of succulents (usually known, incorrectly, as Mesembryanthemums) the DROS-ANTHEMUMS are also the most charming, and a very useful ground cover for rocks or steep banks. Planted a foot or so apart in the poorest soil, they will quickly trail to form dense mats of sparkly pale-green leaves. In spring, these almost disappear under an icing of delicate pale pink daisy flowers.

337   DROSANTHEMUM floribundum
REDONDO CREEPER
SUCCULENT   6 in trailing
CAPE PROVINCE   SPRING

DRYANDRA
PROTEACEAE

Yet another spectacular genus of flowering shrubs from Western Australia, related to Proteas and Banksias. Nearly all winter-flowering in various shades of yellow and orange, DRYANDRAS last well when cut and make striking arrangements. The leaves are generally stiff and saw-toothed, and the plants should be grown in a sheltered place with acid sandy soil and left to their own devices. They do not like cultivation or root disturbance and will not abide lime. Most of them are easily propagated from cuttings, struck in damp soil.

338   DRYANDRA nobilis
GREAT DRYANDRA
SHRUB   8 ft
WESTERN AUSTRALIA   WINTER

339   DRYANDRA polycephala
SHRUB   8 ft
WESTERN AUSTRALIA   WINTER

DURANTA
VERBENACEAE

A useful fast-growing shrub often used as a hedge or windbreak, the DURANTA is attractive at any time of year but breathtaking in late summer when its branches are literally bowed down with orange-yellow berries. The flowers, which are seen at any time, are a delicate china-blue. DURANTA is easy to strike from cuttings and grows in any climate.

340   DURANTA repens
PIGEON BERRY
GOLDEN DEWDROP
GOLDEN TEARS
SHRUB   15 ft
TROPICAL AMERICA   SUMMER

118

341

342

DYCKIA
BROMELIACEAE

A spectacular group of Bromeliads that grow well in the same open sunny aspect that suits Agaves and Yuccas; the DYCKIAS spread from rhizomes like Flag Iris and produce dense rosettes of spiny leaves. The flower stalks are single or many-branched, in the form of candelabra—the flowers themselves are orange or yellow. Perfect drainage is vital, regular watering is required in summer only.

341   DYCKIA altissima
PERENNIAL   4 ft
BRAZIL   SPRING
SUBTROPICAL

ECHEVERIA
CRASSULACEAE

Favourite rockery plants, both for their spreading clusters of succulent leaf-rosettes and useful red and yellow winter flowers. The 150 species of ECHEVERIA are very difficult to identify as they tend to hybridize quite indiscriminately, both with each other and with different succulent species. All natives of the southern states of America and Mexico, they are completely sun and drought proof.

342   ECHEVERIA X hybrida
HEN AND CHICKENS
SUCCULENT   12 in
MEXICO   WINTER

343

344

ECHINACEA
COMPOSITAE

Closely related to Rudbeckias, from which they differ in a few minor botanical details, the ECHINACEAS are showy perennial daisies for the mixed border. Grow them from autumn-planted divisions or seed; they enjoy a deep rich loam and full sun. The rosy-purple flowers are up to 4 in across on tall stems, and ideal for cutting. ECHINACEAS may need staking or tying, particularly in exposed positions.

343 ECHINACEA purpurea
PURPLE CONE FLOWER
PERENNIAL   4 ft
UNITED STATES OF AMERICA
SUMMER

ECHINOPSIS
CACTACEAE

Like strange little spiky balls scattered around haphazardly, ECHINOPSIS produce unbelievably large and fragrant trumpet flowers in dazzling shades of yellow, pink and red. South American in origin, they grow easily in full sun anywhere, but to make them flower is a little more difficult. They need good quality, fast-draining soil with regular water and feeding. If grown in the open rockery, a pebble mulch will prove both beneficial and attractive. ·

344 ECHINOPSIS multiplex
SEA URCHIN CACTUS
HEDGEHOG CACTUS
EASTER LILY CACTUS
CACTUS   3 in
SOUTH BRAZIL   SPRING

ECHIUM

345

346

EICHHORNIA

347

ENKIANTHUS

348

ECHIUM
BORAGINACEAE

Striking blue or pink-flowered biennials and perennials from the Mediterranean and several Atlantic islands—ECHIUMS are all easy to grow; though flowering best in poor quality, well-drained soil. The Pride of Madeira (ECHIUM fastuosum) is a splendid feature plant for seaside gardens, producing tall spikes of blue-purple flowers from spreading mounds of grey foliage. Similar but taller is E. pinin-iana (the twelve-foot Pride of Teneriffe). E. vulgare, a useful biennial for the sea-side garden, is altogether too well-known in inland areas of Australia, where it has become a rampantly spreading weed known as Patterson's Curse. All ECHIUMS have the habit of scattering seed far and wide. The old flower spikes should therefore be pruned and burned.

345　ECHIUM fastuosum
PRIDE OF MADEIRA
TOWER OF JEWELS
PERENNIAL　4 ft
CANARY ISLANDS　SUMMER

346　ECHIUM vulgare
VIPER'S BUGLOSS
PATTERSON'S CURSE
SALVATION JANE
BIENNIAL　3 ft
MEDITERRANEAN　SUMMER

EICHHORNIA
PONTEDERIACEAE

This unusual floating aquatic plant is native to tropical America but has become naturalized in many warm countries with disastrous results. Grow it only where it can be controlled and never in open water-courses, for the plants, kept afloat by bladder-like stems, can drift for miles and take root. The many-flowered spikes of yellow-spotted lilac are attractive right through the warm weather.

347　EICHHORNIA crassipes
WATER HYACINTH
AQUATIC　12 in
TROPICAL ASIA　SUMMER

ENKIANTHUS
ERICACEAE

Grow Azaleas and Ericas—you can grow the delicate ENKIANTHUS, a slow-moving lover of acid mountain soil and semi-shaded places. A background of evergreen shrubbery helps disguise the rather spidery habit and accent the pale flowers and vivid autumn colour. ENKI-ANTHUS is hardy provided the soil acidity is right, but does really well only in cool winter areas. Flowers are white, yellow, pink or red according to species.

348　ENKIANTHUS campanulatus
CHINESE BELL FLOWER
SHRUB　10 ft
ASIA　LATE SPRING

121

EPACRIS

349

EPIDENDRUM

350

351

EPIPHYLLUM

352

EPACRIS
EPACRIDACEAE

The showy Australian or Native Fuchsia is not a Fuchsia at all but an EPACRIS, one of 40-odd species of heath-like shrubs requiring open acid soil rich with leafmould and lightened with sand. Like most Australian natives, it resents disturbance or cultivation. By all means, cut the flower stems as they last well, in fact a hard pruning in late spring will greatly improve flowering the following season.

349   EPACRIS longiflora
NATIVE FUCHSIA
AUSTRALIAN FUCHSIA
SHRUB   5 ft
EASTERN AUSTRALIA   AUTUMN—
SPRING

EPIDENDRUM
ORCHIDACEAE

Popular cane-stemmed orchids for the open garden, EPIDENDRUMS are often seen in the mixed border or rockery where they flower all through the warm weather. Though enjoying full sun, they do best with a cool root run and plenty of dilute liquid fertilizer in the growing season. EPIDENDRUM flowers are exactly like miniature Cattleyas (with which they hybridize) and are available in shades of red, pink, orange, yellow, white and mauve.

350   EPIDENDRUM ibaguense
CRUCIFIX ORCHID
ORCHID   3 ft
COLOMBIA   SUMMER

351   EPIDENDRUM o'brienianum
TREE ORCHID
ORCHID   3 ft
COLOMBIA   SUMMER

EPIPHYLLUM
CACTACEAE

An attractive group of flowering Cacti with spineless flattened stems and a graceful arching habit. The dozen-odd species have been widely crossed and hybridized to produce gorgeous flowers in almost every colour and up to 9 in across. EPIPHYLLUMS are jungle-dwellers, needing semi-shade and a rich, fast-draining compost of sand, leafmould and peat. They strike easily from cuttings and can be grown in large pots, hanging baskets or on the branches of trees in frost-free areas. Slugs and snails find them irresistible—so keep watch!

352   EPIPHYLLUM hybrid
ORCHID CACTUS
EPIPHYTIC CACTUS   2 ft
SOUTH AMERICA   SPRING

122

EREMURUS

ERICA

353

354

356

355

EREMURUS
LILIACEAE

The 30-odd species of EREMURUS are not seen as often as they deserve, for the six-foot spikes of flowers make a fine display in any garden. They like full sun, well-drained soil and must not be disturbed, for the fleshy roots break easily. Flower colours are yellow, pink and white; and the illustrated variety EREMURUS robustus may bear 100 or more peach-coloured blossoms on a single dark-reddish stem.

353   EREMURUS robustus
DESERT CANDLE
FOXTAIL LILY
BULB   6 ft
WEST ASIA   SUMMER

ERICA
ERICACEAE

Charming acid-loving shrubs for full sunlight in cooler districts, ERICAS include many hundreds of natural species and countless hybrids, improved both in size and colour. All of them have fine needle-like leaves, densely clustered on woody stems; and bear masses of bell or tube-shaped flowers. The plants vary from 1 to 15 ft high according to species, and there are some varieties to flower every month of the year; though late winter is the peak. All ERICAS like sandy, well-drained soil, rich in leaf-mould and cannot abide lime or animal manure.
They are usually grown in raised beds by themselves where these special requirements can be sustained. The Spanish Heath (ERICA lusitanica) is easiest to grow and has become naturalised in many parts of Australia. Prune ERICAS after flowering to preserve shapeliness.

354   ERICA X 'Aurora'
SHRUB   4 ft
HYBRID   WINTER

355   ERICA holosericea
SHRUB   2 ft
SOUTH AFRICA   SPRING

356   ERICA lusitanica
SPANISH HEATH
SHRUB   6 ft
SPAIN   WINTER

123

357

359

360

358

ERIGERON
COMPOSITAE

A group of North American daisies which vary from most others in one important point—the flowers have 2 or more rows of fine thread-like petals, generally in shades of violet or pink. They like sandy soil and good drainage; and with the exception of ERIGERON karvinskianus enjoy filtered sun. Plant from divisions in autumn and cut well back after flowering. E. karvinskianus is a popular rockery plant, but rather invasive. It prefers full sun and likes to get its roots under stones. Cut right back periodically to prevent it seeding too freely.

357   ERIGERON karvinskianus
VITTADENIA
FLEABANE
SEASIDE DAISY
PERENNIAL   6 in
MEXICO   SUMMER—AUTUMN

358   ERIGERON speciosum
FLEABANE
PERENNIAL   18 in
UNITED STATES OF AMERICA
SUMMER—AUTUMN

ERIOBOTRYA
ROSACEAE

A tall handsome tree, much favoured for its leathery leaves and juicy aromatic fruit, Loquats are grown from grafted plants. Give them good drainage and plenty of water, preferably in full sun. New shoots are woolly and rust-coloured, autumn flowers are white. The fruit appears in winter clusters and should be sprayed to prevent over-wintering of fruit flies.

359   ERIOBOTRYA japonica
LOQUAT
TREE   20 ft
CHINA   WINTER

ERIOCEPHALUS
COMPOSITAE

A useful South African shrub with deli-cate foliage and inconspicuous purple-centred daisy flowers that expand into woolly balls after flowering. The flower heads are often dried for decoration. ERIOCEPHALUS can be grown from cuttings of young shoots and do best in full sun in a sandy acid soil. There are 20-odd species but only ERIOCEPHA-LUS africanus is widely grown.

360   ERIOCEPHALUS africanus
WOOL FLOWER
SHRUB   6 ft
SOUTH AFRICA   WINTER

ERIOSTEMON

361

362

ERVATAMIA

363

ERYSIMUM

364

ERIOSTEMON
RUTACEAE

Not easy to grow without a deal of attention, the delightful native Wax-flowers of Australia produce masses of waxy pink stars in spring. A well-drained acid compost of leafmould and silver sand suits to perfection and they should be cut back after flowering. Overseas gardeners help both growth and lifespan by grafting cuttings on to shoots of Correa alba, another native shrub.

361   ERIOSTEMON lanceolatus
PINK WAXFLOWER
SHRUB   3 ft
NEW SOUTH WALES   SPRING

362   ERIOSTEMON myoporoides
LONGLEAF WAXFLOWER
SHRUB   4 ft
EASTERN AUSTRALIA   WINTER—SPRING

ERVATAMIA
APOCYNACEAE

Semi-tropical shrubs resembling but not related to Gardenias, the ERVATAMIAS are strictly for the warmer climate. They grow from cuttings, flourish in a soil mixture rich in sand and peat. ERVATA-MIA coronaria is the most popular, its glossy laurel leaves attractive at all times. The snowy-white single or double Gardenia flowers appear in warm weather, are faintly fragrant in the evening.

363   ERVATAMIA coronaria
FLEUR d'AMOUR
ADAM'S APPLE
NERO'S CROWN
CRAPE JASMINE
SHRUB   4 ft
INDIA   SUMMER

ERYSIMUM
CRUCIFERAE

Closely related to the Wallflowers, this dainty creeping perennial produces sheets of tiny golden flowers throughout summer and autumn. Plant in rockeries or at the edge of paving and use as ground cover with Moss Phlox and Aubrieta. It forms quite dense mats, but can be clipped back to shape in winter: new growth will soon appear.

364   ERYSIMUM kotschyanum
BLISTER CRESS
PERENNIAL   6 in
ASIA MINOR   SUMMER—AUTUMN

365

367

366

368

369

ERYTHRINA
LEGUMINOSAE

Favourite specimen trees in temperate to sub-tropical climates, the vividly-flowered Coral Trees are easy to propagate from cuttings or seeds, and mostly grow like wildfire. They are deciduous and often untidy; but come late winter the branches light up with an abundance of brilliantly coloured pea flowers. Favourite varieties include the Indian Coral tree (ERYTHRINA indica); the shrubby E. acanthocarpa (Tambookie Thorn) a dwarf with masses of red and cream flowers in spring; the ubiquitous E. crista-galli (Cockscomb Coral) which dies back to a rather ugly stump each winter; the variegated E. parcelli which does not often flower outside the tropics but has vivid green and yellow leaves throughout most of the year.

365   ERYTHRINA acanthocarpa
TAMBOOKIE THORN
TREE   6 ft
AFRICA   SPRING

366   ERYTHRINA crista-galli
COCKSPUR THORN
COCKSCOMB CORAL
TREE   20 ft
BRAZIL   SPRING—SUMMER

367   ERYTHRINA indica
CORAL BEAN CORAL TREE
INDIAN CORAL TREE
TREE   30 ft
INDIA—AUSTRALIA   WINTER

368   ERYTHRINA parcellii
VARIEGATED CORAL TREE
TREE   20 ft
PACIFIC ISLANDS   SPRING
ALL TROPICAL

ERYTHRONIUM
LILIACEAE

The dog's tooth of the popular name refers to the shape of the bulb rather than the flower. ERYTHRONIUM dens-canis is the only widely cultivated species of many from all over the northern hemisphere. The bulbs are planted in autumn in partial shade. The two-inch mauve and white flowers appear in early spring and the entire plant dies down to rest in summer.

369   ERYTHRONIUM dens-canis
DOG'S TOOTH VIOLET
FAWN LILY
BULB   8 in
EUROPE—ASIA   SPRING

ESCALLONIA

370

ESCHSCHOLTZIA

371

ESCALLONIA
SAXIFRAGACEAE

All 60 species of ESCALLONIA are evergreen and come from Chile and nearby regions. They are hardy, glossy shrubs; at home in sun or shade. They resist wind and drought; look and flower better with adequate water. Most species can be pruned to hedge or specimen shape though this sacrifices many flowers. These are usually quite small and of open bell shape; they vary from white to red.

370   ESCALLONIA macrantha
SHRUB   6 ft
CHILOE   SUMMER
SUBTROPICAL

ESCHSCHOLTZIA
PAPAVERACEAE

Splendid for naturalizing on banks or in country gardens, Californian Poppies give brilliant colour in the mass, but in close-up are inclined to look raggy and discoloured unless dead flowers are trimmed. Broadcast seed where you want them permanently—they will self-sow for years to come. Give Californian Poppies well-drained soil and water regularly till flowering time.

371   ESCHSCHOLTZIA californica
CALIFORNIAN POPPY
ANNUAL   18 in
CALIFORNIA   SPRING—SUMMER

372

374

376

373

375

EUCALYPTUS
MYRTACEAE

Eucalypts are the most obvious feature of Australian vegetation in all states; and some 700 species have been recorded, varying from three-hundred-foot forest giants to the small scrubby Mallee types. Drought-resistance, speed of growth and beauty of form and flower have also led to their export to many other lands; and acceptance as the most widely grown non-native trees in California, Israel and many other arid places. Care should be taken at planting time that the young tree has not become rootbound in its nursery container—a small free-rooting seedling will grow faster than a larger rootbound one. Plant in a shallow hole wider than the widest roots; stake carefully and turn soil in, leaving a slight depression around the trunk. Water well and regularly and protect from frost damage the first year or so. White-flowered weeping EUCALYPTUS niphophila (the Snow Gum) is a good type for cooler areas. Scarlet E. ficifolia the most spectacular for temperate climates. Cream-flowered, red-stemmed E. corymbosa (the Blood-wood) is eye-catching too—as is the tall silver-barked E. citriodora (Lemon-Scented Gum). Many Western Australian shrubby species have large flowers.

372   EUCALYPTUS   corymbosa
BLOODWOOD
TREE   30 ft
NEW SOUTH WALES   SUMMER

373   EUCALYPTUS ficifolia
RED-FLOWERING GUM
TREE   40 ft
WESTERN AUSTRALIA   SUMMER

374   EUCALYPTUS globulus
TASMANIAN BLUE GUM
TREE   75 ft
TASMANIA   ALL YEAR

375   EUCALYPTUS racemosa
NARROWLEAF IRONBARK
TREE   50–80 ft
NEW SOUTH WALES–QUEENSLAND
SUMMER

EUCOMIS
LILIACEAE

Set out bulbs of EUCOMIS in early spring for autumn flowers, and be sure to plant them in a group for striking effect most of the year. From the centre of a clump of crisp, wavy leaves will come purple-spotted stems bearing hundreds of greenish flowers, sometimes tinged with mauve—and to top them all off a tuft of leaves just like a pineapple. They are popular cut flowers, lasting for weeks in water. Grown in greenhouses in colder climates.

376   EUCOMIS comosa
PINEAPPLE LILY
BULB   2 ft
SOUTH AFRICA   AUTUMN
SUBTROPICAL

377

379

380

378

EUGENIA
MYRTACEAE

A large genus (some 700 species) of trees and shrubs grown largely for their ornamental and often edible fruit. There are species from Africa, South America and Asia as well as Australia; though the tropical types need a warm climate to be worthwhile. The Australian natives can be grown from seed or cuttings. They like a sheltered frost-free position with acid soil and develop into neat symmetrical trees with dense evergreen foliage. They are decorative in spring when the new leaves appear in vivid colours, in summer when they are sprinkled with starry white blossom and in autumn when the berry fruits appear in shades of red, pink, violet or blue according to species. Of the tropical EUGENIAS, the best known is the Malay Apple (EUGENIA malaccensis) a rangy grey-barked tree which produces pom-poms of crimson-purple stamens direct from the branches and trunk. These are followed by edible rose-coloured fruits, the size of an egg. The Malay Apple does not flourish more than 30° from the equator.

377   EUGENIA australis
ROSE APPLE
BRUSH CHERRY
SCRUB CHERRY
TREE   20 ft
QUEENSLAND   AUTUMN

378   EUGENIA luehmanii
SMALL-LEAF LILLY-PILLY
TREE   20 ft
NORTH-EASTERN AUSTRALIA
AUTUMN

379   EUGENIA malaccensis
MALAY APPLE
TREE   15 ft
MALAYA   SUMMER
SUBTROPICAL

EUPATORIUM
COMPOSITAE

An enormous genus of shrubs and herbs, mostly from the Americas, EUPATOR-IUMS are frequently mistaken for over-grown Ageratums which they strongly resemble. The Violet Mist Flower makes a splendid contrast to pink spring blossom and is often planted in the mixed border. Grow from spring cuttings and give them a soil well-drained and rich in leafmould, regular water and liquid manure at flowering time. For warm climates.

380   EUPATORIUM sordidum
VIOLET MIST FLOWER
SHRUB   3 ft
MEXICO   SPRING

129

381

383

385

382

384

386

EUPHORBIA
EUPHORBIACEAE

More than 1,000 annuals, perennials, shrubs and succulents—many with little or no resemblance one to the other, and coming from the four corners of the world. All EUPHORBIAS—but what do they have in common? Firstly an unpleasant milky sap, usually poisonous. Secondly, spectacular flower-like arrangements which are not flowers at all, but a series of highly-coloured bracts or modified leaves surrounding a group of tiny simple flowers; some male; some female. The Poinsettia (EUPHORBIA pulcherrima) is the showiest; and the spiny E. milii (Crown of Thorns) can make a good display as well. Lime-coloured E. wulfenii and green and white E. marginata are valued for flower arrangements. Many of the succulent species such as E. caput-medusae are often mistaken for Cacti. All succulent EUPHORBIAS dislike winter frost, and are best grown in warmer climates.

381   EUPHORBIA caput-medusae
MEDUSA'S HEAD
GORGON'S HEAD
SUCCULENT   15 in
SOUTH AFRICA

382   EUPHORBIA milii
CROWN OF THORNS
SHRUB   4 ft
TROPICS   ALL YEAR

383   EUPHORBIA pulcherrima
POINSETTIA
SHRUB   10 ft
MEXICO   WINTER

384   EUPHORBIA pulcherrima 'Alba'
WHITE AND PINK POINSETTIAS
SHRUBS   10 ft
HYBRID   WINTER

385   EUPHORBIA pulcherrima
'Plenissima'
DOUBLE POINSETTIA
SHRUB   10 ft
MEXICO   WINTER

386   EUPHORBIA wulfenii
PERENNIAL   4 ft
EUROPE   SUMMER

EURYOPS

387

FAGUS

388

EURYOPS
COMPOSITAE

Shrubby evergreens from South Africa,
producing brilliant yellow daisy flowers
over a long season centring on winter
in warm climates. Easy to strike from
cuttings, they need perfect drainage but
little water. Windy coastal positions suit
them to perfection, but heavy frosts will
cut them right back. Give EURYOPS full
sun and cut off all faded blooms.

387   EURYOPS athanasiae
MARGUERITE OTHONNA
SHRUB   3 ft
SOUTH AFRICA   WINTER

FAGUS
FAGACEAE

Magnificent deciduous trees for lime-
rich soils, the European Beeches feature
astonishing variations of leaf colour
(green, copper, gold, purple and variegated); leaf form (smoothly-rounded,
toothed or deeply-lobed); habit (tall,
spreading or weeping). They enjoy
shade and make decorative container
plants. The purple-leafed FAGUS sylvatica 'Purpurea' is most popular. Propagation is by grafting. The American Beech
is FAGUS grandifolia, now used where
a large tree is practical.

388   FAGUS sylvatica 'Purpurea'
COPPER BEECH
PURPLE BEECH
TREE   30 ft
EUROPE   SPRING—AUTUMN

FATSHEDERA

389

FATSIA

390

FEIJOA

391

FATSHEDERA
ARALIACEAE

A natural cross between the European Ivy and the Japanese Fatsia, FATSHEDERA has giant Ivy leaves and flowers; can be grown as a shrub or a vine. It makes a very hardy house plant. FATSHEDERA is frost-tender and likes partial shade and protection from wind. Best trimmed and shaped regularly for it tends to become bare and leafless when grown too tall. Watch out for snails and aphis.

389   FATSHEDERA X lizei
JAPANESE IVY
VINE-SHRUB   6 ft
HYBRID   AUTUMN

FATSIA
ARALIACEAE

Hardy evergreen shrubs for full-shade—the FATSIAS help create an exciting tropical effect in mild climates with their lush fan-shaped leaves. Growing in any soil, FATSIA is a good container plant but needs regular water and feeding to retain a healthy appearance. It is propagated from suckers and can be cut back in late winter when too leggy. Plain and variegated leaf varieties are obtainable.

390   FATSIA japonica 'Variegata'
JAPANESE ARALIA
SHRUB   6 ft
JAPAN   ALL YEAR

FEIJOA
MYRTACEAE

Though it fruits sparingly away from the Tropics, FEIJOA is perfectly hardy, and can be grown in almost any type of climate for charming red, white and yellow perfumed flowers. Prune it, shape it, espalier it; train it as a hedge or tree; it will thrive anywhere, particularly if the soil is on the chalky side. Most varieties require cross-pollination to fruit at all.

391   FEIJOA sellowiana
PINEAPPLE GUAVA
SHRUB   6 ft
BRAZIL   SUMMER

FELICIA

392

393

FICUS

394

395

396

397

FELICIA
COMPOSITAE

FELICIAS add blue and mauve to the spectrum of daisy flowers. Best known is the Blue Marguerite (FELICIA amelloides), so hardy and quick growing it is often treated as an annual. Three-inch tip cuttings will root quickly and make a three-foot wide bush in little over a month. Shape regularly and remove dead flowers. F. angustifolia is a splendid choice for large rockeries or sunny banks.

392   FELICIA amelloides
BLUE MARGUERITE
BLUE DAISY
AGATHEA
SHRUB   18 in
SOUTH AFRICA   ALL YEAR

393   FELICIA angustifolia
KINGFISHER DAISY
SHRUB   4 ft
SOUTH AFRICA   SPRING

FICUS
MORACEAE

A large and useful genus of evergreen and deciduous trees, shrubs and vines. Most of them are grown for tropical effect and leaf interest of one sort or another, and although all bear fruit, only that of the Common Fig (FICUS carica) is considered edible. Popular decorative species include the graceful F. benjamina, a hardy tree with weeping branches and one-inch glossy leaves. F. elastica, probably the most popular of all as the India Rubber Plant has some charmingly variegated forms, notably variety 'Doescheri'. F.lyrata (the Fiddleleaf Fig) has particularly dramatic leaf shape for indoor effects. F. macrophylla (Queensland's enormous Moreton Bay Fig) may grow to 150 ft wide and is right out of favour for modern gardens. F. pumila (the dainty Creeping Fig) is useful so long as its vigour is respected. The invasive roots attach themselves to stone or brick and ultimately destroy it if not cut right back every few years. Delicate young shoots can easily develop into heavy branches if not watched.

394   FICUS benjamina
WEEPING FIG
WEEPING CHINESE BANYAN
TREE   60 ft
TROPICAL ASIA   ALL YEAR

395   FICUS elastica 'Doescheri'
INDIA RUBBER PLANT
TREE   8–100 ft
TROPICAL ASIA   ALL YEAR

396   FICUS lyrata
FIDDLELEAF FIG
BANJO FIG
SHRUB   10 ft
AFRICA   ALL YEAR

397   FICUS pumila 'Minima'
CREEPING FIG
CLIMBER
JAPAN–CHINA   ALL YEAR

398

399

FITTONIA
ACANTHACEAE

Reliable hothouse or tropical perennials from South America, the FITTONIAS grow easily in sheltered, shady places provided they are given a fast-draining peaty soil and plenty of water. They are propagated from cuttings which root easily. Pink-veined FITTONIA verschaffeltii is slightly less hardy than its white-veined variety Argyroneura. Both flower, but the leaves are the main interest.

398   FITTONIA verschaffeltii
FITTONIA verschaffeltii var. Argyroneura
NERVE PLANT
PERENNIAL   12 in
PERU   WARM SEASON
TROPICAL

FORSYTHIA
OLEACEAE

Golden-flowered deciduous shrubs that light up the cool-climate garden at the first hint of spring. Grown easily from cuttings, they must have rich, well-drained soil to flower well, and should be cut back and fertilized as soon as the flowers have dropped. Six species are recognized, but almost all the garden varieties are hybrids of FORSYTHIA suspensa.

399   FORSYTHIA suspensa
GOLDEN BELLS
SHRUB   10 ft
CHINA   WINTER
HARDY

FORTUNELLA

400

FRAGARIA

401

402

FRAXINUS

403

404

FORTUNELLA
RUTACEAE

Grown mostly for the decorative value of its winter fruits like perfect one-inch oranges, FORTUNELLA can be trained to formal globular shape for tub planting or allowed to assume its natural weeping habit in the open garden. Leaves and flowers too are just like a miniature orange; and the plant requires warm sun, plenty of water and fertilizer to fruit well. Spray against white wax scale.

400   FORTUNELLA japonica
MARUMI KUMQUAT
SHRUB   4 ft
JAPAN   WINTER

FRAGARIA
ROSACEAE

The delicious strawberry in its many species and varieties is grown not only for the fruit but for its decorative effect as a ground cover and rock garden plant. FRAGARIA chiloensis, the original South American parent of the edible fruit, spreads fast from runners, has charming white flowers, small sweet fruits and colours brilliantly in autumn. Its variety 'Ananassa' is the edible berry. Japanese F. indica has yellow flowers and insipid fruit of interest only to birds.

401   FRAGARIA chiloensis 'Ananassa'
STRAWBERRY
PERENNIAL   TRAINING
SOUTH AMERICA
SPRING—SUMMER

402   FRAGARIA indica
WILD STRAWBERRY
TRAILING PERENNIAL   4 in
INDIA—JAPAN   SPRING—AUTUMN

FRAXINUS
OLEACEAE

The northern hemisphere's indigenous Ash Trees are represented in southern gardens only by their more ornamental species with coloured leaves. In cooler mountain areas with deep soil and not too drying winds these are among the most delightful of summer specimens. FRAXINUS excelsior (the European Ash) has many varieties with leaves golden, variegated, blotched and fringed—the slimmer F. oxycarpa is usually seen with foliage in a range of rich claret shades. Both are slow growers.

403   FRAXINUS excelsior
EUROPEAN ASH (COLOURED LEAF VARIETIES)
TREE   30 ft
EUROPE   SUMMER—AUTUMN

404   FRAXINUS excelsior
(flowers)

405

407

408

406

409

FREESIA
IRIDACEAE

Once prized solely for their unique fragrance, dainty Freesias now have a long flowering season and a wide variety of colourful hybrids. Freesias grow outdoors or in pots from autumn-sown seed or bulbs; and begin to produce their leaves with the first winter rain. They like moisture and good drainage and need protection from hot afternoon sun, particularly the coloured types, which are inclined to fade.

405   FREESIA refracta
BULB   12 in
SOUTH AFRICA   SPRING

406   FREESIA X 'Flame'
BULB   15 in
HYBRID   SPRING

407   FREESIA mendota
ORANGE FREESIA
BULB   10 in
SOUTH AFRICA   SPRING

FUCHSIA
OENOTHERACEAE

Today's garden FUCHSIAS are almost all hybrids from a number of South American species and impossible to sort out botanically. Over 500 named varieties are listed, and they flower continuously from late spring well into winter. Cool, semi-shaded positions suit FUCHSIAS best; the soil lightened and enriched with sand, leafmould and bone meal. FUCHSIAS are ideal subjects for the shady border but can also be grown in bushhouses and hanging baskets. Training on supporting pillars shows off the graceful hanging flowers to perfection. Winter pruning improves flower yield, and the cuttings taken can be struck to form new plants.

408   FUCHSIA X magellanica
'Tom Thumb'
SHRUB   6 ft
CHILE   SPRING

409   FUCHSIA X 'Pink Ballet Girl'
SHRUB   3 ft
HYBRID   AUTUMN

410

411

410   FUCHSIA X 'Lena'
SHRUB   3 ft
HYBRID   AUTUMN

411   FUCHSIA triphylla X
'Gartenmeister Bonstedt'
SHRUB   2 ft
WEST INDIES   SUMMER
SUBTROPICAL

412

GAILLARDIA
COMPOSITAE

Grown as annuals in cold climates
GAILLARDIAS are sun-loving perennials from the south-west of the United
States. GAILLARDIAS romp through
heat and drought producing flowers in
the gay but gaudy colours of an Indian
blanket. Single or double hybrids of the
species GAILLARDIA aristata are available, and most can be grown from seed
in a light well-drained soil. The leaves
are grey-green and rough to the touch,
the flowers appear from early summer
to winter.

412   GAILLARDIA aristata
BLANKET FLOWER
PERENNIAL   18 in
UNITED STATES
WARM WEATHER

137

GALTONIA

413

GAMOLEPIS

414

GARDENIA

415

416

GALTONIA
LILIACEAE

South Africa again is home to this tall summer beauty; closely related to the hyacinth, and resembling it in everything except size and perfume. A splendid feature behind lower plants, its large bulbs are planted 6 in deep in autumn and resent disturbance. In cooler districts they need a deep winter mulch, for they are frost-sensitive. Keep watch for slugs and snails which love the juicy leaves.

413   GALTONIA candicans
SUMMER HYACINTH
BERG LILY
BULB   4 ft
SOUTH AFRICA   SUMMER

GAMOLEPIS
COMPOSITAE

An untidy, straggly shrub that needs regular pruning and pinching to maintain any sort of shape at all. GAMOLEPIS is virtually indestructible; resists sun, frost and drought to produce gay yellow flowers throughout the year; re-seeding as it grows. GAMOLEPIS strongly resembles Euryops (see: EURYOPS) but the leaves are larger and toothed.

414   GAMOLEPIS chrysanthemoides
PARIS DAISY
SHRUB   6 ft
SOUTH AFRICA   ALL YEAR
NOT HARDY

GARDENIA
RUBIACEAE

Sweet-scented, snowy-white GARDENIAS are cherished in every part of the world for bridal bouquets and decorative work, but a hot summer is their prime requirement. In addition, they need plenty of water and feeding with an acid plant food at least once a month. Spraying the leaves (but not flowers) in the early morning is a good way of keeping up their humidity requirements. Most garden types are varieties of GARDENIA jasminoides: variety 'Radicans' is 12 in high with one-inch flowers and spreads rapidly: variety 'Florida' has double three-inch flowers: variety 'Professor Pucci' has showy semi-double blossoms up to 5 in. G. thunbergii is quite a different plant, taller and more tolerant of cold. It bears single periwinkle-type flowers, usually in autumn.

415   GARDENIA jasminoides 'Florida'
SHRUB   4 ft
CHINA   SPRING—AUTUMN

416   GARDENIA thunbergii
SHRUB   10 ft
SOUTH AFRICA   AUTUMN

138

GARRYA

GAZANIA

417

418

420

419

GARRYA
GARRYACEAE

The male form of this small evergreen tree from California produces spectacular curtains of greyish-yellow nine-inch catkins during winter. The less attractive female plant has smaller green catkins followed by purple fruits when trees of each sex are planted. GARRYA is difficult to propagate, although layers are usually successful. Any soil suits, so long as the position is shaded.

417   GARRYA elliptica
SILK TASSEL
CURTAIN BUSH
FRINGE TREE
QUININE BUSH
TREE   20 ft
CALIFORNIA   WINTER
SUBTROPICAL

GAZANIA
COMPOSITAE

South Africa's showy GAZANIAS include 24 species which have been widely hybridized to produce the varieties we know today. There are two main types; trailing and clump-forming. Best of the former is apricot-bronze GAZANIA uniflora with silver-grey leaves. The orange G. splendens is the only original clumping species seen these days—the others are hybrids sold under the general name of G. hybrida. Colours include white, yellow-green, pink, tan and orange: double or single; striped, ringed and splashed. Plant in any soil, water occasionally and feed with a slow-acting fertilizer before spring flowering. GAZANIAS are unsurpassed for summer colour whether in rockeries, borders or footpath planting.

418   GAZANIA hybrida
TREASURE FLOWER
PERENNIAL   12 in
SOUTH AFRICA   SPRING—SUMMER

419   GAZANIA splendens
BLACK EYED SUSAN
PERENNIAL   12 in
SOUTH AFRICA   SPRING—SUMMER

420   GAZANIA uniflora
TRAILING GAZANIA
PERENNIAL   12 in
SOUTH AFRICA   SUMMER

GELEZNOWIA

421

GELSEMIUM

422

GENISTA

423

424

GELEZNOWIA
RUTACEAE

Australian native shrubs for the hot sandy position—GELEZNOWIAS are closely related to both Boronia and Citrus. When drainage is perfect and soil to the plant's liking, it branches heavily, each woody stem becoming crowded with round grey-green leaves. The small yellowish flowers cluster in dense masses at stem tops, and last for weeks when cut.

421   GELEZNOWIA verrucosa
SHRUB   2 ft
WESTERN AUSTRALIA   WINTER
SUBTROPICAL

GELSEMIUM
LOGANIACEAE

Shiny yellow trumpet flowers, pleasantly fragrant, are the trademark of this useful climbing shrub: they appear in late winter. GELSEMIUM is not self-supporting and needs a trellis or wire mesh to twine upwards so it can fall in delicate green curtains. It is also useful as a ground cover, spilling down banks and walls; but should be kept away from children as the entire plant is poisonous.

422   GELSEMIUM sempervirens
CAROLINA JASMINE
CLIMBER   20 ft
SOUTHERN UNITED STATES
WINTER

GENISTA
LEGUMINOSAE

Once given space in your garden, you have the delightful Canary Island Broom for a lifetime; it seeds continuously and pops up everywhere. GENISTA is frost-tender, but indifferent to soil quality. The small yellow pea-flowers appear throughout spring and summer. GENISTA monosperma is more delicate both in habit and perfume—the graceful branches an unforgettable sight in spring, literally bending under the weight of tiny white pea-flowers which appear from end to end. Not fussy about soil, it appears to do better than other species in areas where there is a winter chill. The shrub tends to become top-heavy and early staking is advisable.

423   GENISTA canariensis
CANARY ISLAND BROOM
SHRUB   8 ft
CANARY ISLANDS   SPRING—
SUBTROPICAL

424   GENISTA monosperma
WHITE WEEPING BROOM
SHRUB   8 ft
NORTH AFRICA   SPRING
SUBTROPICAL

GENTIANA

425

GERANIUM

426

427

GERBERA

428

429

GENTIANA
GENTIANACEAE

Although Gentians have given their name to the most brilliant of all blues, the range does include mauve, red, white and even yellow. They are rather finicky alpine plants, requiring winter cold, full sun and absolutely no trace of lime whatever. Give them sharp drainage, a damp soil and a pebble mulch to ensure a cool root run. Tiny GENTIANA acaulis with great trumpet-shaped blue flowers is the best variety.

425   GENTIANA acaulis
GENTIAN
PERENNIAL   4 in
EUROPE   LATE SPRING

GERANIUM
GERANIACEAE

The popular range of plants known as Scented, Fancyleaf and Ivy Geraniums do not belong to this genus at all, and you will find them listed correctly as Pelargoniums. We are dealing with the true GERANIUMS or Cranes Bills; hardy alpine plants for the rockery or sunny slope; most of them with an attractive trailing habit. The colour range is limited; pink, mauve and blue with open five-petalled flowers and deeply-lobed leaves. GERANIUMS like well-drained soil in full sun and need no maintenance beyond regular removal of seed pods to keep them tidy. Pink GERANIUM ibericum, cerise G. wallichianum and hybrid 'Johnson's Blue' are good types.

426   GERANIUM X 'Johnson's Blue'
CRANES BILL
PERENNIAL   12 in
HYBRID   SUMMER

427   GERANIUM wallichianum
PERENNIAL   12 in
HIMALAYAS   SUMMER

GERBERA
COMPOSITAE

Unequalled as a cut flower, the splendid GERBERA is surely the most decorative of daisies, with a wide colour range of crimson, red, orange, pink, yellow and many pastel tones. Both single and double hybrids have been bred from the original Barberton Daisy, a smaller orange-coloured species from the Transvaal. GERBERAS hate really cold weather, like full sun and must have perfect drainage. Regular watering and feeding are essential for good flower quality. Plant out from divisions in autumn, or grow from seed. GERBERAS rapidly form clumps and have a wide leaf spread— 2 ft between plants is not too much.

428   GERBERA jamesonii
AFRICAN DAISY
BARBERTON DAISY
TRANSVAAL DAISY
PERENNIAL   18 in
TRANSVAAL   SPRING–SUMMER

429   GERBERA X jamesonii hybrid
PERENNIAL   18 in
HYBRID   SPRING–SUMMER

141

430

431

432

433

434

GEUM
ROSACEAE

Not seen often in these days of mini-gardens; old-fashioned GEUMS sprawl and scramble in the toughest of conditions to produce lots of red and yellow flowers for cutting. But they do require valuable room to produce a good display. The foliage is rather like a straw-berry's—the flower like a small single ranunculus. The once popular bedding species in mixed colours is GEUM chiloense. GEUMS are planted from divisions in autumn or raised from spring-sown seed. They prefer full sun and good drainage and the bedding varieties need protection from wind.

430　GEUM X borisii
PERENNIAL　6 in
BULGARIA　SPRING–SUMMER

431　GEUM chiloense
AVENS
PERENNIAL　2 ft
CHILOE　SPRING–SUMMER

GLADIOLUS
IRIDACEAE

Florists' favourites for presentation sheafs, the tall multi-coloured spikes of Gladiolus are hybrids of many species, mostly from Africa. Many of these older species, though smaller plants, are still grown for their charming flowers. These include GLADIOLUS psittacinus (the Parrot Gladiolus) and G. nanus. All Gladioli are easy to grow from flat corms which can be planted any time for a regular succession of bloom throughout the year. Corms should be dipped in fungicide before planting, and sprayed against the many insects which find them attractive.

432　GLADIOLUS X Hybridus
'Cherbourg
SWORD LILY
BULB　5 ft
AFRICA　ALL YEAR

433 GLADIOLUS nanus 'The Bride'
DWARF GLADIOLUS
BULB　12 in
SOUTH AFRICA　SPRING

434　GLADIOLUS psittacinus
PARROT GLADIOLUS
BULB　3 ft
EAST AFRICA　AUTUMN

435

436

GODETIA
OENOTHERACEAE

Carmine, white, crimson and salmon in many combinations and graduations place GODETIAS among the most useful summer annuals. Grow them in good soil, keep them damp, and they will produce a long succession of flowers for cutting. GODETIAS are native to the United States where many named varieties are available—elsewhere they are usually seen in mixed colours.

435   GODETIA grandiflora
ANNUAL   2 ft
CALIFORNIA   SUMMER

GOMPHOLOBIUM
LEGUMINOSAE

Showy summer-flowering Australian shrubs, belonging to the gigantic pea family, GOMPHOLOBIUMS are more widely cultivated overseas than in their native land, perhaps because of a reputation for being poisonous to stock. Sandy soil, perfect drainage and not too much water are the prime requirements —and they are frost-tender, preferring a warm coastal climate. GOMPHOLO-BIUM flowers are noteworthy for their golden brilliance and can be propagated from seed.

436   GOMPHOLOBIUM grandiflorum
GOLDEN GLORY PEA
LARGE WEDGE PEA
SHRUB   4 ft
EASTERN AUSTRALIA   SUMMER
SUBTROPICAL

GOMPHRENA

437

GORDONIA

438

GREVILLEA

439

440

GOMPHRENA
AMARATIIACEAE

Purple clover might be the first impression of dainty Globe Amaranths—but the plants are stiffer and more branching, and vary from 3 to 12 in high according to variety. GOMPHRENAS are planted out in late spring, flower throughout most of the hot weather. Dried carefully, they retain full colour for winter arrangements

437   GOMPHRENA globosa
GLOBE AMARANTH
ANNUAL   12 in
INDIA   SUMMER

GORDONIA
THEACEAE

Related to the Camellia which it greatly resembles, the handsome GORDONIA is a tall fast-growing evergreen shrub with dark lustrous leaves and snowy-white three-inch flowers all winter long. It is native to the more tropical parts of China and frost-tender. Strike from cuttings and grow in a lime-free, open sandy soil.

438   GORDONIA axillaris
GORDONIA
SHRUB   15 ft
CHINA—FORMOSA   AUTUMN

GREVILLEA
PROTEACEAE

A showy Australian genus: Grevilleas vary widely from prostrate ground covers to giant trees. They have slender flowers in large spidery clusters, often blooming in winter. Grevilleas must have good drainage, full sun and light, humus-rich soil. They prefer an acid balance but will tolerate lime to some extent. They will not tolerate root disturbance. Those illustrated are only a handful of the 230-odd recognized species and in addition there are countless colourful named hybrids, including 'Olympic Flame', 'Poorinda Queen' and 'Poorinda Constance'. The most spectacular tree form is GREVILLEA robusta (the Silky Oak) often used as a houseplant because of its silvery divided leaves.

439   GREVILLEA banksii 'Forsteri'
TREE   20 ft
QUEENSLAND   SPRING

440   GREVILLEA biternata
WOOLLY GREVILLEA
SHRUB   5 ft
WESTERN AUSTRALIA   AUTUMN

144

441

443

442

444

441   GREVILLEA juniperina 'Rubra'
JUNIPER GREVILLEA
SHRUB   4 ft
NEW SOUTH WALES   SPRING

442   GREVILLEA punicea
RED SPIDER FLOWER
SHRUB   5 ft
NEW SOUTH WALES   SPRING

443   GREVILLEA robusta
SILKY OAK
SILVER OAK
SILK BARK OAK
TREE   80 ft
NEW SOUTH WALES   SUMMER
SUBTROPICAL

GYPSOPHILA
CARYOPHYLLACEAE

A short life but a gay one is the story of
GYPSOPHILA. It grows from seed,
reaches flowering size and dies all
within 2 months or so, and for this
reason is re-sown every 3 weeks for
continuous warm weather bloom. Not
used much for cutting these days, it
contrasts well with dark shrubbery.
G. paniculata is grown as a hardy perennial, reaching a height of 3 feet.

444   GYPSOPHILA elegans
BABY'S BREATH
CHALK PLANT
ANNUAL   1-3 ft
ASIA MINOR   SPRING

HAEMANTHUS

445

446

HAKEA

447

448

HAEMANTHUS
AMARYLLIDACEAE

A vividly coloured genus of bulbous flowers (over 50 species) from tropical Africa. They are easy to grow though they do require summer moisture and a dry winter. The large bulbs cannot abide waterlogging so must be planted in light soil with good drainage, preferably in a partially shaded position—pot culture solves many problems. The Ox-tongue Lily (HAEMANTHUS coccineus) blooms without leaves; the flower compressed into a flat shape. H. multiflorus resembles a six-inch dandelion puff-ball, all bright red. The flower is followed by a tall vase-shaped spike of leaves.

445 HAEMANTHUS coccineus
OX-TONGUE LILY
MARCH LILY
APRIL FOOL
BLOOD FLOWER
WITCHES' PAINT BRUSH
BULB   15 in
SOUTH AFRICA   AUTUMN

446   HAEMANTHUS multiflorus
BLOOD LILY
SCARLET STARBURST
BULB   2½ ft
TROPICAL AFRICA   SUMMER

HAKEA
PROTEACEAE

Tough Australian shrubs that do not like coddling, HAKEAS flower better the harder they are treated. Acid soil, plenty of sun and sharp drainage are ideal, and HAKEAS really take off close to the coast. Ungainly HAKEA laurina (the Pincushion Tree) has a willowy habit, but needs staking in an open position. The glorious red and gold flowers appear like sunbursts in the cold months. The more common H. tenuifolia (syn. H. sericea) produces a mass of silky white or pink flowers in spring to soften its formidable array of stiff spiky needle leaves. Woody seed pods remain on the branches all year after scattering their seed.

447   HAKEA laurina
SEA URCHIN TREE
PINCUSHION FLOWER
PINCUSHION HAKEA
TREE   20 ft
WESTERN AUSTRALIA   WINTER

448   HAKEA tenuifolia
SHRUB   8 ft
EASTERN AUSTRALIA   SPRING

HAMAMELIS

449

HARDENBERGIA

450

HEBE

451

HAMAMELIS
HAMAMELIDACEAE

Valuable for winter flower arrangements, the strap-like golden petals of Chinese Witch Hazel resist frost and icy winds to drape the bare zig-zag branches all through the cold months. Grow them among deciduous trees where the full winter sunlight can reach down, and choose a moist acid soil, enriched with plenty of ground bark and leafmould. American H. Virginiana blossoms in the fall but the capsules do not ripen for a further year.

449   HAMAMELIS mollis
CHINESE WITCH HAZEL
SHRUB   8 ft
CHINA   WINTER

HARDENBERGIA
LEGUMINOSAE

A dainty evergreen climber that twines delicately around twigs, patio columns or wire fences, the Sarsaparilla flowers in a particularly vivid shade of violet–though less common white and pink varieties exist. Light, drained soil; planting in semi-shade avoids the temptation to over-water, which is the most common cause of failure.

450   HARDENBERGIA violacea
(syn. monophylla)
SARSAPARILLA
SHRUBBY VINE   10 ft
AUSTRALIA   SPRING

HEBE
SCROPHULARIACEAE

Useful for landscape work away from frost and dry heat—the HEBES produce showy racemes of violet, blue or white flowers; most usefully in winter. They are densely leafed and can be pruned as hedges and wall plants. Fast-growing; like many other New Zealand plants they are quite resistant to salt air and sea winds. Good drainage required.

451   HEBE speciosa
VERONICA
SHOWY HEBE
SHRUB   5 ft
NEW ZEALAND   WINTER

452

454

455

453

456

HEDERA
ARALIACEAE

Tough dependable climbers for every use; Ivies are great for ground cover; quick as climbers; decorative as house-plants. Ivy also acts as a soil binder on steep banks, and as it spreads along the ground completely smothers weeds and other small plants. Plant Ivy ground covers in early spring from rooted plant-lets, but make sure the soil is thoroughly dug over and enriched with plant food—there will not be a chance to improve it later. Water regularly in hot weather and feed with nitrogen fertilizer twice a year. Many dozens of fancy leaf Ivies are sold, but the hardiest are: HEDERA canarien-sis (the Algerian Ivy), has leaves widely spaced: H. colchica (the Persian Ivy) is heat-resistant and ideal for ground cover. H. helix, the dense-growing English Ivy with its many attractive leaf varieties is much hardier.

452   HEDERA colchica
PERSIAN IVY
CLIMBER   40 ft
ASIA MINOR   ALL YEAR

453   HEDERA helix
ENGLISH IVY
COMMON IVY
CLIMBER   40 ft
EUROPE   ALL YEAR

454   HEDERA helix 'Marginata'
CLIMBER   10 ft
HYBRID   ALL YEAR

HEDYCHIUM
ZINGIBERACEAE

Plant the beautiful White Ginger Blos-som in rich, semi-shaded soil during winter (it grows from shooting sections of rhizome like Flag Iris). It sends up juicy five-foot stems in the spring. The white and lemon butterfly flowers appear among luxuriant leaves at the top of each stalk. Pick them singly for float bowls or cut the whole stem for large floor vases. The related Kahili Ginger (HEDYCHIUM gardnerianum) is easy to grow and certainly more spectacular, producing eighteen-inch spikes of scarlet and yellow blossom all through summer. Kahili Ginger may grow to 8 ft and needs no water in winter.

455   HEDYCHIUM coronarium
WHITE GINGER BLOSSOM
GARLAND FLOWER
BUTTERFLY FLOWER
PERENNIAL   5 ft
INDIA   SUMMER   TROPICAL

456   HEDYCHIUM gardnerianum
KAHILI GINGER
GINGER LILY
YELLOW GINGER
PERENNIAL   8 ft
INDIA   SUMMER   TROPICAL

HEERIA

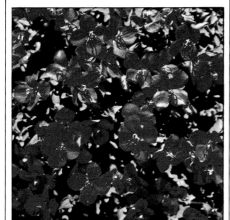

457

HELENIUM

458

HELIANTHEMUM

459

HEERIA (syn. SCHIZOCENTRON)
MELASTOMACEAE

Gayest of all the smaller ground covers, especially in filtered sun, the modest HEERIA of tiny green leaves bursts suddenly into a dazzling sheet of cerise-purple for a few weeks in midsummer. Its popular names are misleading; it is not a Lasiandra or a Fuchsia at all. Pop in a few rooted cuttings and watch them go over rocks or flat areas... or in hanging baskets—magnificent!

457   HEERIA elegans
SPANISH SHAWL
TRAILING LASIANDRA
CREEPING FUCHSIA
PERENNIAL   1 in
MEXICO   SUMMER

HELENIUM
COMPOSITAE

Brownish pom-pom centres set HELE-NIUMS apart from other daisy-flowers, and they enjoy hot summers. Plant from seeds or divisions in late autumn to get them established for summer flowers in a full range of subdued autumn shades. HELENIUMS are useful for the holiday or weekend garden where they suffer neglect happily.

458   HELENIUM autumnale
SNEEZEWEED
PERENNIAL   3 ft
CANADA, UNITED STATES
SUMMER
HARDY

HELIANTHEMUM
CISTACEAE

Small relations of the handsome Cistus or Rock Rose; the HELIANTHEMUMS are spreading shrublets that romp in alkaline soil. Plant out in autumn and let them ramble over rocks, slopes or well-drained raised beds. They will begin to flower in late spring (each bloom lasting one day only) in warm reds, pinks, oranges and yellows. Trim after they fade for more flowers.

459   HELIANTHEMUM nummularium
'Venustum Plenum'
SUNROSE
SHRUBLET   8 in
EUROPE   SUMMER

149

460

461

462

HELIANTHUS
COMPOSITAE

Giants among the annuals, Sunflowers are possibly the easiest of all to grow. Just take some seeds, scatter in good weed-free soil, rake in, water regularly and wait for results. Thinning out or transplanting may be necessary later for a good spacing would be at least 18 in. Plenty of rotted manure or liquid fertilizer helps the plants grow tall and bear flowers up to 14 in across. Sow any time from spring to early summer. HELIANTHUS annuus is the real giant of the family. H. decapetalus is bushier with flowers up to 6 in across, and comes in many double and quilled varieties.

460   HELIANTHUS annuus
SUNFLOWER
ANNUAL   12 ft
UNITED STATES
SUMMER

461   HELIANTHUS decapetalus
Multiflorus'
DOUBLE SUNFLOWER
ANNUAL   6 ft
UNITED STATES
AUTUMN

HELICHRYSUM
COMPOSITAE

One of the few Australian native plants to be successfully improved for garden bedding, the annual HELICHRYSUM is now available in startling colour combinations of red, pink, brown, yellow and white. Seed should be sown direct in spring, or started earlier under glass and the seedlings watered regularly. The flowers can be used fresh, or hung to dry, when they will keep shape and colour for many months.

462   HELICHRYSUM bracteatum
STRAW FLOWER
IMMORTELLE
ANNUAL   2½ ft
HYBRID   SPRING–SUMMER

463

464

465

HELICONIA
MUSACEAE

A remarkably beautiful group of plants
from the Banana family, Heliconias are
strictly for the warm-climate garden or
glasshouse. They prefer filtered sun,
winter warmth and summer humidity.
The flowers are generally insignificant,
hidden inside dazzlingly coloured bracts.
HELICONIA collinsiana produces an
eight-foot stalk which bends over under
a weight of scarlet, yellow and green.
Related H. humilis sends up a four-foot
flower stalk among broad paddle-shaped
leaves—its popular name Lobster Claw
is perfectly descriptive of the red and
green bracts. Individual 'claws' may be
5 in long and cluster heavily right up the
stem. All Heliconias may be grown in
large pots in the warm greenhouse.

463   HELICONIA collinsiana
HANGING HELICONIA
FISHPOLE HELICONIA
PERENNIAL   8 ft
SOUTH AMERICA   SUMMER
TROPICAL

464   HELICONIA humilis
LOBSTER CLAW
PERENNIAL   4 ft
BRAZIL   SUMMER–AUTUMN
TROPICAL

HELIOTROPIUM
BORAGINACEAE

Sweetly fragrant, the old-fashioned
Heliotrope or Cherry Pie of Europe and
America is actually an exotic South
American import—tender to frost and
fast-growing in mild climates. So fast
that many people set out cuttings in
early spring and treat them as annuals.
HELIOTROPIUM rapidly develops a rag-
gedy habit and with its wrinkled leaves
and quick fading lilac flowers can only
be considered for perfume value.

465   HELIOTROPIUM peruvianum
CHERRY PIE
HELIOTROPE
SHRUB   4 ft
PERU   SUMMER

HELIPTERUM

466

HELLEBORUS

467

HELXINE

468

HELIPTERUM
COMPOSITAE

Fifty or sixty species of Paper Daisies can be found somewhere in the vast Australian continent; many of them suitable for cultivation. One of the most charming is the Alpine Paper Daisy (HELIPTERUM albicans) a prostrate perennial with greyish foliage that romps in full sun of a cool climate. It grows easily from seed or cuttings and demands the acid gravelly-type soil of its native alps.

466   HELIPTERUM albicans 'Alpina'
PAPER DAISY
AUSTRALIAN EVERLASTING FLOWER
PERENNIAL   8 in
AUSTRALIAN ALPS   SPRING

HELLEBORUS
RANUNCULACEAE

Useful winter-flowering perennials for the cooler climate, Hellebores provide unusual and exciting colourations for the flower arranger. Apple-green, greenish-white, and many shades of purple are the principal tones. Plant them in masses in the semi-shade of deciduous trees, adding plenty of organic material to the soil. Feed in autumn and give them a year or two to become established.

467   HELLEBORUS orientalis
WINTER ROSE
LENTEN ROSE
HELLEBORE
PERENNIAL   18 in
GREECE   WINTER
HARDY

HELXINE
URTICACEAE

Daintiest and most lushly green of ground covers for cool moist places, HELXINE roots easily from stem cuttings and rolls steadily in all directions; a juicy green carpet, far too delicate to be walked on. Try it around pools, under rocks, in the fernery, even around potted plants. It becomes very untidy in cold weather, turning quite black, but comes to life in spring.

468   HELXINE soleirolli
BABY'S TEARS
ANGEL'S TEARS
PERENNIAL   1 in spreading
CORSICA   ALL YEAR
SUBTROPICAL

HEMEROCALLIS

469

470

HERMODACTYLIS

471

HEUCHERA

472

HEMEROCALLIS
LILIACEAE

A useful genus of perennial bulbs for any climate or type of soil; old-fashioned Daylilies need little care but should be planted on the south side of the garden as flowers turn toward the light. Individual blooms last only one day, but as they come in clusters, a single flower head may be in bloom for weeks. Daylilies are of two principal types; evergreen and deciduous. The evergreen HEMEROCALLIS aurantiaca produces lush clumps of pale-green leaves and has been hybridized to include lemon, pink and purple with the original orange. The deciduous H. fulva is usually seen in double form; orange flowers beautifully marked with mahogany. Daylilies are planted from divisions in winter, and brighter colours are best planted in part-shade to prevent fading.

469   HEMEROCALLIS aurantiaca
DAYLILY
PERENNIAL   3 ft
JAPAN   YEAR ROUND

470   HEMEROCALLIS fulva 'Flore Pleno'
DOUBLE DAYLILY
PERENNIAL   3 ft
JAPAN   SUMMER

HERMODACTYLIS
IRIDACEAE

Rather sinister both in name and colouring, the Snakes' Head Iris is not a real Iris at all, for reasons that interest only serious botanists. It is a hardy little bulb, much valued for flower arrangements, and will grow anywhere the climate is not tropical. Raise it in any soil, sun or shade, so long as the drainage is good. Best planted in clumps to naturalize.

471   HERMODACTYLIS tuberosus
WIDOW IRIS
SNAKES' HEAD IRIS
BULB   12 in
LEVANT   SPRING

HEUCHERA
SAXIFRAGACEAE

A dainty plant for rock garden or border-edgings; HEUCHERA forms neat evergreen clumps of scalloped leaves, rather like Geraniums. But in spring and early summer, the tall wiry stems appear, laden with nodding bell-flowers from white to crimson; but commonly coral pink. Damp sweet soil suits best with full sun except in hot districts. Divide every three years.

472   HEUCHERA sanguinea
CORAL BELLS
ALUM ROOT
PERENNIAL   18 in
MEXICO–SOUTH-WEST UNITED
STATES OF AMERICA   SPRING

473

476

475

477

HIBBERTIA
DILLENIACEAE

Golden Guinea Flowers are one of the showiest genera of Australian native plants, 70 or more species being found in the continent. They include both shrubs and climbers, and HIBBERTIA scandens in particular has become popular all over the world. It is a shrubby vine with evergreen leaves and likes sandy well-drained soil. It thrives on sand dunes, covers rocks and will climb a heavy wall or fence.

473 HIBBERTIA scandens
GUINEA GOLD VINE
SHRUBBY CLIMBER 8 ft
AUSTRALIA SUMMER–AUTUMN

HIBISCUS
MALVACEAE

In the warm-climate garden, Hibiscus is the connoisseur's flower; with as many fans as the Rose, the Camellia and the Azalea all put together. There are over 150 accepted species native to every continent except Europe: shrubs, trees and perennials among them. The named hybrids between these would fill a large encyclopedia. Perennial HIBISCUS moscheutos in pink, red and white is suitable for cooler areas and can be cut right back in winter. Shrubby H. syriacus, mostly with mauve or blue flowers; and both single and double varieties of H. mutabilis can also be grown away from the sub-tropics... the latter fading from white to red. The Tree Hibiscus, (H. tiliaceus) is found by water in every hot part of the world, its golden flowers turning to bronze and crimson as the days pass. Fragrant white H. arnottianus from Hawaii, and cream H. venustus from Tahiti have been crossed with H. rosa-sinensis to produce flowers of incredible size—up to 10 in across! Literally every known colour is represented among them. Hibiscus flowers last only a day (or two at the most) whether left in the garden or picked, and it makes little difference whether you put them in water or not. Scatter them on tables or stick them on a spiky branch. The shrubs are easy to grow in coastal areas, enjoying full sun and well-drained soil. Protect them from frost and wind and feed regularly in the warm weather. You can prune them as hedges—train them as espaliers or let them have their heads.

Hibiscus need spraying against aphis; pruning in spring to keep the flower production up. Plant or move them only in warm weather.

474 HIBISCUS coccineus
ROSE MALLOW
PERENNIAL HIBISCUS
PERENNIAL 5 ft
UNITED STATES OF AMERICA
SUMMER

475 HIBISCUS mutabilis
CONFEDERATE ROSE
SHRUB 8 ft
CHINA SUMMER

476 HIBISCUS rosa-sinensis
BLACKING PLANT
ROSE OF CHINA
CHINESE HIBISCUS
SHRUB 15 ft
CHINA SUMMER

478

480

482

479

481

477   HIBISCUS X 'Tropic Hybrids'
SHRUBS   6 ft
HYBRID   SUMMER

478   HIBISCUS rosa-sinensis
'D. J. O'Brien'
SHRUB   8 ft
HYBRID   SUMMER

479   HIBISCUS schizopetalus
SKELETON HIBISCUS
CORAL HIBISCUS
SHRUB   8 ft
EAST AFRICA   SUMMER

480   HIBISCUS syriacus
ROSE OF SHARON
SHRUB   ALTHAEA
SHRUB   8 ft
SYRIA   SUMMER

481   HIBISCUS tiliaceus
TREE HIBISCUS
HAU TREE
TREE   15 ft
TROPICS   ALL YEAR

HIPPEASTRUM
AMARYLLIDACEAE

Often seen as pot plants, the colourful hybrid HIPPEASTRUMS really enjoy life in the open garden. Fist-sized bulbs should be planted in autumn, the neck at soil level: and the flower stalks will appear before the leaves in late spring and summer. Most of the brightly coloured HIPPEASTRUMS seen are hybrids of the Peruvian HIPPEASTRUM vittatum. Individual flowers are 9 in across, open progressively on two-foot stems.

482   HIPPEASTRUM amaryllis
BARBADOES LILY
GIANT AMARYLLIS
FIRE LILY
ROYAL DUTCH AMARYLLIS
BULB   2 ft
PERU   SUMMER

HOLMSKIOLDIA

483

HOSTA

484

485

HOUSTONIA

486

HOLMSKIOLDIA
VERBENACEAE

A gay little shrub for warm coastal climates or sunny sheltered positions further inland; HOLMSKIOLDIA is evergreen, fast-growing and flowers right through the warm weather, its blossoms a pleasant shade of orangy brick-red. It likes a light, rich soil; and in very hot areas should be planted in semi-shade to prevent the flowers fading. Grow from cuttings in sharp sand.

483   HOLMSKIOLDIA sanguinea
CHINESE HAT PLANT
PARASOL FLOWER
SHRUB   6 ft
INDIA   SUMMER
SUBTROPICAL

HOSTA
LILIACEAE

For shady, moist positions, the elegant Plantain Lilies provide a touch of luxuriant tropic vegetation. Dying down in autumn, the fresh leaves (glossy, heavily-veined, sometimes crimped and variegated) are produced abundantly in spring and are great favourites with flower arrangers. Small bell-like flowers in white or lilac sometimes appear in summer, but these are of secondary interest. Good for poolside or shrubbery —but watch out for slugs!

484   HOSTA fortunei var. albopicta
VARIEGATED PLANTAIN LILY
PERENNIAL   12 in
JAPAN   SUMMER

485   HOSTA plantaginea
FUNKIA
PLANTAIN LILY
PERENNIAL   20 in
CHINA   SUMMER

HOUSTONIA
RUBIACEAE

The starry lilac blue flowers are a delightful surprise when they appear on this tiny mat plant—no taller or more interesting than a sheet of Moss. Give them loose sandy soil in a semi-shaded part of the rockery, or between paving stones, and let them spread. North America is its original home, but now it is found everywhere. The flowers open in late winter in a warm position.

486   HOUSTONIA caerulea
BLUE CUSHION
INNOCENCE
BLUETS
QUAKER LADIES
PERENNIAL   2 in
EASTERN NORTH AMERICA
SPRING

HOVEA

487

HOYA

488

489

HUMEA

490

HOVEA
LEGUMINOSAE

Pea-flowers in brilliant shades of blue, pink and purple deck the branches of HOVEA, a small genus of dwarf ever-green Australian shrubs. Any light sandy soil suits, so long as the drainage is good; and you can grow them from cuttings or seed soaked in hot water. Most vivid species is the Mountain Beauty (HOVEA longifolia) with violet-purple flowers in spring.

487   HOVEA longifolia
MOUNTAIN BEAUTY
SHRUB   5 ft
EASTERN AUSTRALIA   SPRING

HOYA
ASCLEPIADACEAE

Natives of Australia, Asia and the Pacific Islands, HOYAS are summer-blooming climbers with superbly scented flowers like wax dipped in powdered sugar. The twining HOVA carnosa flowers best when completely potbound and must not be pruned as new flowers always appear from the remains of the old. H. bella is a hanging basket subject with flower clusters beneath the branches.

488   HOYA bella
BEAUTIFUL HONEYPLANT
WEEPING SHRUB   3 ft
BURMA   SUMMER

489   HOYA carnosa
WAXFLOWER
WAX PLANT
CLIMBER   30 ft
SOUTH CHINA   SPRING

HUMEA
COMPOSITAE

Few commonly grown biennials are Australian in origin. HUMEA is the exception, though probably best appre-ciated outside its native land. Tall and stately, it shoots up to 6 ft before producing delicate drooping flowers with a delicious incense perfume. Sow seeds in early summer for flowers 18 months later, and plant away from wind. Any soil suits, but manure and charcoal are helpful.

490   HUMEA elegans
INCENSE PLANT
BIENNIAL   6 ft
AUSTRALIA   SUMMER

491

493

495

492

494

HYACINTHUS
LILIACEAE

Most deliciously fragrant of the spring-flowering bulbs, Dutch Hyacinths are the result of hybridizing the old-fashioned Roman Hyacinth (HYACINTHUS orientalis). The original single whites and blues have been improved to include pinks, purples, creams and reds; many of them double-flowered. Buy the largest bulbs available for autumn planting (6 in deep) or grow indoors in bulb fibre or special hyacinth glasses. Hyacinths are best seen in mass-planting rather than rows; and to ensure good flowers in succeeding years it is necessary to feed and water until leaves die away completely.

491   HYACINTHUS orientalis X hybridus
DUTCH HYACINTH
BULB   12 in
HYBRID   SPRING

492   HYACINTHUS orientalis Albulus
ROMAN HYACINTH
FRENCH HYACINTH
BULB   9 in
SOUTH FRANCE   WINTER

HYDRANGEA
SAXIFRAGACEAE

Rewarding shrubs for the shady border or sunless aspect, Hydrangeas produce big showy flower heads and are often used for Christmas decoration in the southern hemisphere. They need rich porous soil and heavy watering all through the hot weather, as they make massive leaf growth. Commonly grown HYDRANGEA macrophylla hybrids are noted for one very striking peculiarity—they do equally well in acid or alkaline soil, *but* in acid conditions they flower in shades of blue and mauve—in alkaline, red or pink. And it is possible to switch from one colour range to the other by chemical addition to the soil. Aluminium sulphate turns them blue—lime turns them pink—it is as simple as that! There are also naturally white and greenish varieties. Other Hydrangea species grown are H. paniculata (the Plumed Hydrangea) with long clusters of fragrant white flowers and leaves that colour in autumn. H. quercifolia (the cream flowered Oak-Leaf Hydrangea) and H. petiolaris (the Climbing Hydrangea) which clings to walls and rocks with aerial roots.

493   HYDRANGEA X macrophylla
FRENCH HYDRANGEA
CHINESE HYDRANGEA
SHRUB   6 ft
HYBRID   SUMMER

494   HYDRANGEA X macrophylla 'Hortensia'
HORTENSIA
BIGLEAF HYDRANGEA
GARDEN HYDRANGEA
SHRUB   12 ft
HYBRID   SUMMER

495   HYDRANGEA paniculata
PLUMED HYDRANGEA
SHRUB   15 ft
CHINA   SUMMER

HYLOCEREUS

496

HYMENOCALLIS

497

HYMENOSPORUM

498

HYLOCEREUS
CACTACEAE

This loveliest of warm-climate flowers is seen at its best on moonlit nights in summer, when it occasionally bursts into breathtaking bloom—the individual flowers like enormous waxy cups brimming with gold stamens may be up to 10 in across. The cactus itself is a rambler with triangular fleshy stems which twine up the highest trees and walls. It needs deep rich soil to perform really well.

496   HYLOCEREUS undatus
NIGHTBLOOMING CEREUS
CACTUS   40 ft
MEXICO   SUMMER

HYMENOCALLIS
AMARYLLIDACEAE

A valuable bulbous plant from South America, fragrant HYMENOCALLIS is hardy in almost every district—cold or hot, wet or dry. Bulbs are planted out in early spring—choosing a sunny position in cold districts. The bulbs demand good drainage and summer water; rapidly develop into a large clump. Broad strap-like leaves are a rich green; the spidery white flowers 4 in across on two-and-a-half-foot stems.

497   HYMENOCALLIS littoralis
SPIDER FLOWER
ISMENE
SPIDER LILY
FILMY LILY
BASKET FLOWER
BULB   2½ ft
SOUTH AMERICA   SUMMER
SUBTROPICAL

HYMENOSPORUM
PITTOSPORACEAE

The heavily perfumed flowers of this lovely Australian native are more often smelled than picked for it has a tall sparse habit and bears its flowers in loose bunches high above the ground. It is a very fast grower, suited to both coastal and cool districts, and is easily propagated from seeds or suckers. The rich butter-yellow flowers fade to cream and their scent is noticeable blocks away.

498   HYMENOSPORUM flavum
SWEETSHADE
NATIVE FRANGIPANI
TREE   40 ft
AUSTRALIA   SPRING

159

HYPERICUM

499

HYPOESTES

500

HYPOXIS

501

HYPERICUM
GUTTIFERAE

A widespread genus represented in the wild on every continent, HYPERICUMS provide all year round colour in mild temperate climate. Over 100 species are in cultivation, mostly shrubs and perennials. All have the typical five-petalled golden flower with prominent stamens. HYPERICUM chinense is a species of medium height: H. leschenaultii grows to 6 ft H. coris is a useful ground cover.

499 HYPERICUM chinense
GOLD FLOWER
ST JOHN'S WORT
AARON'S BEARD
SHRUB   3 ft
CHINA   SUMMER

HYPOESTES
ACANTHACEAE

An attractive foliage plant for the warm climate garden or greenhouse in cool areas—and perfectly described by either of its popular names. HYPOESTES likes a loose acid soil and needs regular feeding and frequent cutting back or renewal from cuttings to look its best. Not often seen in flower, it does sometimes sprout pale purple and white blossoms in midsummer.

500 HYPOESTES sanguinolenta
FRECKLE FACE
PINK POLKA DOT PLANT
PERENNIAL   2 ft
MADAGASCAR   ALL YEAR
SUBTROPICAL

HYPOXIS
AMARYLLIDACEAE

Too seldom seen in the average garden, the many species of HYPOXIS are worthwhile searching out for the brilliant glossy yellow of their starry flowers which tend to green on the underside. HYPOXIS prefers a rough sandy loam slightly on the acid side and is fairly drought-resistant. The flowers appear on short stems in autumn, but are not fragrant.

501 HYPOXIS longifolia
BULB   1½ ft
SOUTH AFRICA   AUTUMN
SUBTROPICAL

IBERIS

502

IBOZA

503

IBERIS
CRUCIFERAE

Free-flowering Candytuft is often mistaken for a large form of Sweet Alice, but is a much showier plant with a wide range of colours and varieties. Sow in autumn or plant in spring with part-shade and regular water. IBERIS amara is the popular hyacinth-flowered white strain: the bushier pink, lilac and crimson types are hybrids of I. umbellata (the Globe Candytuft).

502 IBERIS amara
CANDYTUFT
WRYFLOWER
ANNUAL 15 in
EUROPE SUMMER

IBOZA
LABIATAE

Softly-flowered, spicily-scented, the tender South African IBOZA is of great winter value in a mild climate. Cuttings taken in early spring and struck in sandy, well-drained soil will flower the following winter. The shrubs bear velvety sage-like leaves, and produce long sprays of silvery blossom sprinkled with purple anthers. IBOZA should be cut back hard after winter flowering.

503 IBOZA riparis
MOSCHOSMA
NUTMEG BUSH
SHRUB 5 ft
SOUTH AFRICA WINTER

504

505

506

507

508

ILEX
AQUIFOLIACEAE

The very spirit of Christmas in the northern hemisphere, Hollies include 300 species of shiny-leafed, brightly-berried shrubs that bring cheer to the coldest winter day. They prefer rich, slightly acid soil, but should be grown away from other plants as they do not take to cultivation. Most Holly bushes are either male or female; and berries will not appear on the female plant unless a male plant is nearby, or a male branch has been grafted on. Hollies fruit best in a cold climate and withstand the most freezing temperatures, but they are also popular for their dramatic shapes and foliage in warmer areas. Hollies can be clipped to make splendid hedges or formal container plants.

504   ILEX aquifolium 'Aureo Marginata'
VARIEGATED HOLLY
TREE   30 ft
HYBRID   WINTER

505   ILEX aquifolium 'Fructu Luteo'
YELLOW HOLLY
TREE   30 ft
WINTER

506   ILEX cornuta
HORNED HOLLY
SHRUB   10 ft
CHINA   WINTER

IMPATIENS
BALSAMINACEAE

Wonderful perennials for moist shade in the warmer climate, the many Balsam species are virtually indestructible. Their Botanic name is an allusion to the impatience with which they spread—their many common names are evidence of their popularity. The two most wide-spread types, the Busy Lizzies, are IMPATIENS holstii and I. sultanii. Very similar, they cross readily and have produced brilliant hybrids in shades of carmine, orange, scarlet, rose and lilac. The flowers are followed by elastic pods which scatter seed; but individual varieties can be propagated from cuttings or division, for the branches take root wherever they touch ground. I. Oliveri (the Poor Man's Rhododendron) is a taller plant for cooler areas, producing two-and-a-half-inch flowers in lilac and white. The annual species, I. balsamina 'Camelliaeflora' is much favoured in public gardens and parks.

509

510

511

507   IMPATIENS balsamina
'Camelliaeflora'
BALSAM
ANNUAL   12 in
AFRICA   SPRING

508   IMPATIENS oliveri
POOR MAN'S RHODODENDRON
OLIVER'S SNAPWEED
PERENNIAL   8 ft
EAST AFRICA   SUMMER
SUBTROPICAL

509   IMPATIENS sultanii
SNAPWEED
PATIENCE PLANT
BUSY LIZZIE
PATIENT LUCY
ZANZIBAR BALSAM
SULTAN'S BALSAM
PERENNIAL   18 in
ZANZIBAR   ALL YEAR
SUBTROPICAL

INCARVILLEA
BIGNONIACEAE

Beautifully marked trumpet flowers in pink and mauve are an attractive feature of this perennial from the high places of Tibet. Growing from a mass of fleshy roots, INCARVILLEA sends up ferny leaves and eighteen-inch flower stems in spring. It needs deep, rich soil with perfect drainage, for the roots rot easily; and in really cold places should be lifted and stored each winter.

510   INCARVILLEA delavayi
PRIDE OF CHINA
PERENNIAL   18 in
TIBET   SPRING

INDIGOFERA
LEGUMINOSAE

Long sprays of Wistaria-type blossom appear throughout the warm weather on this dainty weeping shrub. It is highly drought-resistant and very useful in dry coastal gardens where the soil is poor but well-drained. Grow it in full sun or sheltered pockets of large rockeries; and cut back to the ground each winter in cold areas.

511   INDIGOFERA decora
(syn. incarnata)
SUMMER WISTARIA
WEEPING SHRUB   2 ft
CHINA,   JAPAN   SUMMER

IOCHROMA

IPHEION

512

513

IOCHROMA
SOLANACEAE

Long tubular flowers of rich purple hang in heavy clusters throughout the summer on this fast-growing shrub. Raise from cuttings in a warm sheltered spot and give it plenty of water. IOCHROMA will send up succulent stems and felty eight-inch leaves and unless kept in shape can quickly become straggly and untidy. Try it as an espalier or wall shrub and cut back hard during winter.

512   IOCHROMA cyanea
SHRUB   8 ft
COLOMBIA   SUMMER

IPHEION
LILIACEAE

Useful small bulbs for ground cover in neglected areas; IPHEIONS multiply and spread with astounding speed, both from bulb and seed. The leaves are flat and blueish-green with a distinct onion smell, and the star-shaped blue and white flowers appear profusely on six-inch wiry stems in spring. They grow literally in any soil, sunny or shaded. Plant in autumn.

513   IPHEION uniflorum
TRITELEIA
SPRING STAR FLOWER
GLORY OF THE SUN
BULB   6 in
ARGENTINA   SPRING

164

IPOMOEA

514

515

IRESINE

516

IPOMOEA
CONVOLVULACEAE

Morning Glories are the most trouble-free of climbers, both annual and perennial; and can be relied on absolutely to cover a bank or drape an old fence in a single season. Notch seeds with a file, soak in warm water for 2 hours then plant where you want them; once in, they stay for a lifetime. IPOMOEA leari (the Blue Dawnflower) is most popular, and is covered with flashy bright-blue trumpets all summer—each flower opens at dawn, fades by sunset. Its less rampant cousin I. palmata is native to the eastern coast of Australia. The scarlet I. horsfalliae (Brazilian Glory) is seen mostly in warmer climates, as is I. tuberosa (the Wood Rose) so beloved of flower arrangers.

514   IPOMOEA leari
**PURPLE WINDER
BLUE DAWN FLOWER
MORNING GLORY
CLIMBER   20 ft
TROPICAL AMERICA   SUMMER**

515   IPOMOEA palmata
**NATIVE MORNING GLORY
TWINER   20 ft
EASTERN AUSTRALIA   SUMMER**

IRESINE
AMARANTHACEAE

Quick-growing shrubby perennials for milder climates, best treated as annuals if there is any chance at all of winter frosts. They do have spikes of greenish-yellow flowers, but are grown particularly for the brilliant red and violet shades of the leaves. Take cuttings in autumn and grow on indoors till the cold weather is over. Plant IRESINE in the mixed border, or even in containers. They can be shaped to improve branching.

516   IRESINE herbstii
**BLOODLEAF
PERENNIAL   2½ ft
SOUTH AMERICA   SUMMER**

IRIS

517

519

521

518

520

522

IRIS
IRIDACEAE

A vast group of bulbous plants with stiff, sword-like leaves, the Irises include both desert and water plants; grow from true bulbs or tuberous rhizomes. They may also be evergreen or die down completely each winter. The flowers, while differing widely in shape and colour, do have a family similarity, which is three vertical petals (called standards) alternating with three dropping ones (called falls). The flowers may appear singly or in groups: many of them are highly perfumed.

For convenience they are often grouped into three classes: (A) Bulbous. (B) Bearded. (C) Beardless. The *Bulbous* Iris, planted in autumn, are represented in most gardens by the English, Dutch and Spanish types, all hybrids of species IRIS reticulata, I. xiphium and I. xiphioides. They are early-spring flowering in tones of white, blue, yellow and bronze.

The *Bearded* Iris—popularly known as Flags, are further divided into dwarf, intermediate and tall types. Modern varieties are very much ruffled, with broad falls. Colours now include pink, red, yellow, bronze, purple and tan in addition to the original mauves and whites. They grow from rhizomes; flower early summer.

Beardless Iris include most other species and vary too widely for general description. Notable are the gorgeous I. kaempferi which loves boggy conditions, winter-flowering I. stylosa, and quickly-spreading I. sibirica which also loves water.

517   IRIS kaempferi
JAPANESE IRIS
RHIZOME   5 ft
JAPAN   SUMMER

518   IRIS ochroleuca
RHIZOME   4 ft
ASIA MINOR   SPRING

519   IRIS X ('Orange Glint') ('Golden Dream')
DWARF BEARDED IRIS
RHIZOMES   6 in
HYBRID   SPRING

520   IRIS X 'Minnie Colquit'
BEARDED OR FLAG IRIS
RHIZOME   3 ft
HYBRID   SPRING

521   IRIS stylosa
WINTER IRIS
ALGERIAN IRIS
RHIZOME   1½ ft
ALGERIA   WINTER

522   IRIS X xiphium
SPANISH IRIS
BULB   18 in
SPAIN   SPRING

166

523

524

525

523 IRIS X xiphioides 'Imperator'
DUTCH IRIS
BULB 18 in
HYBRID SPRING

ISOLOMA (syn. KOHLERIA)
GESNERIACEAE

A spectacular perennial for the warm climate, or greenhouses in colder areas, KOHLERIA belongs in the same family as African Violets, Achimenes and Gloxinias. It can be struck from top cuttings, or raised from seed, and produces showy tubular flowers of fire-orange with spotted throats. These and the red-edged velvety leaves make it a real show plant for any warmer garden.

524 ISOLOMA (syn. KOHLERIA)
hirsuta
PERENNIAL 4 ft
COLOMBIA SUMMER
SUBTROPICAL

ISPOGON
PROTEACEAE

A small group of evergreen Australian shrubs producing cone-shaped flower heads right through the warm weather in varying shades of yellow, pink, purple and white. These cut well and are useful for large arrangements. Conebushes like acid sandy soil and regular water in the growing season. ISPOGON anemoni-folius is the most commonly seen.

525 ISPOGON anemonifolius
CONEBUSH
DRUMSTICKS
SHRUB 6 ft
NEW SOUTH WALES SPRING–
SUMMER

IXIA

526

527

IXORA

528

529

IXIA
IRIDACEAE

Delicate spring-flowering bulbs for all but the coldest areas, Ixias naturalize well in lawns and can be left in the ground season after season. Planted in late summer, they bloom in early spring on tall wire-like stems. The flowers, heavily-clustered, are in shades of cerise, pink, orange and cream; often with darker centres. The less common tur-quoise-flowered species, IXIA viridiflora, reaches about 3 ft in height.

526   IXIA maculata
AFRICAN CORN LILY
BULB   18 in
SOUTH AFRICA   SPRING

527   IXIA viridiflora
GREEN IXIA
BLUE IXIA
BULB   3 ft
SOUTH AFRICA   SPRING

IXORA
RUBIACEAE

Colourful shrubs and small trees from all over Asia, Africa and the Pacific Islands, IXORAS are striking plants for gardens where the humidity is high. Grow them in a sandy soil rich with leafmould and give plenty of summer water. Let IXORAS dry out a little during the winter and cut back to shape. IXORA chinensis 'Prince of Orange' is often used as a mass bedding plant in the tropics; but the flowers fade badly and it is more brilliant in semi-shade. The large I. coc-cinea is a handsome shrub indeed: the leaves golden-green, the flowers a striking shade of deep scarlet.

528   IXORA chinensis 'Prince of Orange'
SHRUB   4 ft
CHINA   SUMMER

529   IXORA coccinea
SHRUB   8 ft
EAST INDIES   SUMMER

530

531

JACARANDA
BIGNONIACEAE

Sydney's summer pride and joy; the beautiful Jacaranda is actually from the high deserts of Brazil—which explains why it flowers better in a dry year and goes to leaf in a rainy season. Simple to grow from seed, it flowers as young as 3 years and grows to a massive size. But careful here—it is a surface-rooter and few other plants will grow around it. There is no perfume at all, but with the brilliance of the flowers that is a small fault. White, pink and red varieties exist, but are not commonly seen.

530   JACARANDA mimosaefolia
JACARANDA
FERN TREE
BRAZILIAN ROSEWOOD
BEAUTIFUL BLUE BRAZILIAN
TREE   40 ft
BRAZIL   SUMMER

JACOBINIA
ACANTHACEAE

In the semi-tropical garden or shaded sunny aspect in frost-free areas, the Brazilian Plume Flower produces spikes of rose, pink or red flowers all through the summer. Well-drained acid soil, regular water and fertilizer keep it covered with large handsome leaves; neglect makes it grow tall and scruffy. Prune back hard in early spring to encourage branching.

531   JACOBINIA carnea
BRAZILIAN PLUME FLOWER
SHRUB   5 ft
BRAZIL   LATE SUMMER

169

532

534

536

533

535

JASMINUM
OLEACEAE

Think of fragrance—think of Jasmine. Delicate starry flowers in yellow, white or pink according to species, and native to all the fabled lands of the East. You can have Jasmines in flower all year round if you pick the right varieties. Just give them a partially shaded or sunny position, reasonable soil and an occasional going over with the secateurs to keep them in bounds. JASMINUM nudiflorum flowers in winter on bare branches and is called in Japan 'The Flower that Welcomes Spring'. J. mesneyi follows at the first sign of warm weather, and spring is really here when the fast-growing J. polyanthum bursts into bloom. Give it a wire or two for support; it will cover a wall in no time. J. officinale and the larger-flowered J. rex keep up the fragrance throughout summer, and last of all comes dainty J. azoricum which blooms to winter.

532   JASMINUM azoricum
VINE   6 ft
AZORES   AUTUMN

533   JASMINUM mesneyi
PRIMROSE JASMINE
CHINESE JASMINE
SHRUB   10 ft
CHINA   SPRING

534   JASMINUM nudiflorum
WINTER JASMINE
SHRUB   8 ft
CHINA   WINTER

535   JASMINUM polyanthum
CLIMBER   20 ft
CHINA   SPRING

536   JASMINUM rex
KING JASMINE
CLIMBER   8 ft
SIAM   WINTER
TROPICAL

JUNIPERUS

537

JUSTICIA

538

539

JUNIPERUS
CUPRESSACEAE

North America's gift to the modern pebble garden, the Prostrate Juniper is a mountain plant and likes the perfect drainage and cool root run it finds under a pebble mulch, or in large rock pockets where it can spread over the stones. Though extremely hardy, it is subject to a number of small pests that make homes among the dense branches. Malathion or other contact sprays will fix most of them.

537 JUNIPERUS horizontalis
CREEPING JUNIPER
PROSTRATE JUNIPER
SHRUB   12 in
NORTH AMERICA   ALL YEAR

JUSTICIA
ACANTHACEAE

Outside the tropics, a warm patio or sheltered sunny aspect is necessary to bring out the best in Justicias, a shrubby group of perennials with showy spikes of tubular flowers in white, violet and red. The Red Justicia (JUSTICIA coccinea) is a favourite in warm-climate gardens anywhere for its large glossy leaves. The scarlet flowers are spectacular, but useless for cutting as they open irregularly and drop all over the place. Mauve J. peruviana is a tidier plant altogether, with white-throated violet flowers appearing all the way up the stems. Justicias grow easily from spring cuttings and enjoy a soil rich with leafmould.

538 JUSTICIA coccinea
RED JUSTICIA
PERENNIAL   8 ft
TROPICAL AMERICA   AUTUMN

539 JUSTICIA peruviana
PERENNIAL   2½ ft
PERU   SUMMER

KALANCHOE

540

542

541

KALANCHOE
CRASSULACEAE

Popular winter-flowering succulents, KALANCHOES require subtropical conditions for all year round growing outdoors. Raise from seed or leaf cuttings, and plant in a rich well-drained soil for best results. In warm sheltered positions, KALANCHOES can become something of a problem, for every leaf that drops will form a new plant right away. KALANCHOE blossfeldiana is one of the best winter houseplants, especially in its miniature varieties. Popular subtropical garden species include K. pinnata (the Air Plant) and K. beharensis (the Felt Plant).

540   KALANCHOE blossfeldiana
SUCCULENT   6–18 in
MADAGASCAR   WINTER
SUBTROPICAL

541   KALANCHOE fedtschenkoi
SUCCULENT   2 ft
MADAGASCAR   WINTER
SUBTROPICAL

542   KALANCHOE flammea 'Yellow'
SUCCULENT   15 in
SOMALILAND   SPRING
SUBTROPICAL

KALMIA

543

KENTRANTHUS

544

KERRIA

545

KALMIA
ERICACEAE

A garden treasure outside its native American Mountains, the slow-growing KALMIA does well in exactly the same conditions as its Rhododendron relatives. Part-shade, humidity, an acid soil rich in leafmould. The laurel-like leaves are dark and glossy, the flowers apple-blossom pink with a curious sticky feel. It is completely cold-hardy and will survive below zero temperatures.

543   KALMIA latifolia
MOUNTAIN LAUREL
CALICO BUSH
SHRUB   6 ft
UNITED STATES OF AMERICA
SPRING

KENTRANTHUS
VALERIANACEAE

Easy to grow from seed, the old-fashioned Valerian is still very useful for bright colour in tough, dry situations. Use it in sun or shade; on clay, sand or rock; it will succeed anywhere except in a damp position. The common variety has deep-pink flowers, but there are also reds and whites. No worry about replacements, Valerian self-seeds regularly.

544   KENTRANTHUS ruber
RED VALERIAN
JUPITER'S BEARD
PERENNIAL   2 ft
EUROPE   SPRING–SUMMER

KERRIA
ROSACEAE

A decorative deciduous member of the Rose family, KERRIA lights up the shaded garden corner with a profusion of golden blooms. Grown from cuttings, layers or divisions, it does well in any good soil but needs at least a six-foot spread to display its graceful arching branches. Prune out old flowering branches and dead wood just as you would with Roses. Double and single varieties.

545   KERRIA japonica 'Pleniflora'
GLOBE FLOWER BUSH
JEW'S MALLOW
SHRUB   6 ft
JAPAN   SPRING–SUMMER

KLEINIA

546

KNIPHOFIA

547

KOLKWITZIA

548

KLEINIA
COMPOSITAE

Flowering succulents belonging to the Daisy family, KLEINIAS are propagated from cuttings and make useful ground covers on sandy porous soil. Like most KLEINIAS, the succulent leaves of KLEINIA repens are a vivid blue-grey and contrast particularly well with other foliage in gold, dark-green or bronze. The white Daisy flowers are quite uninteresting and are usually pulled off. Sun or shade.

546   KLEINIA repens
SUCCULENT   2 ft
CAPE PROVINCE   SUMMER

KNIPHOFIA
LILIACEAE

A coarse but stately plant native to South Africa, the KNIPHOFIA is greatly valued for cold weather colour in the mixed border or background planting. Propagate by seed or spring root-division; it prefers a light soil with plenty of water in hot weather. Modern hybrids include every shade of red, yellow, orange and cream and bear a twelve-inch mass of tubular untidy flowers atop tall stems. These last for many months and are attractive to birds.

547   KNIPHOFIA uvaria
RED HOT POKER
TORCH LILY
PERENNIAL   2–9 ft
SOUTH AFRICA   SPRING

KOLKWITZIA
CAPRIFOLIACEAE

Closely related to the Abelias, for which it is sometimes mistaken, KOLKWITZIA is surely one of the loveliest of garden plants. Grow it in well-watered part-shade with good drainage; the tall arching stems will soon grow to full height, draping themselves in spring with spicily fragrant masses of palest-pink trumpet flowers, their throats spotted orange-yellow. Bristly fruits and autumn colour come later.

548   KOLKWITZIA amabilis
CHINESE BEAUTY BUSH
SHRUB   8 ft
CHINA   SPRING

549

550

KOPSIA
APOCYNACEAE

Beautiful three-inch Periwinkle-type flowers coloured like strawberry ice-cream assure Kopsia a favoured place in warm humid climates. Firm young shoots can be struck fairly easily under glass and plants should be grown in an acid sandy soil, rich in humus. Keep up the humidity all year, and do not even try it in cold-winter areas.

549   KOPSIA fruticosa
SHRUB   8 ft
MALAYA   SUMMER
TROPICAL

KUNZEA
MYRTACEAE

Closely related to Bottlebrush and Tea-tree, the KUNZEAS are a small Australian genus of evergreen shrubs with tiny heath-like leaves and showy masses of long-stamened flowers. KUNZEA ambigua (the Tick Bush) is easy to grow, provided the soil is light and the drainage good. The fragrant creamy white flowers persist for months. K. baxteri has scarlet flowers; K. pomifera yellow and K. recurva lilac.

550   KUNZEA ambigua
TICK BUSH
SHRUB   10 ft
SOUTH-EASTERN AUSTRALIA
SUMMER

LABURNUM

551

LACHENALIA

552

553

LABURNUM
LEGUMINOSAE

Handsome anytime as a specimen tree or background shrub, LABURNUM is a stunner in spring when the branches are festooned with chains of golden flowers. But the pods that follow are poisonous and should be removed. LABURNUM can be grown tall or pruned to a shrubby habit. It is deciduous and needs shade in warmer areas. Well-drained acid soil and regular water bring out its best.

551   LABURNUM anagyroides
GOLDEN RAIN
GOLDEN CHAIN
TREE   20 ft
SOUTHERN EUROPE   LATE SPRING

LACHENALIA
LILIACEAE

A large and useful genus of bulbs for early bloom in all but the coldest areas, and pot culture where the winters are hard. LACHENALIAS are instantly recognizable by their succulent brown-spotted stems and leaves and stiff spikes of bell-flowers for all the world like rows of brightly-garbed soldiers. The commonly grown LACHENALIA aloides has many colour varieties in shades of yellow, bronze, red, green and purple— sometimes banded all on the same flowers. There are also plain coloured species in red, purple, green and yellow.

552   LACHENALIA aloides 'Aurea'
CAPE COWSLIP
BULB   9 in
SOUTH AFRICA   SPRING

553   LACHENALIA tricolor
SOLDIER LILY
BULB   9 in
SOUTH AFRICA   SPRING

LACHNOSTACHYS

554

LAELIOCATTLEYA

555

LAGERSTROEMIA

556

LACHNOSTACHYS
VERBENACEAE

More woolly than hairy, the stems and floppy leaves of remarkable LACHNO-STACHYS contrast wonderfully with other darker foliage; and the spikes of cottonwool flowers with showy violet centres are wonderful in flower arrangements. Grow from seed and give a fully sun-drenched aspect with sandy well-drained soil. Keep the plant moist during autumn and winter.

554　LACHNOSTACHYS verbasci-folia
LAMB'S TAILS
SHRUB　6 ft
WESTERN AUSTRALIA　WINTER

LAELIOCATTLEYA
ORCHIDACEAE

This magnificent genus of orchids—naturally occurring hybrids of the two species Laelia and Cattleya—includes over 2,000 named varieties. They are epiphytic and can only be grown where the temperature and humidity can be kept high. Pot in a commercially prepared compost and water only when it dries out. Place the pots on a tray of moistened gravel to keep up the humidity.

555　LAELIOCATTLEYA X HYBRID
ORCHID　18 in
HYBRID　SOUTH AMERICA

LAGERSTROEMIA
LYTHRACEAE

A favourite flowering tree in sub-tropical climates, the Crepe Myrtle does well in mild coastal areas further south—but as a more compact deciduous shrub, with autumn leaf colour. The showy panicles of blossom appear in late summer, all crinkly like crepe paper. The colours are pink, mauve, white and red, and the shrubs flower best when cut right back to the trunk every winter.

556　LAGERSTROEMIA indica
CREPE MYRTLE
PRIDE OF INDIA
SHRUB—TREE　to 20 ft
CHINA　AUTUMN

LAGUNARIA

557

LAMBERTIA

558

LAMPRANTHUS

559

560

LAGUNARIA
MALVACEAE

Native to Australia as well as its name-sake Norfolk Island the LAGUNARIA is ideal for coastal areas, being completely resistant to salt air and wind. The felty leaves are attractive all year and almost hidden in midsummer by masses of small Hibiscus flowers in pink or mauve. The tree is big: may grow to 75 ft in good soil, and self-seeds regularly.

557   LAGUNARIA patersoni
COW-ITCH TREE
PRIMROSE TREE
NORFOLK ISLAND HIBISCUS
PYRAMID TREE
TREE   75 ft
AUSTRALIA   SUMMER

LAMBERTIA
PROTEACEAE

Clusters of Red Honeysuckle flowers top LAMBERTIA's branches throughout the spring and summer and are very attractive to honeyeating birds and butterflies. The flowers are followed by curious woody pods like horned heads. The shrub is handsome, with serrated evergreen leaves, and grows from cuttings. Pamper it with a sandy soil, rich in humus.

558   LAMBERTIA formosa
HONEY FLOWER
MOUNTAIN DEVIL
HONEYSUCKLE
SHRUB   6 ft
NEW SOUTH WALES
SPRING—SUMMER

LAMPRANTHUS
AIZOACEAE

Winter and spring flowering succulents that literally disappear under a dazzling blanket of flowers, LAMPRANTHUS are the most brilliant of all the iceplants usually tossed together under the catch-all name of Mesembryanthemums. (You will find others listed under Carpobrotus, Dorotheanthus and Drosanthemum.) All species are very hardy and need summer water only when the juicy leaves begin to look droopy. Iceplants grow easily from cuttings and should be planted at eighteen-inch intervals for ground cover work—but not where they will be trodden on. Most species have cylindrical or triangular one-inch leaves and two-inch flowers. Apart from those illustrated, there are purple-flowered LAMPRANTHUS productus; golden-yellow L. aurea, and many others.

559   LAMPRANTHUS
(in rock garden)

560   LAMPRANTHUS aurantiacus
ORANGE TRAILING ICEPLANT
TRAILING SUCCULENT   6in
CAPE PROVINCE   WINTER

561

562

563

564

565

561   LAMPRANTHUS coccineus
SCARLET PIGFACE
SUCCULENT   30 in
CAPE PROVINCE   SPRING

562   LAMPRANTHUS spectabilis
PINK ICEPLANT
TRAINING SUCCULENT   18 in
CAPE PROVINCE   WINTER

LANTANA
VERBENACEAE

Posies of tiny Verbena flowers in mixed or separate colours make Lantana a favourite in all mild winter districts. But many species quickly become unwelcome guests if not watched constantly. The cheery mauve-flowered creeping shrub LANTANA montevidensis is the exception—its dainty habit and delicately-arched stems make a wonderful ground cover or small hedge and never become troublesome. The more robust L. camara can quickly take over the garden if not pruned back regularly. Any soil will suit, but warmth and full sun are musts. Named hybrids like 'Cloth of Gold' and orange-red 'Radiation' are more beautiful and less rampant.

563   LANTANA camara
 Cloth of Gold'
CLOTH OF GOLD
SHRUB   3 ft
HYBRID   SUMMER

564   LANTANA montevidensis
TRAILING LANTANA
GROUND SHRUB   2 ft
URUGUAY   SUMMER

565   LANTANA camara var. nivea
WHITE LANTANA
SHRUB   6 ft
EAST INDIES   SUMMER

LATHYRUS

566

568

LAVANDULA

569

567

LATHYRUS
LEGUMINOSAE

Now greatly improved, annual Sweet Peas can be flowered any time of the year, even in winter. Modern hybrids produce more flowers to a stem in a remarkable range of colours. Sweet Peas demand loose well-drained soil, lime and a fertilizer rich in phosphorus and potash. They should be grown from seed in rows running north and south so sun can reach all parts of the plants. If this is not possible, well-staked wire cylinders will give adequate support in the open. A dwarf non-climbing type is now available for planting in mixed beds. The older Perennial Pea (LATHYRUS latifolius) has its admirers too. Plant seeds in autumn for summer flowers in shades of cerise, purple and white.

566   LATHYRUS latifolius
PERENNIAL PEA
ARGENTINE PEA
EVERLASTING PEA
PERENNIAL   8 ft
SPRING

567   LATHYRUS odoratus
SWEET PEA
ANNUAL   6 ft
SICILY   ALL YEAR

568   LATHYRUS odoratus 'Bijou'
DWARF SWEET PEA
ANNUAL   2 ft
HYBRID   SPRING

LAVANDULA
LABIATAE

Lavender's Blue, dilly, dilly; and in mild areas it blooms continuously. Not spectacular, Lavender is valued more for its grey aromatic foliage than the flowers, though these can be dried for refreshingly perfumed sachets. The English species (LAVANDULA spica) has stronger perfume and silver leaves. The dark purple type is L. stoechas (the Spanish Lavender).

569   LAVANDULA dentata
FRENCH LAVENDER
SHRUB   4 ft
MEDITERRANEAN   ALL YEAR

570

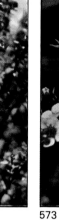

571

573

572

LEONOTIS
LABIATAE

Striking whorls of velvety white or orange flowers crowd right up the stems of this quick-growing hardy perennial. Cut LEONOTIS back after the flowers fade and more appear throughout the warm weather. A mild to warm climate suits best although the plant is fairly frost-resistant; and it stands up well to dry conditions too. LEONOTIS needs regular summer watering.

570   LEONOTIS leonurus
LION'S TAIL
LION'S EAR
PERENNIAL   3–5 ft
SOUTH AFRICA   SUMMER

LEPTOSPERMUM
MYRTACEAE

Since Captain Cook brewed a beverage from tiny leaves of a LEPTOSPERMUM, the whole family has been blessed with the name of Teatree, though nobody seems eager to repeat the good Captain's experiment. Between 30 and 40 species are recognized, all of them natives of Australia and New Zealand. LEPTO-SPERMUMS are deservedly popular shrubs of graceful habit, their profusion of flowers resembling peach blossom. Grown in full sun, they resist drought, wind and even salt spray. In fact the larger forms thrive on coastal cliffs where they assume a graceful contorted shape. Most widely cultivated are the named varieties of Australian LEPTO-SPERMUM laevigatum and the New Zealand L. scoparium.

571   LEPTOSPERMUM scoparium X 'Ruby Glow'
MANUKA
SHRUB   6 ft
HYBRID   WINTER–SPRING

572   LEPTOSPERMUM squarrosum
SOUTH SEA MYRTLE
PORT JACKSON TEATREE
SHRUB   5 ft
NEW SOUTH WALES–QUEENSLAND
LATE SUMMER

573   LEPTOSPERMUM X 'Walkeri'
SHRUB   5 ft
HYBRID   SPRING–SUMMER

LESCHENAULTIA

574

LEUCADENDRON

575

LEUCOJUM

576

LESCHENAULTIA
GOODENOVIAE

Delicate Western Australian shrubs much valued for their brilliant flowers of scarlet, yellow, orange, green and blue, the Leschenaultias are easy to grow anywhere the soil is gravelly, the drainage perfect and the sunlight brilliant. Grow them from spring cuttings; mulch with Eucalyptus and other acid leaf matter and leave well alone except for an occasional light watering.

574   LESCHENAULTIA biloba
BLUE LESCHENAULTIA
SHRUB   12 in
WESTERN AUSTRALIA   SPRING

LEUCADENDRON
PROTEACEAE

Silvery, silky grey leaves shining in the sunlight could only belong to South Africa's handsome LEUCADENDRON. The sandy well-drained soil of seaside gardens suits perfectly and it is highly resistant to salt air. But inland, frosts disagree with it except in sunny sheltered mountain places. Other LEUCADENDRON species have colourful flower-like bracts in red, pink or gold.

575   LEUCADENDRON argenteum
SILVER TREE
TREE   20 ft
SOUTH AFRICA   SPRING

LEUCOJUM
AMARYLLIDACEAE

Delicate green-tipped snowy bells, freshly fragrant, appear by the hundred in earliest spring among clumps of stiff green leaves. The more crowded they are, the better they seem to flower. Plant Snowflake clumps in heavy soil beneath deciduous trees where the winter sun can reach them. Divide after leaf dieback only when desperately overcrowded.

576   LEUCOJUM vernum
SNOWFLAKE
BULB   12 in
MEDITERRANEAN   WINTER

LEUCOSPERMUM

577

578

LEUCOTHOE

579

LEYCESTERIA

580

LEUCOSPERMUM
PROTEACEAE

Many species of the beautiful South African LEUCOSPERMUM have been introduced to Australia where they are proving perfectly at home. The sandy coastal soil, free of lime and rich in leaf-mould, is just what they need. Wonderful for cutting, the flowers vary widely from species to species as you would expect from variable members of the Protea family—but most of them are 3 in to 4 in across in shades of green, yellow, pink, orange and scarlet. The leathery leaves are slightly toothed at the tips which distinguishes them from the true Proteas.

577   LEUCOSPERMUM tottum
FIREWHEEL PINCUSHION
SHRUB   4 ft
SOUTH AFRICA   SPRING

578   LEUCOSPERMUM reflexum
ROCKET PINCUSHION
SHRUB   8 ft
SOUTH AFRICA   SPRING

LEUCOTHOE
ERICACEAE

The graceful arching branches of LEU-COTHOE are quite unique with their reflexed leathery leaves and pendant showers of pearly-cream blossom. LEU-COTHOE spreads rapidly in rich, lime-free soil, via a system of underground stems; and in the cool climate it prefers, the leaves turn bronze, purple and even scarlet in the autumn. Cut whole flowering branches for indoor decoration.

579   LEUCOTHOE axillaris
PEARL FLOWER
DOG HOBBLE
FETTER BUSH
SHRUB   6 ft
UNITED STATES OF AMERICA
SPRING

LEYCESTERIA
CAPRIFOLIACEAE

Rich woodland temperate zones are home to the deciduous LEYCESTERIA. Though frosts tend to cut it right back in winter, spring sees fast-growing hollow stems shoot up many feet. These produce hanging clusters of peculiar reddish-purple flowers surrounded by bracts. The bracts remain to hide black berries, which are a favourite of many birds. Grow from seed or cuttings.

580   LEYCESTERIA formosa
HIMALAYA HONEYSUCKLE
SHRUB   8 ft
HIMALAYAS   LATE SPRING

LIATRIS

581

LILIUM

582

584

583

585

LIATRIS
COMPOSITAE

Really only a daisy in disguise, LIATRIS is a wonderfully hardy perennial for the mixed border. The woody rootstock shows only a tuft of grassy leaves until summer, when tall fine-leafed spikes of rose-purple flowers shoot up to two-and-a-half ft. They are indifferent to heat and cold but do best away from high humidity areas.

581   LIATRIS spicata
BLAZING STAR
BUTTON SNAKEROOT
SPIKE GAYFEATHER
GAYFEATHER
SNAKEROOT
PERENNIAL   30 in
UNITED STATES OF AMERICA
SUMMER

LILIUM
LILIACEAE

Longer in cultivation than any other plant, the tall and stately Lily was known in gardens 3,000 years ago. This was the still popular LILIUM candidum. But most of today's popular LILIUMS were developed in the last 40 years. Many are hybrids of the two Japanese species L. auratum and L. speciosum—others cross a number of North American natives. LILIUMS grow from scaly bulbs, and are planted deep in rich well-drained soil, preferably on the acid side. They like shade around the roots and filtered sun at flowering height. Most LILIUMS do extremely well in large containers which can be moved about when the flowers come into bloom—anywhere from spring to autumn according to type. Modern LILIUMS are quite expensive—a little study of their specialized needs will be amply repaid in flower quality.

582   LILIUM X auratum 'Pictum'
GOLDEN RAYED LILY OF JAPAN
BULB   6 ft
JAPAN   SUMMER

583   LILIUM X aurelian 'Limelight'
BULB   6 ft
HYBRID   SUMMER

584   LILIUM X 'Stookes' aurelianense
BULB   6 ft
HYBRID   SUMMER

585   LILIUM candidum
MADONNA LILY
BULB   3 ft
ASIA MINOR   SPRING

184

586

588

590

587

589

586   LILIUM formosanum
FORMOSA LILY
BULB   7 ft
FORMOSA   AUTUMN

587   LILIUM X 'Adventure'
ORIENTAL HYBRID LILY
BULB   4 ft
HYBRID   SUMMER

588   LILIUM X Parkmanii
'Jillian Wallace'
BULB   6 ft
SUMMER

589   LILIUM speciosum
PINK TIGER LILY
BULB   4 ft
JAPAN   SPRING–SUMMER

590   LILIUM speciosum 'Album'
WHITE TIGER LILY
BULB   4 ft
JAPAN   SUMMER

LIMONIUM

591

LINARIA

592

LIQUIDAMBAR

593

LIMONIUM
PLUMBAGINACEAE

Once a popular dried subject for winter arrangements, Statice is easily grown in the mixed border from seeds or seedlings, both planted out in autumn. Full sun and well-drained soil suit best, and no special cultivation is required beyond a sprinkling of packaged fertilizer in the spring while flower heads are developing. The true flowers are white, but surrounded by bracts in shades of blue, mauve, pink, yellow and white.

591   LIMONIUM sinuatum
SEA LAVENDER
STATICE
ANNUAL   2 ft
MEDITERRANEAN   SPRING

LINARIA
SCROPHULARIACEAE

A weak and wispy plant that must be grown *en masse* for a colourful effect, LINARIA is sown in autumn precisely where you want it to grow. The soil should be sprinkled with lime and broken down weeks beforehand, and weeds must be removed regularly, for LINARIA dislikes competition. Mixed colours only, but they include every shade imaginable.

592   LINARIA maroccana
EGGS AND BACON
TOADFLAX
BABY SNAPDRAGON
ANNUAL   18 in
MOROCCO   SPRING

LIQUIDAMBAR
HAMAMELIDACEAE

Most colourful of autumn trees, the North American Sweet Gum has a tall pyramid shape and produces leaf colours in every shade through yellow to red and purple. Generally a slow-grower, it really takes on speed in swampy surroundings when it may reach 80 ft. It produces fruits or 'conkers' which fall and sprout readily, and is often root-pruned to improve autumn colour.

593   LIQUIDAMBAR styraciflua
SWEET GUM
TREE   40 ft
NORTH AMERICA   AUTUMN

186

LIRIODENDRON

594

LIRIOPE

595

LIRIODENDRON
MAGNOLIACEAE

A fast-growing tree that is beautiful any time of year, the Tulip Tree is also a giant of the vegetable kingdom, best limited to large country gardens. The attractive four-cornered leaves are magnificent in both summer and autumn, and the flowers exquisite Tulips in lime-green and apricot. But they are often hard to see, for the tree may be bare of branches to 60 ft above the ground.

594   LIRIODENDRON tulipifera
TULIP TREE
TULIP WOOD
TREE   200 ft
NORTH AMERICA   SPRING

LIRIOPE
LILIACEAE

Often confused with the similar Ophio-pogon, LIRIOPE is an extraordinarily versatile plant, equally at home in hot or cold climates. It forms dense tufts of striped green and white leaves that are valued as ground cover, border-edgings and pot plants. During summer and autumn LIRIOPE produces eighteen-inch violet stems of mauve flowers similar to large grape hyacinths. These are good for cutting.

595   LIRIOPE muscari
LILY TURF
BULB   18 in
CHINA   SUMMER

LOBELIA

596

598

LOBIVIA

599

597

LOBELIA
CAMPANULACEAE

A very large and variable genus with showy flowers and juicy leaves and stems, Lobelias need a cool semi-shaded position to survive hot summers. Best known is the tiny LOBELIA erinus that grows from seed scattered in spring and flowers in many shades of blue from ice to navy. The much taller L. cardinalis is a bog-loving perennial grown from divisions. Its leaves are dark-red and its flowers a vivid flame. More suited to tropical conditions, the Mexican L. laxiflora sends up six-foot woody stems of scarlet and yellow tubular flowers all year. A spectacular specimen plant, but useless for picking.

596   LOBELIA cardinalis
CARDINAL FLOWER
PERENNIAL   3 ft
UNITED STATES OF AMERICA
SUMMER

597   LOBELIA erinus
LOBELIA
ANNUAL   6 in
SOUTH AFRICA   SUMMER

598   LOBELIA laxiflora
PERENNIAL   6 ft
MEXICO   SPRING—AUTUMN

LOBIVIA
CACTACEAE

South American Cacti with growth like ribbed, spiky cucumbers, LOBIVIAS are popular house plants but do best in rockeries with sandy well-drained soil. Give them plenty of water and monthly feeding in warm weather to produce the vivid flowers—purple, yellow, orange, pink or red, according to species. LOBIVIAS quickly form large colonies and do well in pots of gravelly compost.

599   LOBIVIA huascha
CACTUS   12 in
ARGENTINA   SPRING

LOBULARIA

600

601

602

603

604

LOBULARIA
CRUCIFERAE

Quick and dependable, Sweet Alice produces masses of tiny honey-scented flowers in 6 weeks from seed, and can be sown absolutely anywhere at any time outside the frostiest days. White 'Carpet of Snow' and Purple 'Violet Queen' are the hardiest and most common varieties, but the delicate pink strain named 'Rosie O'Day' is gaining in popularity.

600   LOBULARIA maritima
'Lilac Queen'
MADWORT
SWEET ALICE
SWEET ALYSSUM
ALYSSUM
ANNUAL   9 in
MEDITERRANEAN   ALL YEAR

601   LOBULARIA maritima
Procumbens, 'Violet Queen', 'Carpet of Snow'.
ANNUAL   3 in
HYBRID   ALL YEAR

LONICERA
CAPRIFOLIACEAE

A garden without Honeysuckle? Unthinkable! The scented honey-rich flowers bring birds and bees and small children all eager for a taste. And the twining evergreen stems and leaves of most types make useful cover for sheds and fences. Grow them from cuttings or layers taken in late summer and shop around for interesting species of which there are literally hundreds. The smaller golden-leafed LONICERA japonica 'Aurea' is a splendid ground cover; L. serotina's mulberry and yellow flowers are fine for cutting; L. hildebrandiana is a giant with stems as thick as your arm and six-inch tubular flowers of rich cream, fading to orange. L. fragrantissima is a different type of plant altogether. Deciduous, it flowers in midwinter on long arching canes of previous year's wood.

602   LONICERA fragrantissima
WINTER HONEYSUCKLE
WOODBINE
SHRUB   8 ft
CHINA   WINTER

603   LONICERA hildebrandiana
GIANT HONEYSUCKLE
BURMESE HONEYSUCKLE
CLIMBER   60 ft
BURMA   SUMMER

604   LONICERA periclymenum
'Serotina'
LATE DUTCH HONEYSUCKLE
TWINING SHRUB   20 ft
EAST AFRICA–ASIA   SUMMER

LOROPETALUM

605

LOTUS

606

LUCULIA

607

LOROPETALUM
HAMAMELIDACEAE

Obviously related to the Witch Hazel (Hamamelis), the Chinese Fringe Flower differs in several respects. It is evergreen, it prefers a mild frost-free climate and the spidery flowers are much paler; a creamy white. It likes rich acid soil and filtered sun and is particularly handsome when young, older shrubs tending to become leggy.

605   LOROPETALUM chinense
FRINGE FLOWER
SHRUB   4–12 ft
CHINA   WINTER

LOTUS
LEGUMINOSAE

A silvery grey waterfall of fine needle leaves and hanging stems, the Lotus is a great favourite for rock pockets and hanging baskets where it finds the perfect drainage it needs. Give warmth and shelter or else winter cold will play havoc with its appearance and spoil the spring and summer display of scarlet pea-flowers; borne in heavy clusters all down the trailing branches.

606   LOTUS bertholetii
CORAL GEM
SCARLET LOTUS
PROSTRATE SHRUB   6 in
CANARY ISLANDS   SPRING

LUCULIA
RUBIACEAE

Most desirable and infuriating of winter-flowering shrubs, the Himalayan beauty we call LUCULIA has broken many gardeners' hearts. Just why does it die out so suddenly? Every expert has his own opinion. It will not stand cultivation or competition from other roots. It does not like hot winds (or cold ones either). Maybe you gave it too much lime or not enough. Cut it right back after flowering, and do not water till new growth begins in spring.

607   LUCULIA gratissima
SHRUB   5–10 ft
HIMALAYAS   WINTER

LUNARIA

608

LUPINUS

609

610

LYCORIS

611

612

LUNARIA
CRUCIFERAE

A rather old-fashioned biennial that can become a bit of a pest unless grown in a shady unused part of the garden. The coarse heart-shaped leaves flop easily in hot weather unless watered regularly— the flowers are a pretty pink, but the seed pods quite spectacular—masses of silvery translucent discs that are dried for bouquets. Grow from seeds in autumn.

608 LUNARIA biennis
HONESTY
MONEY PLANT
BIENNIAL 2½ ft
SWEDEN SUMMER

LUPINUS
LEGUMINOSAE

Dense spikes of pea-flowers in a variety of colours identify the showy Lupin genus which includes several hundred annual, perennial and even shrubby plants, mostly natives of America. All species are easy to grow and the annuals often raised as a first crop in new gardens, to be dug in as soil enrichment. These include blue LUPINUS hartwegii and yellow L. sulphureus. Pride of the family are the magnificent perennial Russell Hybrids, with flower spikes up to 5 ft in every shade from white to yellow and orange—from purple to red through blue and pink. These are usually planted from crowns like Delphiniums.

609 LUPINUS polyphyllus
RUSSELL LUPIN
PERENNIAL 4 ft
UNITED STATES OF AMERICA
LATE SPRING

610 LUPINUS sulphureus
GOLDEN LUPIN
ANNUAL 18 in
OREGON SUMMER

LYCORIS
AMARYLLIDACEAE

A beautiful bulb species from China and Japan, strongly resembling Nerines but with backward curling petals and long spidery stamens. The bulbs are planted in early autumn in a sheltered place and may not flower the first year. When they do, the flower stems pop out of the bare soil before the leaves. Showy, golden LYCORIS aurea is the most spectacular but does not like cold winter areas. The smaller L. radiata is a superb cut flower, lasting well in all sorts of containers. Unlike others of the Amaryllis family, LYCORIS bulbs should be planted well under the soil, generally twice their own depth.

611 LYCORIS aurea
GOLDEN SPIDER LILY
BULB 2 ft
CHINA AUTUMN

612 LYCORIS radiata
RED SPIDER LILY
ORIENTAL SPIDER LILY
BULB 18 in
JAPAN AUTUMN

191

LYTHRUM

613

MACADAMIA

614

LYTHRUM
LYTHRACEAE

Here is a showy plant for that damp,
hard-to-drain area! The water-loving
Loosestrife soaks it all up and bursts into
showy spikes of flowers that are grand
for picking. Colours are rose, crimson
and red violet. Plant from divisions in
autumn and expect flowers from early
summer to winter.

613   LYTHRUM salicaria
PURPLE LOOSESTRIFE
PERENNIAL   5 ft
EUROPE   SUMMER—AUTUMN

MACADAMIA
PROTEACEAE

Slow-growing, but very beautiful, the
MACADAMIA is strikingly ornamental
at any time. The magnificent foliage is
ideal for large arrangements: it bears
dense clusters of white flowers in early
summer: and to crown it all, delicious
nuts that ripen in winter are much sought
after as a delicacy. Hawaii claims them
as its own, but the tree is as Australian
as the Kangaroo.

614   MACADAMIA ternifolia
QUEENSLAND NUT
AUSTRALIAN NUT
TREE   25 ft
QUEENSLAND   SUMMER

615

617

619

616

618

MAGNOLIA
MAGNOLIACEAE

The sort of picture conjured by the name Magnolia depends on where you live. If home is a warm humid climate, you naturally think of the overpoweringly perfumed Evergreen Magnolia from America's deep south. Shiny laurel leaves, rusty stems and shoots, tremendous ten-inch flowers that look as if they were carved from cream wax. It is a giant of a tree, magnificent as a solitary specimen—but also useful trained as a fast-growing espalier in cooler districts. If on the other hand, you live in a cold winter area, you are more familiar with the gorgeous oriental Magnolias, deciduous, mostly coloured, and more delicately perfumed. The Yulan Tree, earliest flowering with gorgeous creamy cups spread over dark branches, hard to propagate and expensive to buy; the Lily Magnolia with longer bell-shaped flowers, dark outside, pale within: and the result of crossing them both—M. Soulangeana. The Star Magnolia is different altogether, a complicated spreading shrub with white and rose flattened flowers borne early. All Magnolias like rich acid soil, loathe lime and the deciduous kind need shelter from wind.

615   MAGNOLIA denudata
YULAN TREE
TREE   25 ft
CHINA   WINTER

616   MAGNOLIA grandiflora
EVERGREEN MAGNOLIA
SOUTHERN MAGNOLIA
BULL BAY
TREE   60 ft
SOUTHERN UNITED STATES OF
AMERICA   SUMMER

617   MAGNOLIA liliflora 'Nigra'
LILY MAGNOLIA
SHRUB   12 ft
CHINA   SPRING

618   MAGNOLIA X soulangeana
SOULANGE BODIN'S MAGNOLIA
SAUCER MAGNOLIA
SHRUB   18 ft
HYBRID   SPRING

619   MAGNOLIA stellata
STAR MAGNOLIA
SHRUB   10 ft
JAPAN   SPRING

MAHONIA

620

MALCOMIA

621

MALPIGHIA

622

MAHONIA
BERBERIDACEAE

Clean-looking shrubs with spiky holly-like leaves and plumes of golden flowers in spring or even earlier; the MAHONIAS are useful plants for hard conditions. Frosty or hot, shady or dry, any position seems to suit them and the flowers are usually followed by blue-black berries. MAHONIA lomariifolia is one of the larger species, but M. japonica and M. aquifolia are equally attractive and half the height.

620   MAHONIA lomariifolia
SHRUB   10 ft
YUNNAN   WINTER

MALCOMIA
CRUCIFERAE

For fast, fast, fast colour; rely on Virginian Stock—only 6 weeks from seed-sowing to full bloom in a warm sunny spot. Rich open soil is helpful but not essential, and you can use them in emergency anytime except the hottest months...the tiny root system does not upset other plants at all, so plant as a cover round potted shrubs. Sold in mixed colours only.

621   MALCOMIA maritima
VIRGINIAN STOCK
FRENCH FORGET-ME-NOTS
ANNUAL   8 in
MEDITERRANEAN   SPRING

MALPIGHIA
MALPIGHIACEAE

Not a Holly, nor from Singapore either; this fine example of botanical misnaming is a very worthwhile plant for the warm climate garden, where it can be clipped into shape as a neat hedge or border. The leaves are sharp and prickly; the feathery flowers white to pink and some-times there are tiny red fruits to follow.

622   MALPIGHIA coccigera
SINGAPORE HOLLY
SHRUB   5 ft
WEST INDIES   SUMMER
TROPICAL

623

625

624

626

627

MALUS
ROSACEAE

A shower of delicate white, pink or red blossom in early spring is only the first of many blessings from the Flowering Crabapple. Summer shade of profuse green or purple leaves is another—the autumn leaf colours are often gorgeous —and the best is yet to come! Small tangy apple fruits in yellow, red, purple and orange. Cut sprays of them for decoration—pick for jams and jellies, and if the birds leave any after that you will have them hanging on the tree all winter long. All in all, the Crabapples are among the most attractive and trouble-free of flowering trees for the cooler or hilly districts. Well-drained soil is best; whether acid or alkaline; but they are really not too fussy. Only remember to spray the fruit or strip the tree altogether if you live in a fruitfly area.

623   MALUS floribunda
JAPANESE FLOWERING CRABAPPLE
JAPANESE CRAB
TREE   20 ft
JAPAN   SPRING

624   MALUS X pumila
HYBRID   CRABAPPLES
TREE   12 ft
HYBRID   SPRING—AUTUMN

625   MALUS ioensis 'Plena'
FLORAL APPLE
BECHTEL CRABAPPLE
TREE   8 ft
UNITED STATES OF AMERICA
LATE SPRING

626   MALUS X purpurea 'Eleyi'
ELEY'S FLOWERING CRAB
TREE   15 ft
HYBRID   SPRING

MALVA
MALVACEAE

Showy annuals and perennials related to the Hibiscus but with smaller flowers; MALVAS are useful hardy border plants for average soil. Grow from seed or cuttings (in the case of the perennials) and plant in full sun with plenty of water. The Musk Mallow (MALVA moschata) is a perennial species with pink and white flowers in summer.

627   MALVA moschata
MUSK MALLOW
PERENNIAL   2 ft
EUROPE   SUMMER

MALVAVISCUS

628

MANDEVILLA

629

MANETTIA

630

MALVAVISCUS
MALVACEAE

If your scarlet-flowered Hibiscus fails to open, but produces many vivid hanging buds, it is probably not a Hibiscus at all, but the related MALVAVISCUS. Peaty well-drained soil brings the best results, and MALVAVISCUS is strictly a warm-climate shrub needing summer humidity and filtered sun. There are several species, all with bright red flowers; but MALVAVISCUS mollis is the most commonly seen.

628   MALVAVISCUS mollis
TURK'S CAP
WAX MALLOW
SHRUB   6 ft
SOUTH AMERICA   SUMMER—
AUTUMN
SUBTROPICAL

MANDEVILLA
APOCYNACEAE

Gardenia-scented white trumpet flowers on stems you can pick are an attractive feature of the fast-climbing Chilean Jasmine. To get them in summer profusion you should plant in the open soil and not a pot, giving rich sandy loam and regular water. Though quite frost-hardy, MANDEVILLA is usually cut back in winter to sort out the tangles it makes when twining around itself and everything else in sight.

629   MANDEVILLA suaveolens
CHILEAN JASMINE
TWINING CLIMBER   15 ft
ARGENTINA   SUMMER

MANETTIA
RUBIACEAE

Gay little tubular flowers, made out of scarlet and gold velvet, shine like Christmas baubles among the felty leaves and stems of this attractive small twiner. Evergreen and tropical in origin, MANETTIAS flourish in any warm to temperate climate provided you give them sun for at least part of the day. Sandy acid soil is a help.

630   MANETTIA bicolour
(syn. inflata)
CLIMBING SHRUB   6 ft
BRAZIL   ALL YEAR

196

MANGIFERA

631

MANIHOT

632

MARANTA

633

MANGIFERA
ANACARDIACEAE

More commonly seen in the tropics, the handsome Mango tree can safely be grown in cooler areas—although it may not bear fruit. The tree is evergreen and beautiful at many times of the year. In spring it is decked with new foliage of shining copper-pink—in early summer with sprigs of deep-pink blossom—and for the rest of the year hung with fruits of many shades from green to pink and orange.

631   MANGIFERA indica
MANGO
TREE   30 ft
ASIA   SUMMER
SUBTROPICAL

MANIHOT
EUPHORBIACEAE

Like many spectacular foliage plants, MANIHOT is tropical and suited only to the warm climate garden or greenhouse. The beautifully-marked green and cream leaves with scarlet stems have made it popular, but it is also an important plant. The poisonous sap becomes both a useful antiseptic and your tapioca pudding! Grow from cuttings in sharp sand under glass.

632   MANIHOT utilissima 'Variegata'
CASSAVA
TAPIOCA PLANT
MANDIOC
PERENNIAL   3 ft
SOUTH AMERICA   SUMMER
TROPICAL

MARANTA
MARANTACEAE

This perennial greenhouse or tropical garden plant has the curious habit of folding its leaves together at night—hence the popular name Prayer Plant. MARANTA prefers filtered light; must have moisture and regular feeding to produce its beautifully-marked leaves. The uninteresting white flowers appear in summer. Away from the sub-tropics, MARANTAS are often seen growing under greenhouse benches where they revel in the damp shady conditions.

633   MARANTA leuconeura
PRAYER PLANT
RABBIT TRACKS
PERENNIAL   12 in
BRAZIL   SUMMER
SUBTROPICAL

MATTHIOLA

634

635

MAURANDIA

636

MEDINILLA

637

MATTHIOLA
CRUCIFERAE

Deliciously-scented Stock, so popular as cut flowers, are rarely grown to good quality in the home garden because their needs are difficult to fill. Firstly, they should never be grown where Stock have been grown before. Plant in new soil, deeply dug and enriched with lime, plant food and all the old manure you can lay hands on. They must have good drainage, regular watering and feeding to develop champion-sized flower spikes. There is no such thing as a guaranteed double Stock seedling. Selected varieties will give up to 80% doubles.

634   MATTHIOLA incana
'Branching type'
STOCK
GILLYFLOWER
BIENNIAL   18 in
SOUTHERN EUROPE   WINTER

635   MATTHIOLA incana
'Column type'
STOCK
BIENNIAL   3 ft
HYBRID   SPRING

MAURANDIA
SCROPHULARIACEAE

Here is a lightweight climber you can grow from seed: dainty leaves and mauve trumpet flowers appear in profusion as it twines rapidly around supports all through the warm weather. Rich, well-drained soil will do the trick, and give them sun with plenty of water. Cut back in autumn, where climate is warm enough, or throw away and grow new plants from seed the next spring.

636   MAURANDIA barclaiana
PERENNIAL CLIMBER   6 ft
MEXICO   SUMMER

MEDINILLA
MELASTOMATACEAE

Most gorgeous of tropical plants, MEDINILLAS are fussy growers outside the tropics but worth every effort when the fantastic hanging flower clusters appear in late spring. These combine strawberry-pink flowers and mauve-pink bracts with purple and yellow stamens. The stems are woody and angular, the leaves glossy and large. MEDINILLAS demand a warm winter, a humid summer, and should be watched for red spider. Grow in large pots of sand, peat and powdered charcoal.

637   MEDINILLA magnifica
JAVANESE RHODODENDRON
SHRUB   5 ft
JAVA–PHILIPPINES   LATE SPRING
TROPICAL

MELALEUCA

638

640

MELIA

642

639

641

MELALEUCA
MYRTACEAE

This vigorous group of shrubs and trees from all parts of Australia are particularly noted for their showy flowers and decorative peeling bark. Melaleucas are evergreen and provided drainage is reasonable are not particular as to soil. MELALEUCA armillaris has weeping branches of bright-green needle leaves and fluffy bottlebrush flowers from spring on. It can be clipped to a dense hedge. The more colourful M. hypericifolia has red bottlebrushes and coppery leaves, and blooms more heavily unclipped. M. linariifolia is one of the loveliest of all trees with needle leaves and feathery spikes of white summer blossom. The hardy M. leucadendra has shiny oval leaves and yellowish bottlebrush flowers in autumn. It is often found in Australian coastal swamps and is an exception to the good drainage rule. Other species have mauve, pink or green flowers.

638   MELALEUCA armillaris
DROOPING MELALEUCA
BRACELET HONEYMYRTLE
TREE   15 ft
VICTORIA—NEW SOUTH WALES
SPRING—AUTUMN

639   MELALEUCA hypericifolia
DOTTED MELALEUCA
SHRUB   6 ft
NEW SOUTH WALES   LATE SPRING

640   MELALEUCA leucadendra
BROADLEAF PAPERBARK
SWAMP PAPERBARK
CAJEPUT TREE
TREE   30 ft
AUSTRALIA—MALAYSIA   SUMMER

641   MELALEUCA linariifolia
FLAXLEAF PAPERBARK
SNOW IN SUMMER
TREE   20 ft
NEW SOUTH WALES—QUEENSLAND
SUMMER

MELIA
MELIACEAE

Not, as many believe, an Australian native, the attractive White Cedar is found in almost every country, and its origin is iost. It grows anywhere; as popular in the hot outback as in moist semi-tropical gardens. The pale mauvish flowers appear in summer, followed by yellow-orange fruits which remain on the branches throughout winter. In Australia many good trees have been cut down due to their infestation with the irritating procession caterpillar.

642   MELIA azederach
TEXAS UMBRELLA TREE
WHITE CEDAR
CHINA BERRY
BEAD TREE
PRIDE OF PERSIA
PERSIAN LILAC
TREE   25 ft
WORLD-WIDE   SUMMER

MESPILUS

643

METROSIDEROS

644

MICHELIA

645

MESPILUS
ROSACEAE

Favourite fruits in southern Europe, the popularity of Medlars is not universal. They ripen in autumn and are kept through winter until thoroughly squashy; then used for making cheeses and spreads. Medlars grow on a quaint crooked tree with dull-green deciduous leaves. The flowers are like white single roses with red anthers. They do best in cold winter areas.

643   MESPILUS germanica
MEDLAR
TREE   20 ft
SOUTHERN EUROPE   AUTUMN

METROSIDEROS
MYRTACEAE

A most useful flowering tree for the coastal area—resisting salt spray, wind and even the sea itself—METROSIDE-ROS has been seen with some of its roots right in salt water! Slow-growing, it has a most attractive leaf colouring of dark-green and silver and may reach 40 ft in time. In its native southern hemisphere the flowers, Bottlebrush in style and dark red, appear almost exactly at Christmas every year. The tree also resists industrial fumes and grows proli-fically in polluted city air.

644   METROSIDEROS tomentosa
POHUTUKAWA
NEW ZEALAND CHRISTMAS TREE
TREE   40 ft
NEW ZEALAND   SUMMER

MICHELIA
MAGNOLIACEAE

When it comes to fragrance, one man's Port Wine is apparently another man's Banana: if the popular names of this charming shrub mean anything. A glossy evergreen; its tiny beige and purple flowers fill the garden with fruity fra-grance in spring. Grow MICHELIA in filtered sun for best appearance and make sure it is near the house to get the maxi-mum from the perfume.

645   MICHELIA fuscata
PORTWINE MAGNOLIA
BANANA SHRUB
SHRUB   8 ft
CHINA   SPRING

MILTONIA

646

MIRABILIS

647

MISCANTHUS

648

MILTONIA
ORCHIDACEAE

Vibrant South American Orchids that can be flowered successfully without heat; MILTONIAS include unusual colour combinations of crimson, purple, pink, white, gold and brown. The single Pansy flowers last well on the plant, often appearing twice a year. Grow in a fine ground-bark compost and keep moist except in winter. MILTONIAS take cool conditions but more heat makes better flowers develop.

646   MILTONIA X hybrid
PANSY ORCHID
ORCHID   18 in
SOUTH AMERICA
SPRING–AUTUMN

MIRABILIS
NYCTAGINACEAE

For warmer climates only; this interesting tuberous perennial grows like a weed and makes a colourful display on summer afternoons. Plant where the evening light can unfurl the marvellously vivid flowers of cerise or yellow—sometimes mixed on the one plant! Grow from seed (once planted you will have it always). MIRA-BILIS can be raised in cold winter areas if you lift and store the tubers like Dahlias.

647   MIRABILIS jalapa
MARVEL OF PERU
FOUR O'CLOCK
PERENNIAL   2 ft
TROPICAL AMERICA   SUMMER

MISCANTHUS
GRAMINEAE

Closely related to Sugar Cane, this Chinese grass is grown from divisions and forms clumps about 3 ft across. MIS-CANTHUS survives in any soil and makes a decorative addition to the mixed border, while the feathery flower heads are used for summer arrangements. Illustrated variety 'Variegata' has blue-green leaves striped with creamy yellow. Variety 'Zebrina' has yellow stripes *across* the leaves; Variety 'Gracil-limus' is a soft grey-green.

648   MISCANTHUS sinensis
'Variegata'
EULALIA
PERENNIAL GRASS   4 ft
CHINA   SUMMER

MOLUCCELLA

649

MONARDA

650

MONSTERA

651

MOLUCCELLA
LABIATAE

A favourite of the flower arrangement fans; unusual Molucca Balm is easy to grow in almost any soil—but must be sown direct in its flowering position and kept well watered. The two-foot stems flower their entire length—although the showy green part is really an overgrown calyx, almost hiding the tiny white flowers. MOLUCCELLA lasts weeks in water, and the flowers are often dried for winter arrangement.

649   MOLUCCELLA laevis
SHELL FLOWER
BELLS OF IRELAND
MOLUCCA BALM
IRISH BELLFLOWER
ANNUAL   2 ft
SYRIA   SUMMER

MONARDA
LABIATAE

Fragrant summer-flowering perennials that naturalize well in damp shady areas; MONARDAS spread rapidly and send up masses of flower-crowned stems in summer and autumn. Colours are scarlet, carmine, rose and pink, usually surrounded by red bracts. Cut back every year, water well in summer and divide periodically for better bloom. Butterflies and honeyeating birds dote on them.

650   MONARDA didyma
OSWEGO TEA
BEE BALM
PERENNIAL   3 ft
NORTH AMERICA   SUMMER

MONSTERA
ARACEAE

One of the world's great houseplants, MONSTERAS are really seen at their best outdoors, in the humid shade of a warm climate. There, the deeply-divided leaves are twice as large and the plant assumes its natural habit and climbs with aerial roots. In warm districts it will produce ten-inch, Arum-type flowers of rich yellow, and in the semi-tropics these ripen into delicious fruit with a wonderfully rich flavour.

651   MONSTERA deliciosa
CERIMAN
MONSTERIA
FRUIT SALAD PLANT
VINE   20 ft
MEXICO   ALL YEAR

MORAEA

652

653

MORUS

654

MURRAYA

655

MORAEA
IRIDACEAE

Great resembling Irises, MORAEAS are a bulb genus from South Africa, Madagascar and Australia. Only two of some 40 species are commonly grown: MORAEA spathulata; a rich butter-yellow, three-inch flower which blooms equally well in wet or dry and survives cold winters, and M. pavonia (the Peacock Iris); a dainty plant with fine grass-like leaves and flowers of white, mauve or orange, all of them stamped with glossy black and blue peacock eyes. MORAEAS are planted in autumn, need plenty of water during the growing season but a dry summer when they are dormant.

652   MORAEA spathulata
YELLOW MORAEA
BULB   18 in
SOUTH AFRICA   SUMMER

653   MORAEA pavonia
PEACOCK IRIS
PEACOCK FLOWER
BULB   12 in
SOUTH AFRICA   SPRING

MORUS
MORACEAE

The delicious messy fruit beloved of birds and children everywhere comes from a handsome, easy to grow tree that romps in deep rich soil. Plant Mulberries from cuttings—whole branches if you like—in late winter. They strike and grow quickly, producing fruit under the toothed, fragrant leaves. Plant away from paths, for the fruit stains badly when ripe. Mulberry stains can be removed from skin and clothes with the juice of the green fruit.

654   MORUS nigra
BLACK MULBERRY
PERSIAN MULBERRY
TREE   20 ft
PERSIA   SUMMER

MURRAYA
RUTACEAE

Jasmine fragrance and clustered flowers like orange blossom win MURRAYA an important place in any garden. A dense graceful shrub with glossy leaflets, it does best in a semi-shaded position with sun only part of the day. Lots of water and humus-rich soil are musts for heavy flowering, but its beauty suffers badly in a cold winter climate.

655   MURRAYA exotica
ORANGE JESSAMINE
SATIN WOOD
COSMETIC BARK
SHRUB   10 ft
INDIA   AUTUMN

MUSA

656

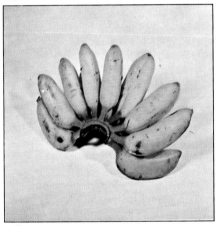

657

MUSCARI

658

MUSSAENDA

659

660

MUSA
MUSACEAE

Though a semi-tropical climate is required to guarantee ripening of fruit, Bananas will grow elsewhere in a sunny sheltered spot. Very rich soil and plenty of water are required, and many ingenious gardeners have discovered that these enormous perennials really flourish in the soakage area of septic tanks—as well as providing a discreet disguise for the plumbing. Bananas are propagated from suckers and grow from 2–20 ft high according to species. The giant pendant flowers are most spectacular and the fruit appears in dense hanging clusters or 'hands'. A Banana trunk that has flowered and fruited will never do so again, and should be cut right back to make room for vigorous new shoots.

656   MUSA paradisiaca
BANANA
PERENNIAL   15 ft
TROPICS   SUMMER

657   MUSA paradisiaca
(fruit)
ADAM'S APPLE
BANANA

MUSCARI
LILIACEAE

A wonderful contrast to Daffodils in cold winter areas, the dainty Grape Hyacinths produce a mass of rich blue flowers in spring. Best left undisturbed, MUSCARI demand well-drained soil rich in compost, and are indifferent to the presence of lime. Planted in clumps in early autumn, Grape Hyacinths produce leaves right away and are rarely without them. They do not like hot sun or mild winters.

658   MUSCARI armeniacum
GRAPE HYACINTH
BULB   9 in
ASIA MINOR   SPRING

MUSSAENDA
RUBIACEAE

Curious tropical shrubs that put on a brilliant summer display. On close inspection though, the colour is largely supplied by an occasional oversized sepal, the flowers being quite uninteresting. Principally grown species are MUSSAENDA erythrophylla with white flowers and scarlet sepals; M. frondosa, yellow flowers and white sepals; M. luteola, orange flowers and yellow sepals. Grow them in warm coastal districts only, in sandy soil. Water well. Cuttings strike easily under glass in summer.

659   MUSSAENDA erythrophylla
CLIMBING SHRUB   20 ft
CONGO   SPRING—AUTUMN

660   MUSSAENDA frondosa
SHRUB   3 ft
TROPICAL ASIA   SUMMER

661

662

MYOPORUM
MYOPORACEAE

Asia, New Zealand, islands of the Pacific and Indian Oceans are all home to more than 20 species of MYOPORUM, but few of them can compare with Australia's beautiful MYOPORUM floribundum. This is a spreading plant, its branches draped with fringes of deep-green hanging leaves and in spring a frosting of tiny white flowers that makes the tree look as if it has been caught in a blizzard. Grow in light acid soil.

661   MYOPORUM floribundum
BOOBIALLA
SHRUB   6 ft
NEW SOUTH WALES   SPRING

MYOSOTIS
BORAGINACEAE

It would be difficult to forget Forget-Me-Nots if only because they keep popping up every year to remind us it is spring again. Very easy to establish from seed in a damp shady spot with morning sun—they will reappear for years to come. Seed is slow to germinate; so best scatter it around late summer. Pink and white varieties are available.

662   MYOSOTIS alpestris
FORGET-ME-NOT
SCORPION GRASS
ANNUAL   9 in
EUROPE   WINTER—SUMMER

MYRIOPHYLLUM

MYRTUS

663

664

MYRIOPHYLLUM
HALORRHAGIDACEAE

Delicate aquatic perennials for the shallow freshwater pool or pond; MYRIOPHYLLUMS are planted from cuttings and spread rapidly, sending up tall flexible stems of feathery green leaves. When the stems reach water level, they produce minute flowers which seed so more plants may appear spontaneously elsewhere. Useful for oxygenating fish tanks.

663   MYRIOPHYLLUM
proserpinacoides
PARROT'S FEATHER
AQUATIC PERENNIAL   8 in
CHILE   SUMMER

MYRTUS
MYRTACEAE

Fragrant fuzzy white flowers in summer are merely an extra added attraction, for the Myrtle's aromatic bright-green leaves are its chief charm. The shrub will grow in any soil, sunny or shaded position, provided drainage is good. It can be clipped to make an informal hedge or trained tall to reveal trunk and branches. Grow it from cuttings.

664   MYRTUS communis
TRUE MYRTLE
SHRUB   6 ft
EUROPE–ASIA MINOR   SUMMER

NANDINA

665

666

NANDINA
BERBERIDACEAE

Deciduous shrubs that are nothing whatever to do with Bamboo in spite of their misleading common name. They grow in rich, well-watered soil and are very popular in modern landscape gardening for the vertical effect of their tall stems and delicate foliage. New growth is a delicate pink, and the leaves tint magnificently in autumn, finally becoming a brilliant scarlet where the frost hits them. Nandinas produce sprays of tiny white flowers in summer, and later shiny red berries. The dwarf variety 'Nana Compacta' is popular as a rock plant because of its vivid autumn colour.

665 NANDINA domestica
SACRED BAMBOO
HEAVENLY BAMBOO
SHRUB 6 ft
CHINA AUTUMN

666 NANDINA domestica 'Nana'
DWARF NANDINA
SHRUB 12 in
CHINA AUTUMN

207

667

669

671

668

670

672

NARCISSUS
AMARYLLIDACEAE

Daffodils, Jonquils and Narcissus are all the one genus so far as botanists are concerned. All grow from autumn-planted bulbs, produce long flat or hollow leaves and a single stem of flowers. Blooms of single varieties have 6 petals and a central trumpet protecting the stamens. The Jonquils (varieties of NARCISSUS tazetta) are early flowering (often in the autumn) and richly fragrant. Narcissus like winter cold and yet enjoy hot drying summers in their dormant season. They are best planted in drifts—the individual bulbs 6 in apart to leave room for natural increase. In warmer climates thought should be given to the planting site—ideally in semi-shade during summer but open to the winter sun. On the shady side of deciduous shrubs is ideal. After flowering, continue to water until the leaves die back naturally—this is the time next season's flowers develop.

667   NARCISSUS bulbicodium
HOOP PETTICOATS
BULB   9 in
MEDITERRANEAN   SPRING

668   NARCISSUS X incomparabilis 'Golden Glow'
DAFFODIL
BULB   15 in
EUROPE   SPRING

669   NARCISSUS odorus rugulosus
CAMPERNELLE
BULB   15 in
SPRING   MEDITERRANEAN

670   NARCISSUS poeticus 'Edwina'
PHEASANT'S EYE
BULB   15 in
MEDITERRANEAN   SPRING

671   NARCISSUS tazetta 'Grand Soleil d'Or'
JONQUIL
BUNCH FLOWERED NARCISSUS
BULB   2 ft
EUROPE–ASIA   WINTER

672   NARCISSUS X 'King Alfred'
TRUMPET TYPE DAFFODIL
BULB   18 in
HYBRID   SPRING

673

675

677

674

676

673   NARCISSUS X 'Texas'
DOUBLE DAFFODIL
BULB   18 in
HYBRID   SPRING

674   NARCISSUS X HYBRID
WIDE CUP DAFFODIL
BULB   18 in
HYBRID   SPRING

NEMESIA
SCROPHULARIACEAE

Showy winter-spring flowering annuals; shallow-rooted and particularly valuable for planting between and over summer-flowering bulbs. They are best put in right after the last frost in an open cool position, and pinched back regularly till they develop a bushy habit. NEMESIA strumosa hybrids are available in mixed colours including many shades from lemon to crimson, while the dwarf N. nana 'Compacta' is a much tinier plant with small flowers in soft shades of blue. It makes an eye-catching contrast to pink Primula or yellow Daffodils.

675   NEMESIA nana 'Compacta'
BLUE GEM NEMESIA
ANNUAL   10 in
SOUTH AFRICA   SPRING

676   NEMESIA strumosa
ANNUAL   18 in
SOUTH AFRICA   SPRING

NEMOPHILA
HYDROPHYLLACEAE

Baby Blue Eyes aptly describes the simple charm of this annual plant which is widely used for ground cover among spring-flowering bulbs. As it is difficult to transplant, NEMOPHILA seed must be broadcast where it is to grow (either in early spring or autumn in frost-free districts). It enjoys full sun and a rich soil and will re-seed for years to come if conditions are right.

677   NEMOPHILA menziesii 'Insignis'
BABY BLUE EYES
ANNUAL   6 in
UNITED STATES OF AMERICA
SPRING

678

679

NEOREGELIA
BROMELIACEAE

An interesting genus of epiphytic Bromeliads, characterized by the vivid colouring
of the centre leaves which gives rise to
the popular name. This colouring is
obviously designed to attract insects to
the tiny blue flowers which are almost
invisible, barely showing above the
water collected and stored in the leaf
funnel. NEOREGELIAS will grow in the
open garden in all but cold-winter
districts.

678 NEOREGELIA concentrica
'Marginata'
HEART OF FLAME
BROMELIAD 12 in
BRAZIL SPRING

NEPENTHES
NEPENTHACEAE

In the semitropical garden, carnivorous
Pitcher Plants are an interesting novelty,
grown either in hanging baskets or
heavy orchid pots. They need filtered
sun, high humidity and a temperature
that does not drop below 60° F. all year.
Pitcher Plants climb via tendrils which
develop on the leaf ends—some of
these later turn into curious lidded
flowers. Insects are attracted into them,
drown in the liquid and are absorbed
by the plant as food.

679 NEPENTHES salpouriana
PITCHER PLANT
VINE 20 ft
INDONESIA SUMMER

210

680

681

682

NEPETA
LABIATAE

Aromatic perennials of the mint family, NEPETAS are grown in the rockery or large border for their delicate mauve flower spikes and attractive greyish leaves. Planted out in light soil in the open sun, they spread rapidly into soft mounds of leaves which will be irresistible to any cat in the family. Water well and cut right back to the roots after flowers fade.

680   NEPETA mussinii
CAT MINT
PERENNIAL   2 ft
PERSIA   SUMMER

NEPHELIUM
SAPINDACEAE

Lovers of Chinese food should consider growing the delicious Lychee fruit in their own gardens. It is borne on an elegant evergreen tree that races ahead in any frost-free district where the soil is rich and acid. It will grow from the seed or nut inside the fruit, when freshly planted, but professionally raised plants are more reliable. Hanging clusters of white flowers in spring precede the fruit.

681   NEPHELIUM litchi
LYCHEE
LITCHI
LICHEE
LEE CHEE NUT
TREE   20 ft
SOUTH CHINA   SUMMER

NEPHROLEPIS
POLYPODIACEAE

Most popular of ferns for indoor use, NEPHROLEPIS has many named varieties with feathery, curled, and finely cut leaves. Grow in baskets or large pots of sandy fibrous soil. Water regularly and feed monthly with liquid fertilizer. Boston Fern should be kept constantly moist and prefers plenty of light without direct sun. A sunless window is probably the ideal position.

682   NEPHROLEPIS exaltata
BOSTON FERN
FERN   18 in
TROPICS   ALL YEAR

211

NERINE

683

685

NERIUM

686

684

687

NERINE
AMARYLLIDACEAE

Similar in appearance to Lycoris, but from South Africa and altogether a hardier genus of bulbs, Nerines enjoy a mild to cool climate and flower best at the end of a wet summer. Plant bulbs with the necks right out of the soil in spring, and make sure the position is open to autumn sun. NERINE bowdenii (the Pink Agapanthus) is most common. Its striped leaves sometimes persist until after flowering. N. filifolia is mass-planted in rockeries where it is evergreen except in a dry winter. The Guernsey Lily (N. sarniensis) is the beauty of the genus, vivid scarlet to cyclamen with an iridescent effect on the petals.

683   NERINE bowdenii
PINK AGAPANTHUS
LARGE PINK NERINE
BULB   18 in
SOUTH AFRICA   AUTUMN

684   NERINE sarniensis
GUERNSEY LILY
RED NERINE
BULB   18 in
SOUTH WEST AFRICA   AUTUMN

685   NERINE filifolia
GRASS LEAFED NERINE
BULB   10 in
SOUTH AFRICA   AUTUMN

NERIUM
APOCYNACEAE

The many-coloured flowers of Oleander would be reason enough for its great popularity in warm climates; but that is only the beginning of the story. These handsome shrubs are almost indestruct-ible and will put on a tremendous show even in drought-stricken areas or grimy industrial streets. Cuttings root easily in pots of sand—or even bottles of water. Plant them out in early spring, give plenty of decayed manure to stimulate growth and watch them go. Mature plants flower right through the warm weather to late autumn. Double and single varieties are available in shades of white, yellow, apricot, pink, red and crimson. The yellow-centred delicate pink 'Punc-tatum' with red buds is the best and hardiest. All parts of the plant are extremely poisonous.

686   NERIUM oleander 'Dr Golfin'
OLEANDER
SHRUB   6 ft
MEDITERRANEAN   SUMMER

687   NERIUM oleander 'Punctatum'
OLEANDER
SHRUB   8 ft
MEDITERRANEAN   SUMMER

689

690

688

688   NERIUM oleander 'Sister Agnes'
WHITE OLEANDER
SHRUB   15 ft
MEDITERRANEAN   SUMMER

NICOTIANA
SOLANACEAE

Closely related to Petunias, which they also resemble, the many species of Tobacco are often grown for their delicate evening fragrance. The flowers, usually in shades of pink, white or lime, are unattractive in themselves, and rarely open fully during the daylight hours. Sun or part-shade suit them equally well, so long as the soil is rich. Best for warm-climate gardens.

689   NICOTIANA tabacum
TOBACCO
ANNUAL   4 ft
TROPICAL AMERICA   SUMMER

NIEREMBERGIA
SOLANACACEAE

Dwarf perennials with fine lacy foliage, NIEREMBERGIAS are sprinkled with violet-blue cup flowers all summer long and widely used for garden and rockery work. They grow from seed or cuttings and prefer a light moist soil in semi-shade. Pinch back regularly in spring to encourage branching and again after flowering. Several named varieties are available in colours varying from palest blue to a true violet.

690   NIEREMBERGIA caerulea
BLUE CUP FLOWER
PERENNIAL   12 in
ARGENTINE   SUMMER

NIGELLA

691

NOPALXOCHIA

692

NYMPHAEA

693

694

NIGELLA
RANUNCULACEAE

Delicate pastel flowers all but hidden in a mist of feathery pale-green foliage give rise to the popular name of this charmer. Sow where it is to grow, particularly among spring bulbs in a sheltered spot. It makes a delicate cut flower, but leave some to re-seed for another year. Pink and white varieties are available as well as the traditional baby blue.

691   NIGELLA damascena
LOVE IN A MIST
DEVIL IN A BUSH
ANNUAL   18 in
TENERIFFE   SPRING

NOPALXOCHIA
CACTACEAE

A truly magnificent plant for basket or pot planting, the tongue-twisting NOP-ALXOCHIA is an epiphytic cactus from the high Mexican mountains. Grown in a rich, well-drained compost and fed regularly, it will produce masses of flowers right along the spineless leaf branches. These shade from rich carmine outside to delicate rose inside. NOPALXOCHIAS strike easily from large leaf cuttings severed with a very sharp knife.

692   NOPALXOCHIA phyllanthoides
EMPRESS CACTUS
CACTUS   2 ft
MEXICO   SPRING

NYMPHAEA
NYMPHAEACEAE

A splendid genus of aquatic plants requiring a considerable depth and area of water to do well, most Waterlilies are a little beyond the range of the average garden. Nevertheless, they are so attractive that flower lovers go to extraordinary lengths to grow them in all manner of containers and small pools. There are two main types, hardy and tropical. The former in shades of white, gold, pink and red—the tropicals adding blue and violet. Hardy Waterlily rhizomes are planted in early spring in boxes or pots of rich soil, at least 12 in below the water surface—they bloom throughout the warm weather, both flowers and leaves floating at water level. Tubers of the tropical type must be lifted and replanted where winters are cold—they bloom later and the flowers are held high above the water on tall stems. Most Waterlilies are richly fragrant.

695

697

696

693 NYMPHAEA alba
WATERLILY
AQUATIC
EUROPE   SUMMER

694 NYMPHAEA X 'Citronelle'
YELLOW WATERLILY
AQUATIC
HYBRID   SUMMER

695 NYMPHAEA caerulea
BLUE LOTUS
AQUATIC
NORTH AFRICA   SUMMER

696 NYMPHAEA capensis
'Zanzibariensis'
AQUATIC
EAST AFRICA   SUMMER

OBERONIA
ORCHIDACEAE

Tiniest of all the native Australian orchids, the minute OBERONIA—named for the King and Queen of the Fairies—is more of curiosity value than anything else—the tiny red and buff flowers are borne literally by the hundreds on a long drooping raceme in summer. The plant itself is epiphytic, growing outdoors on sheltered trees in the sub-tropics—in the bush-house in cooler areas. It is found on many Pacific Islands.

697 OBERONIA titania
FAIRY ORCHID
ORCHID   2 in
AUSTRALIA–PACIFIC   SUMMER

698

699

700

701

OCHNA
OCHNACEAE

From South Africa a hardy, gaily coloured shrub for any climate. No worry about propagating this one—any friend who has an OCHNA will find seedlings everywhere. Bronzy new spring foliage is followed by yellow buttercup flowers which soon fall, leaving the sepals or flower covers which turn vivid scarlet. Within these appear 5 bright green berries, which turn to shiny black.

698 OCHNA serrulata
MICKEY MOUSE PLANT
BIRDS EYE BUSH
CARNIVAL BUSH
SHRUB 5 ft
NATAL SPRING

OENOTHERA
ONAGRACEAE

Colourful perennials for the mixed border, rockery or sunny spot, Evening Primroses mostly open in the late afternoon. Nearly all 200 species are natives of North America and Mexico, but so adaptable that many have become naturalized as seaside and roadside plants in many lands. Any well-drained sandy soil makes them happy and they are easily grown from seed sown on the spot in late spring. The dwarf OENOTHERA speciosa (Rose of Texas) almost disappears beneath a profusion of rose-pink flowers in summer, and dies right back in autumn. O. tetragona displays gay Buttercup yellow flowers on wiry red stems. O. biennis (the true Evening Primrose) grows 4 ft high with a profusion of fragrant yellow blossom on summer evenings.

699 OENOTHERA albicaules
EVENING PRIMROSE
PERENNIAL 2 ft
NORTH AMERICA SPRING

700 OENOTHERA speciosa 'Childsii'
MEXICAN EVENING PRIMROSE
ROSE OF MEXICO
PERENNIAL 12 in
MEXICO SUMMER

701 OENOTHERA tetragona
SUNDROPS
PERENNIAL 3 ft
NORTH AMERICA SUMMER

702

703

ONCIDIUM
ORCHIDACEAE

Splendid epiphytic Orchids, native to the Americas, ONCIDIUMS can be grown in hanging containers or large pots in the sub-tropical garden. Long arching sprays of flowers are produced any time of year; and in the wind, these immediately suggest the popular name of Dancing Ladies. Yellow, brown and red are the most usual colours in this large genus—but pink and white are seen among some of the collectors' hybrids. Plant in fine ground tanbark, water generously.

702 ONCIDIUM crispum
'Grandiflorum'
DANCING LADIES
ORCHID   4 ft
BRAZIL   ALL YEAR

703   ONCIDIUM X 'Phyllis Wells'
BUTTERFLY ORCHID
ORCHID   4 ft
HYBRID   ALL YEAR

OPUNTIA

ORNITHOGALUM

704

705

707

706

708

OPHIOPOGON
LILIACEAE

Popular with landscape gardeners, the tough OPHIOPOGON has great value as ground cover in hard or heavily-shaded areas, although it does tend to become a harbour for snails and other pests. The leaves greatly resemble Liriope to which it is related; but the flowers are borne in loose drooping sprays, and are snowy white instead of mauve. OPHIO-POGON also has fibrous roots rather than bulbs.

704   OPHIOPOGON jaburan
WHITE MONDO GRASS
PERENNIAL   2 ft
JAPAN   SUMMER

OPUNTIA
CACTACEAE

Brilliantly-flowering cactii of dramatic appearance and extremely hardy constitution; the 200-odd species are all from the Americas and grow in any well-drained soil with the addition of a little lime. OPUNTIAS can be struck from one of the flat, oval leaf joints which should be handled with great care. The spines are very irritating and hard to get out of the skin. Spring flowers appear on old plants, but only in warm situations. They are followed on many species (notably the yellow-flowered OPUNTIA ficus-indica) by sweet and juicy red fruits which are most refreshing, but must be peeled carefully. The two species O. vulgaris and O. stricta are proclaimed pests in Australia.

705   OPUNTIA bergeriana
INDIAN FIG
PRICKLY PEAR
CACTUS   3 ft
UNITED STATES OF
AMERICA   SPRING

706   OPUNTIA santa-rita
PRICKLY PEAR
BUNNY EARS
CACTUS   2 ft
ARIZONA   SPRING

ORNITHOGALUM
LILIACEAE

Not the most spectacular of spring-flowering bulbs, ORNITHOGALUMS are nevertheless popular in warm climates because of their extreme reliability. They prefer a light, well-drained position in full sun, and like to be baked dry in the summer. The species ORNI-THOGALUM arabicum is most often sold as a cut flower, the tall stems being capped by regularly shaped white and gold flowers with centres like polished jade. The quaint O. thyrsoides has several useful peculiarities—the flowers last for many weeks, even out of water, and also absorb colour when the stems are rested in a pot of dye or ink. They are often sold in bunches, dyed mixed colours.

707   ORNITHOGALUM arabicum
STAR OF BETHLEHEM
STAR OF AFRICA
BULB   3 ft
AFRICA   SPRING

708   ORNITHOGALUM thyrsoides
CHINCHERINCHEE
CHINKS
INK FLOWER
BULB   15 in
SOUTH AFRICA   SPRING

OSMANTHUS

709

OTHONNA

710

OXALIS

711

OSMANTHUS
OLEACEAE

To many people the most delicious fragrance of all is the unforgettable perfume of Osmanthus, a blend of Jasmine, Gardenia and ripe Apricots. A dense shrub with glossy, toothed leaves that almost hide the minute flowers, it can be trained as a small tree, an espalier or even clipped as a hedge. Osmanthus does best in semi-shade; the soil rich, acid and well-drained.

709   OSMANTHUS fragrans
SWEET OSMANTHUS
SWEET OLIVE
SHRUB   8 ft
HIMALAYAS—CHINA   SUMMER

OTHONNA
COMPOSITAE

A gaily-flowered South African perennial for the warm-climate rockery, OTHONNA grows well from cuttings in sand, and needs perfect drainage at all times. OTHONNA trails rapidly, and more than anything else resembles clusters of juicy green jelly beans. The bright yellow Daisy flowers appear any time, but most heavily in winter. On wiry stems, they can be picked for posies.

710   OTHONNA capensis
TRAILING SUCCULENT   6 in
SOUTH AFRICA   WINTER

OXALIS
OXALIDACEAE

Tell an Australian gardener he should actually plant OXALIS and you are likely to be marked down as mad, for several types have already become the most hated weeds. But there are many charming little species guaranteed not to take over the garden. Among them, OXALIS versicolor, a delicate little plant with red-banded white flowers that open in full sun and close spirally when the clouds come by to look like tiny barbers' poles.

711   OXALIS versicolor
BARBERS' POLES
PERENNIAL   4 in
SOUTH AFRICA   AUTUMN

712

714

713

715

PAEONIA
RANUNCULACEAE

Spectacular shrubs and perennials for cold-winter climates only, Paeonies like semi-shade and deep mountain soil rich with compost. Hybrids of the perennial PAEONIA lactiflora are most often seen, though a good clump takes years to develop. Tubers are planted in autumn, and the flowers, spicily fragrant and up to 6 in across, appear in spring. There are many named varieties. You may also be surprised to see Paeony flowers on a small tree. This is the wonderful P. suffruticosa (or Moutan) from the Himalayas. For winter-cold districts only, it develops an exciting contorted shape. The flowers may be up to 12 in across and vary from single to full double— from white through pink to red and purple. Yellow or partly yellow varieties are hybrids of P. lutea.

712   PAEONIA X lactiflora 'Therese'
PAEONY ROSE
CHINESE PAEONY
PERENNIAL   2 ft
SIBERIA   SPRING

713   PAEONIA X lactiflora
PAEONY
PERENNIAL   2 ft
SIBERIA   SPRING

714   PAEONIA X lactiflora 'Torpillier'
PAEONY
PERENNIAL   2 ft
SIBERIA   SPRING

715   PAEONIA suffruticosa
TREE PAEONY
MOUTAN
SHRUB   6 ft
CHINA–TIBET   LATE SPRING

PAPAVER

716

718

PAPHIOPEDILUM

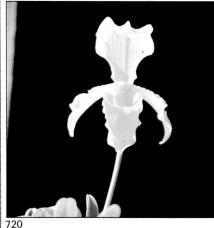
720

717

719

721

PAPAVER
PAPAVERACEAE

Gaily coloured annuals and perennials, Poppies produce open flowers in great profusion, but are adapted best to colder climates. All Poppies are pest-free and easy to grow, provided the soil is prepared in advance. They need a well-drained position with morning sun, and the soil should be dug fine and enriched with well-rotted manure. Sow or plant out seedlings in autumn. The winter-flowering Iceland Poppy (PAPAVER nudicaule) is current favourite, but the large Shirley Poppies flower for a longer period and the grey-leafed Opium Poppy makes a wonderful display in colder districts, particularly in its double form. King of them all is the satiny Oriental Poppy with six-inch flowers in red, pink orange or white.

716   PAPAVER nudicaule
ICELAND POPPY
ANNUAL   2 ft
SUB-ARCTIC   WINTER

717   PAPAVER orientale
ORIENTAL POPPY
PERENNIAL   3 ft
ARMENIA   LATE SPRING

718   PAPAVER rhoeas
SHIRLEY POPPY
FIELD POPPY
CORN POPPY
ANNUAL   4 ft
EUROPE–ASIA   SPRING–SUMMER

719   PAPAVER somniferum
OPIUM POPPY (DOUBLE TYPE)
ANNUAL   4 ft
ASIA   SPRING-SUMMER

PAPHIOPEDILUM
ORCHIDACEAE

Popular terrestrial Orchids from tropical Asia, PAPHIOPEDILUMS are quite hardy and can be grown in the open garden or even indoors. Pots should be small, as the Slipper Orchids enjoy being crowded — and the best compost is a moisture-retaining mixture of sandy soil and ground bark (available from nurserymen). These Orchids bloom in winter or early spring but have no resting period and can be kept moist all year. The shiny flowers are borne usually one to a stem, are long lasting and good for cutting. The background colours are generally white, yellow or green; the markings mahogany, crimson, tan or dark green, often in the form of spots and stripes.

720   PAPHIOPEDILUM insigne
LADIES' SLIPPERS
SLIPPER ORCHID
CYPRIPEDIUM
ORCHID   12 in
ASSAM   WINTER

721   PAHIOPEDILUM X leeanum
ORCHID   12 in
ASSAM   WINTER–SPRING

722

723

724

PARTHENOCISSUS
VITACEAE

A group of woody tendril-climbers native to North America and Asia. The very very popular Boston Ivy is PARTHENOCIS-SUS tricuspidata, actually native to Japan. Some of the leaves are like those in the illustration, others consist of three distinct leaflets. The common American Virginian Creeper is P. quinquefolia. It has five leaflets to the leaf. P. henryana of China also has five leaflets. Its foliage is velvety green above, first with white veins. Leaves are purple beneath. All this colouring other than green disappears when grown in sun.

722 PARTHENOCISSUS henryana
VINE 12 ft
CHINA AUTUMN

723 PARTHENOCISSUS tricuspidata
VIRGINIA CREEPER
BOSTON IVY
JAPANESE IVY
CREEPER 40 ft
JAPAN SPRING—AUTUMN

PASSIFLORA
PASSIFLORACEAE

Imaginative Catholic missionaries of the seventeenth century first brought these glorious flowers out of South America— naming them for a fancied symbolic representation of the passion of Jesus Christ. To them the colourful crown represented the crown of thorns; 5 stamens the Five Wounds; 10 petals the Ten Apostles who remained faithful to the end. Passion Flower vines climb over trees and fences, tangling themselves impossibly in the process. Most will grow in almost any soil with regular feeding. Flowers can be pink, white, blue, purple or scarlet according to species. Many develop delicious fruit, notably PASSIFLORA edulis (the Passionfruit), P. quadrangularis (the Granadilla), and P. mollissima (the Banana Passionfruit).

724 PASSIFLORA alato-caerulea
PASSION FLOWER
CLIMBER 20 ft
SOUTH AMERICA SUMMER
SUBTROPICAL

725

726

727

725   PASSIFLORA mollissima
BANANA PASSIONFRUIT
CLIMBER   15 ft
SOUTH AMERICA
SPRING–SUMMER

PATERSONIA
IRIDACEAE

Delicate mauve Iris flowers that open in
cloudy summer weather are common to
all 20 species of these Australian perennials. They spread from creeping rhizomes, send up evergreen leaf fans and
flower through the warm weather in an
acid sandy soil. PATERSONIA glabrata
has purple flowers; P. glauca very pale
blue; P. sericea deep blue-violet with
woolly bracts.

726   PATERSONIA glauca
WILD IRIS
LEAFY PURPLEFLAG
PERENNIAL   18 in
AUSTRALIA   SUMMER

PEDILANTHUS
EUPHORBIACEAE

Colourful and eye-catching in every part
of its growth, the succulent Zig Zag
Plant should be seen in every warm-
climate garden or indoor collection. The
waxy leaves are beautifully variegated
and tinted with pink; the stems (often
striped) are formed in a perfect zig zag
and the flowers (which only appear in
warmer districts) consist of vivid scarlet
bracts, formed like tiny slippers.

727   PEDILANTHUS tithymaloides
'Variegata'
SLIPPER FLOWER
ZIG ZAG PLANT
RED BIRD
PERENNIAL   4 ft
TROPICAL AMERICA   SUMMER

223

728

730

732

729

731

PELARGONIUM
GERANIACEAE

Wonderfully varied shrubby perennials for gardens everywhere the soil is not too rich and moist . . . then they are so busy making leaf they just never have time to flower. Pelargoniums like the going acid, sandy and quick-draining —just see them in weekend seaside gardens where they romp and flower with minimal attention. Three principal groups are grown: PELARGONIUM domesticum (the Regal Pelargonium) with attractively blotched flowers in a variety of colours including chocolate, mauve and purple; P. zonale (the common Geranium) including all the fancy coloured-leaf varieties and most often grown in pots; P. peltatum (the Ivy Leaf Geranium) has shiny spicy leaves and a trailing habit that makes it useful for walls and large containers. In California it is often seen as a hillside ground cover. All Pelargoniums are irresistible to caterpillars of every sort and should be sprayed with insecticide regularly. Spray Zonal types with Zineb against rust.

728   PELARGONIUMS IN ARRANGEMENT (Zonale, Peltatum & Domesticum types)

729   PELARGONIUM X domesticum
REGAL PELARGONIUM
MARTHA WASHINGTON GERANIUM
PERENNIAL   3 ft
HYBRID   SUMMER

730   PELARGONIUM peltatum
IVY LEAF GERANIUM
PERENNIAL   TRAILER
HYBRID   SUMMER

731   PELARGONIUM zonale
ZONAL GERANIUM
PERENNIAL   6–30 in
HYBRID   ALL YEAR

732   PELARGONIUM quercifolium 'Royal Oak'
OAK LEAF GERANIUM
PERENNIAL   3 ft
SPRING

PENSTEMON

733

PENTAPTERYGIUM

734

PENTAS

735

736

PENSTEMON
SCROPHULARIACEAE

Among the most useful and long flowering perennials, Penstemons enjoy full sun (except in hot climates) and being of mountain origin need good drainage and a loose gravelly soil. Plant out in summer for flowers the following spring, and cut back after flowering to stimulate further bloom. Over 150 species are grown, all of them native to North America, but commonly seen types are hybrids of PENSTEMON gloxinioides.

733　PENSTEMON gloxinioides
BEARD TONGUE
BORDER PENSTEMON
PERENNIAL　2½ ft
NORTH AMERICA　SPRING–
AUTUMN

PENTAPTERYGIUM
ERICACEAE

A delightful shrub with Ericas and Rhododendrons in semi-shade, PENTAPTERYGIUM grows from a rather tuberous rootstock, sending up slender drooping stems lined with tiny bright-green leaves. Heath-type flowers of vivid scarlet hang loosely in pairs beneath the stems, their weight bending them into graceful arches. These are succeeded by pale purple berries.

734　PENTAPTERYGIUM serpens
SHRUB　3 ft
CHINA　SUMMER

PENTAS
RUBIACEAE

A colourful genus of compact shrubs from tropical Africa, grown easily from spring cuttings and somewhat resembling Bouvardia. PENTAS grows in any frost-free climate, but prefers a wet tropical summer and warm winter. Well-drained sandy soil rich with leafmould is necessary, and regular pinching back encourages a neat bushy habit. PENTAS lanceolata var. coccinea has ribbed leaves and brilliant carmine flowers; P. lanceolata flowers in a pale rosy purple—its varieties include 'Alba' (white) and 'Parviflora' (vivid scarlet). In tropical countries PENTAS is often grown as a mass bedding plant on account of its neat compact habit.

735　PENTAS lanceolata var. coccinea
RED STAR CLUSTER
SHRUB　3 ft
AFRICA　SUMMER

736　PENTAS lanceolata
EGYPTIAN STAR CLUSTER
SHRUB　2 ft
AFRICA–ARABIA　SUMMER

PEPEROMIA

737

PERISTROPHE

738

PERSOONIA

739

PEPEROMIA
PIPERACEAE

Useful perennials for home, greenhouse or tropical garden; PEPEROMIAS sprout easily from cuttings and rapidly make a dense mass of decorative leaves, very attractive as a ground cover. All species prefer diffused light and indirect sun and will do well indoors for quite a while. Give them a light potting compost and not too much water. PEPEROMIA obtusifolia (the popular Pepper Face) trails with thick stems and variegated waxy leaves. The green flower spikes are uninteresting.

737   PEPEROMIA obtusifolia
'Variegata'
PEPPER ELDER
PEPPER FACE
PERENNIAL   8 in
WEST INDIES   ALL YEAR

PERISTROPHE
ACANTHACEAE

Vividly flowered perennials to brighten the winter garden, PERISTROPHES enjoy similar conditions to the related Justicia. (See: JUSTICIA). The plants assume a rather floppy habit unless staked, and the flowers (in clusters of 2 or 3), rather resemble Honeysuckle in shades of pink to purple. PERISTROPHE speciosa blossoms profusely in a strong red-violet.

738   PERISTROPHE speciosa
PERENNIAL   4 ft
ASIA   WINTER

PERSOONIA
PROTEACEAE

Attractive Australasian shrubs and trees for the sandy, acid garden; PERSOON-IAS mostly have pine-like leaves, yellow flowers and green berries. The species PERSOONIA pinifolia is particularly lovely, with a weeping habit and spring flowers in long clusters. The principal interest, however, is the bright green berries or Geebungs which turn red in autumn and hang on the tree for many months.

739   PERSOONIA pinifolia
PINELEAF GEEBUNG
SHRUB   10 ft
AUSTRALIA   SPRING

226

740

741

PETRAEA
VERBENACEAE

Cascades of lavender-blue tumbling over fences and trees in warm weather could only be the rampant Sandpaper Vine. The actual flowers are purple and fall quickly, but the lavender calyxes remain for weeks in a spray up to 10 in long. PETRAEA is a tough, woody vine and the leaves are unusually rough to the touch.

740   PETRAEA volubilis
PURPLE WREATH
SANDPAPER VINE
VINE   30 ft
TROPICAL AMERICA   SPRING

PETROPHILA
PROTEACEAE

More members of the Protea family but with less exotic flowers than usual; PETROPHILAS are most often represented by the feathery PETROPHILA sessilis, used by florists to fill out bunches of cut flowers. As plants they have many good qualities; they grow easily (and not too big) in warm sandy soil, have handsome heat-resistant foliage and fine tubular flowers springing from cone-shaped heads which remain when the petals fall.

741   PETROPHILA linearis
DRUMSTICKS
SHRUB   6 ft
WESTERN AUSTRALIA   ALL YEAR

742

744

745

743

PETUNIA
SOLANACEAE

The hotter the summer, the better Petunias produce. Open, cheerful flowers, they do best in a good soil and like lime. Planted from early spring to early summer, they should be pinched back regularly to ensure branching, and fertilized monthly till the hot weather begins. Then, all they need is water and watch them go! Old time single bedding varieties such as 'Rosy Morn' and 'Rose O'Day' are still the cheapest summer colour you can buy but many splendid new Japanese hybrids are available. These include the larger ruffled 'Grandiflora' strain, and the 'Multifloras' which have the old small-sized flowers, but many more of them. 'Multifloras' include many new colours such as 'Butterscotch' and variegated types like pink and white 'Cherry Pie'.

742   PETUNIA X 'Fl Hybrid
 Grandiflora'
ANNUAL   2 ft
HYBRID   SUMMER

743   PETUNIA X 'Fl Hybrid
 Multiflora'
ANNUAL   2 ft
HYBRID   SUMMER

744   PETUNIA hybrida 'Rose O'Day'
BEDDING PETUNIA
ANNUAL   12 in
SOUTH AMERICA   SUMMER

PHALAENOPSIS
ORCHIDACEAE

Like a flight of butterflies quivering in the morning air, PHALAENOPSIS are not difficult to grow if you can assure them of high humidity and a constant winter temperature of around 60°F. to 70°F. Use a coarse compost with plenty of bark chunks into which the plants can run their thick worm-like roots. They are rather sparse plants, with 2 or 3 large leathery leaves and no pseudobulbs.

745   PHALAENOPSIS amabilis
MOTH ORCHID
BUTTERFLY ORCHID
ORCHID   15 in
JAVA   AUTUMN
TROPICAL

PHILADELPHUS

PHILODENDRON

746

747

749

748

PHILADELPHUS
SAXIFRAGACEAE

The overpowering orange blossom fragrance of PHILADELPHUS should be
reason enough for its presence in any
summer garden plan. But when you add
masses of delicate golden-centred
snowy blossom on tall arching canes,
the effect is irresistible. Mockorange
grows readily from cuttings and all old
wood should be cut out after flowering.
It is deciduous and prefers part-shade
in hot areas.

746   PHILADELPHUS coronarius
SWEET MOCKORANGE
SYRINGA
SHRUB   10 ft
ASIA MINOR   SPRING

PHILODENDRON
ARACEAE

The seedy specimens one sees in office
foyers give no hint of the magnificence
of these durable plants growing free in
tropical gardens. The 120 species include
giant-leafed shrubby types and slim
delicate vines that will twine into the
highest tree. All need a rich, loose soil
with good drainage — and prefer broken
sun. Water and fertilize regularly for good
leaf colour and hose the leaves down to
keep them glossy. PHILODENDRON
oxycardium is the most popular twining
type with heart-shaped leaves. P. pertusum, popular for indoor effect is actually
a juvenile leaf form of Monstera. (See:
MONSTERA). P. selloum is hardiest of
the shrubby type; its leaves may be 3 ft
long.

747   PHILODENDRON oxycardium
VINE   30 ft
WEST INDIES   ALL YEAR

748   'PHILODENDRON pertusum'
SPLIT LEAF PHILODENDRON
VINE
SOUTH MEXICO   ALL YEAR

749   PHILODENDRON selloum
SHRUBBY VINE   6 ft
BRAZIL   ALL YEAR

229

PHLOMIS

750

PHLOX

751

753

752

754

PHLOMIS
LABIATAE

This shrubby old-fashioned perennial deserves greater popularity, for it does particularly well in poor soil, by the sea, and even in drought-stricken areas. The bright-yellow flowers appear in circular whorls near the top of tall stems, and make it quite useful for cutting. Its only needs are an occasional staking and cutting back by about half in autumn.

750   PHLOMIS fruticosa
JERUSALEM SAGE
PERENNIAL   4 ft
SOUTHERN EUROPE
SPRING–SUMMER

PHLOX
POLEMONIACEAE

Summer annuals and perennials with showy clustered flowers and little scent. Useful for hot-weather bedding in almost any soil, sunny or shaded. The common annual variety PHLOX drummondii is planted out by millions every spring and shares the summer bedding stakes with Petunias. Its colour range is immense, lacking only a true blue or orange. P. drummondii var. Stellaris has smaller star-shaped flowers; P. paniculata is popular for the perennial border, planted from divisions in late autumn. The prostrate Moss Phlox bloom earlier and are used in rockeries or alpine lawns in cooler climates. They are literally a sheet of colour when grown well.

751   PHLOX drummondii
ANNUAL PHLOX
ANNUAL   12 in
TEXAS   SUMMER

752   PHLOX paniculata
PERENNIAL PHLOX
PERENNIAL   3 ft
NORTH AMERICA   SUMMER

753   PHLOX drummondii var. Stellaris
STAR PHLOX
ANNUAL   10 in
HYBRID   SUMMER

754   PHLOX subulata
ALPINE PHLOX
MOSS PHLOX
PERENNIAL   3 in
UNITED STATES OF AMERICA
SUMMER

230

PHOENIX

755

PHORMIUM

756

PHOTINIA

757

PHOENIX
PALMACEAE

One of the world's great trees of commerce, the Date Palm is also a most attractive garden subject—particularly in desert or coastal areas. Grow it from date stones in sandy soil if you are patient—buy a mature plant if you are not. The fruits are unlikely to develop without trees of both sexes in close proximity.

755   PHOENIX dactylifera
DATE PALM
TREE   30 ft
NORTH AFRICA   ALL YEAR

PHORMIUM
LILIACEAE

Useful accents for the modern garden, New Zealand Flax plants are virtually indestructible—thriving in wet or dry, hot or cold—even exposed to salt spray. Leaf colours vary from green to bronze or red-purple—plain or variegated. The flower spikes appear in summer, dull red or sometimes yellow, but the plant is really grown for the dramatic effect of the stiff, vertical leaves.

756   PHORMIUM tenax 'Variegatum'
NEW ZEALAND FLAX
FLAX LILY
PERENNIAL   8 ft
NEW ZEALAND   SUMMER
SUBTROPICAL

PHOTINIA
ROSACEAE

Spectacular in almost every season, the hardy PHOTINIA produces orange new foliage in early spring; followed by clouds of pungent whitish blossom. Later come red berries and finally (although it is evergreen) brilliant red leaf colouring as the cold weather approaches. It can be clipped as a hedge or specimen bush or allowed to grow tall and rangy. PHOTINIA grows everywhere but looks more showy in cold areas.

757   PHOTINA serrulata
CHINESE HAWTHORN
TREE   15 ft
CHINA   SPRING

PHYLLOSTACHYS

758

PHYSALIS

759

PHYSOSTEGIA

760

PHYLLOSTACHYS
GRAMINEAE

A graceful, dainty Bamboo of manage-able size, PHYLLOSTACHYS spreads from running roots, will stand tempera-tures as low as zero and can be planted out any time of year. Its stems rarely exceed 8 ft in height or three-quarters of an inch in diameter and the delicate leaves are a golden-green. Bamboo is a grass, and like all grasses needs regular water and feeding. Use PHYLLOSTA-CHYS for screens, background planting or tub work.

758   PHYLLOSTACHYS aurea
GOLDEN BAMBOO
BAMBOO   8 ft
CHINA   ALL YEAR

PHYSALIS
SOLANACEAE

The flowers of this perennial are its least interesting feature, white and insignifi-cant. But they are succeeded in late summer by lantern-shaped seed cap-sules which ripen from green to a variety of shades in orange, yellow and scarlet. Entire stems can be cut and dried for winter decoration. Plant from seed in spring, or divisions in autumn, but be warned that it does spread rapidly.

759   PHYSALIS franchetii
CHERRY IN A LANTERN
WINTER CHERRY
CHINESE LANTERN
CAPE GOOSEBERRY
PERENNIAL   2½ ft
JAPAN   AUTUMN

PHYSOSTEGIA
LABIATAE

PHYSOSTEGIA's giant heath flowers bloom vividly in late summer and autumn. They are good for cutting, but more showy left in the open garden where seeding will help them spread rapidly into a dense clump. Grow them in any good soil, in sun or (for brighter flowers) in shade. Very vigorous plants, they can be moved even when in flower, but should be cut back in winter.

760   PHYSOSTEGIA virginiana
'Vivid'
GALLIPOLI HEATH
FALSE DRAGONHEAD
OBEDIENT PLANT
PERENNIAL   2 ft
NORTH AMERICA   SUMMER—
AUTUMN

PICEA

761

PIERIS

762

PILEA

763

PICEA
PINACEAE

Most beautiful of cold-climate conifers, the Colorado Blue Spruce comes tall and straight, a perfect Christmas tree. It grows well from seed, but the leaf colours are variable—the finest blues being propagated by grafting. Variety 'Kosteriana' has needle foliage of a clean blue-grey; Variety 'Aurea' has green needles with a tinge of gold. Grow PICEA in any soil, but spray through the summer against red spider.

761   PICEA pungens 'Kosteriana'
COLORADO BLUE SPRUCE
TREE   20 ft
WESTERN UNITED STATES OF
AMERICA   ALL YEAR

PIERIS
ERICACEAE

Cream Lily-of-the-Valley flowers festoon this lovely shrub in springtime profusion. Grow in tubs or the open garden, but it must have rich lime-free soil and a cool, moist, sheltered position. Andromeda is attractive at all times; the summer foliage in cool deep green; the chains of pink buds in autumn; the magnificent colours of new leaves in winter—white, pink or scarlet according to variety.

762   PIERIS japonica
JAPANESE PEARL FLOWER
LILY-OF-THE-VALLEY SHRUB
PEARL BUSH
ANDROMEDA
SHRUB   4 ft
JAPAN   SPRING

PILEA
URTICACEAE

In the tropical garden (or greenhouse elsewhere) Pileas provide interesting foliage effects. The Aluminium Plant (PILEA cadierei) produces masses of silver-splashed greenery with a distinctive metallic effect—while the Artillery Plant (P. microphylla) is more fern-like, with soft clouds of feathery green that fire pollen in all directions when dry. Both prefer warmth, humidity and semi-shade with porous leafy soil.

763   PILEA cadierei
ALUMINIUM PLANT
WATERMELON PILEA
PERENNIAL   18 in
VIETNAM   SUMMER

PIMELEA

764

PINUS

765

PISTACHIA

766

PIMELEA
THYMELAEACEAE

Related to Daphne, the fragrant Rice Flowers are an important and attractive part of the Australian Flora. All they need for success is a light porous acid soil and plenty of sunshine. PIMELEAS are quite variable in habit and flower colour, but the general form is a dense cluster of starry long-tubed flowers enclosed by four coloured bracts. PIMELEA rosea is a deep pink species; P. suaveolens yellow and green; P. ligustrina creamy white.

764   PIMELEA ligustrina
TALL RICE FLOWER
ALPINE ROSE
SHRUB   6 ft
EASTERN AUSTRALIA   SPRING

PINUS
PINACEAE

Too big, too slow-growing and too pest-ridden for the average garden—the northern hemisphere's beautiful Pines have found little popularity in southern gardens—although they are often seen as windbreaks in country estates. They do however make the most delightful Bonsai plants, where their slow growth and gnarled bark are an advantage. The Japanese White and Red Pines and the European Mugho Pine are favourites for this work because of their relatively small needles. Sandy, well-drained soil is the rule.

765   PINUS parviflora
(as a Bonsai)
JAPANESE WHITE PINE
TREE   50 ft
JAPAN   ALL YEAR

PISTACHIA
ANACARDIACEAE

Most vivid and variable in its autumn colouring, the Chinese Pistachio tree makes an ideal specimen in cold-climate districts. The flowers are hardly notice-able; the leaves a delicate green in warm weather and when autumn comes trans-formed into a fiery rainbow. PISTA-CHIAS enjoy full sun, need plenty of water but are not too particular as to soil.

766   PISTACHIA chinensis
PISTACHIO
CHINESE PISTACHIO
PISTACHE
TREE   25 ft
CHINA   AUTUMN

234

767

768

PITCAIRNEA
BROMELIACEAE

A large genus of terrestrial Bromeliads, only one or two of which are commonly cultivated—PITCAIRNEAS are grown for their tall flower spikes—usually red and yellow, but sometimes green and white. PITCAIRNEAS are from cooler climates than most other Bromeliads and flourish in the open garden, a striking addition to the perennial border. They enjoy a heavy mulch of leaves or garden compost.

767   PITCAIRNEA flammea
PERENNIAL   3 ft
BRAZIL   SUMMER

PITTOSPORUM
PITTOSPORACEAE

A lovely but messy tree from the Victorian forests, PITTOSPORUM undulatum is decked with shiny, wavy-edged leaves all year and makes a splendid background planting away from paths and lawns. Strongly-perfumed cream flowers open in spring and are followed by orange berries which split and drop sticky seeds all over the place. Prune when young to develop a single trunk and spray regularly against aphids and scale insects.

768   PITTOSPORUM undulatum
VICTORIAN BOX
TREE   30 ft
VICTORIA   SPRING

PLATANUS

PLATYCERIUM

PLATYCODON

769

770

771

PLATANUS
PLATANACEAE

The broad fan-like leaves and spreading shape of the London Plane make it a favourite whenever summer shade is needed—yet it will flourish anywhere with deep soil and moisture. A lovely sight when growing naturally, the Plane is unfortunately more often seen cropped and pruned, growing out of asphalt as a street tree. It grows readily from seeds which it drops everywhere.

769   PLATANUS acerifolia
LONDON PLANE
TREE   60 ft
EUROPE   ALL YEAR

PLATYCERIUM
POLYPODIACEAE

Somewhat out of fashion these days, dramatic Stag's Horn Ferns bring a lush tropical touch to the shaded courtyard or in the warmer open garden. Tree-dwellers in nature, they are commonly raised on slabs of treefern or tree trunk where they rapidly increase in size if you keep up the humidity with regular spray-ing. Ensure filtered sun and protection from frosts.

770   PLATYCERIUM bifurcatum
STAG'S HORN FERN
EPIPHYTIC FERN   3 ft
AUSTRALIA   ALL YEAR

PLATYCODON
CAMPANULACEAE

Balloon-like buds swell and pop open into blue star-flowers all summer long when you have established the charming PLATYCODON in your garden. It mixes perfectly with other summer perennials in the open border in all but the hottest districts: then, part-shade is desirable. Plant from divisions in good soil, water regularly. But do not be alarmed when it disappears altogether in winter.

771   PLATYCODON grandiflorum
BALLOON FLOWER
CHINESE BELLFLOWER
PERENNIAL   2 ft
CHINA–JAPAN   SUMMER

PLECTRANTHUS

772

773

PLUMBAGO

774

PLUMERIA

775

776

PLECTRANTHUS
LABIATAE

Frequently mistaken for Coleus or Salvias, PLECTRANTHUS are a variable genus of plants within the same mint family—some shrubby, some trailing perennials. All grow well in frost-free areas and can be propagated by cuttings which root easily. They are native to Africa, Asia and Australasia—the African species being most commonly grown. PLECTRANTHUS eckloni (the Cockspur Flower) is a semi-evergreen shrub for filtered sun, and produces upright spikes of purple blossom in autumn. P. oertendahlii is much favoured as a ground cover in semi-shade. Its velvety leaves are backed with purple, and spikes of delicate mauve-white flowers appear in late summer.

772   PLECTRANTHUS eckloni
COCKSPUR FLOWER
BLUE SPUR FLOWER
SHRUB   4 ft
SOUTH AFRICA   AUTUMN

773   PLECTRANTHUS oertendahlii
PERENNIAL   12 in
NATAL   SUMMER

PLUMBAGO
PLUMBAGINACEAE

Sky blue Phlox flowers in lavish clusters decorate the useful Plumbago right through the warm weather. Any soil will do, provided drainage is good; but the flowers retain their colour best in filtered sun. Be warned that Plumbago spreads rapidly from suckers and quickly becomes sprawling and untidy unless clipped back spring and autumn. Use it as an informal hedge or to disguise ugly walls and fences.

774   PLUMBAGO auriculata
(syn. capensis)
PLUMBAGO
CAPE PLUMBAGO
LEADWORT
SHRUB   6 ft
SOUTH AFRICA   WARM WEATHER

PLUMERIA
APOCYNACEAE

'A set of antlers decked with posies' was one graphic description of this grotesque tropical tree and its bare, blunt branches. But the flowers make it all worthwhile; delicious, fragrant waxy blossoms that open profusely all through the warm weather. Just pick them up as they drop and use them in float bowls—or go Tahitian and pop one behind your ear. The species PLUMERIA. obtusifolia is pure white and evergreen. P. acutifolia is the common white and yellow, and all the coloured varieties are hybrids of P. rubra and P. acutifolia. There are at least 40 different colours by the way, but all are frost-tender.

775   PLUMERIA acutifolia
GRAVEYARD FLOWER
FRANGIPANI
PLUMERIA
MELIA
TREE   10 ft
MEXICO   SUMMER

776   PLUMERIA rubra
RED FRANGIPANI
TREE   10 ft
MEXICO   SUMMER
SUBTROPICAL

POLIANTHES

777

POLYGALA

778

POLYGONATUM

779

POLIANTHES
AMARYLLIDACEAE

A favourite everywhere for bridal bouquets, the deliciously scented Tuberose
can be flowered all year in mild climates.
Tubers are planted anytime but not
watered until leaves begin to appear.
The glorious blossoms show in pairs on
a tall stem, and individual flowers rarely
last more than a day. They are usually
picked singly and wired into bouquets.

777   POLIANTHES tuberosa
TUBEROSE
BULB   3 ft
MEXICO   SUMMER

POLYGALA
POLYGALACEAE

Useful for its masses of brilliant winter
flowers, the Sweet Pea Shrub should be
planted with care as the flower colour
seems to clash with just about everything. A leggy shrub, it is best for background or fence planting and does well
just about anywhere, though the flower
colour lasts better in part-shade. It grows
fast and is often used as a temporary
filler behind slower growing plants.

778   POLYGALA myrtifolia
'Grandiflora'
SWEET PEA SHRUB
SHRUB   6 ft
SOUTH AFRICA   WINTER–SPRING
SUBTROPICAL

POLYGONATUM
LILIACEAE

A charming and graceful flower for
woodland areas or cool shady places,
the old-fashioned Solomon's Seal is
grown from long tuberous bulbs. Planted
out in autumn, these send up a leaf spike
in spring and flower only a few weeks
later. The flower stems are long and
arching with small clusters of green and
white bells hanging at intervals. The
leaves stand out like pairs of green wings.

779   POLYGONATUM multiflorum
SOLOMON'S SEAL
DAVID'S HARP
BULB   2 ft
EUROPE   LATE SUMMER

POLYGONUM

780

781

POPULUS

782

783

PORTULACA

784

POLYGONUM
POLYGONACEAE

For quick cover up jobs in tough places, rely on the Knotweeds or POLY-GONUMS but just be sure they do not take over the whole garden. Unsightly fences, old trees and sheds will look lovelier every day when you plant POLYGONUM aubertii (the Silverlace Vine). Water regularly and the glossy heart-shaped leaves will twine every-way, disappearing in turn under a cloud of frothy summer flowers. The smaller P. capitatum is just as useful for rockshelves and unused banks. The spring and summer flowers are like tiny pink pom-poms and often used in small bouquets. But it seeds freely, especially in damp soil, so watch out for seedling plants and take them out before they take over. POLYGONUMS should be cut right back in winter.

780   POLYGONUM aubertii
SILVERLACE VINE
RUSSIAN VINE
VINE   40 ft
SZECHUAN   SPRING-AUTUMN

781   POLYGONUM capitatum
JAPANESE KNOTWEED
PERENNIAL   10 in
NORTH INDIA   ALL YEAR

POPULUS
SALICACEAE

Blazing torches on the autumn landscape in favoured districts, the Lombardy Poplars colour well only where the autumn nights are cold. They present so many problems they are best raised well away from buildings and drains of any kind. They sucker prolifically; reach and raid drains constantly; feed voraciously; and are host to many pests. They also break easily in storms. Still, if you have a large garden, you will probably plant one anyway—for what other tree is so lovely to look at any time of year?

782   POPULUS nigra 'Italica'
LOMBARDY POPLAR
TREE   100 ft
EUROPE–MIDDLE EAST   AUTUMN

783   POPULUS nigra 'Italica'

PORTULACA
PORTULACACEAE

Vivid waxy blooms in wildly clashing colours appear everywhere on these trailing plants all through summer. Any-where it is hot and open, especially on sandy or gravelly soil, they will flower and flourish to excess. Plant out in spring, even in restricted spots between paving—they will give you no trouble. Just reward them with a little water.

784   PORTULACA grandiflora
ROSE MOSS
PURSLANE
SUN PLANT
PIGFACE
ANNUAL   6 in
BRAZIL   SUMMER

239

PORTULACARIA

785

POSOQUIERIA

786

POTENTILLA

787

PORTULACARIA
PORTULACACEAE

Succulent green leaves and solid red stems make the Jade Plant a favourite everywhere for rockery work or tub planting—even a small specimen having much the appearance of a dwarfed, mature tree. It is very hardy, enjoying sun, shade or salt air equally—but it rarely, if ever, produces its tiny pink flowers away from its native South Africa—and never indoors. Strikes easily from large cuttings.

785   PORTULACARIA afra
JADE PLANT
ELEPHANT'S FOOD
SPEKBOOM
SUCCULENT SHRUB   8 ft
SOUTH AFRICA   ALL YEAR
SUBTROPICAL

POSOQUIERIA
RUBIACEAE

Exaggeratedly long tubular flowers with a strong Gardenia perfume are the notable feature of these exciting shrubs. Grown in the tropics or frost-free coastal climates in part-shade and acid soil; they are handsome at any time of year, with leathery glossy leaves. The flowers may be white, yellow or pink according to species, but in POSOQUIERIA frag-rantissima they have an elegant drooping habit and reflexed petals.

786   POSOQUIERIA fragrantissima
NEEDLE BUSH
SHRUB   6 ft
BRAZIL   SUMMER
SUBTROPICAL

POTENTILLA
ROSACEAE

Hardy perennials and shrubs of the Rose family, POTENTILLAS are useful in the mixed border, shrubbery or rock garden. Almost all of the 350 species have leaves similar to a Delphinium or Strawberry, and panicles of single or semi-double Rose flowers on tall thin stems. The flowers are cream, yellow, white, pink or red. Most of them prefer full sun and lose their looks in cold winters.

787   POTENTILLA hirta
CINQUEFOIL
PERENNIAL   2½ ft
EUROPE–ASIA–AFRICA   SUMMER

PRIMULA

788

790

792

789

791

793

PRIMULA
PRIMULACEAE

A vast botanical genus of over 500
species, mostly from the alps and wood-
lands of the northern hemisphere. They
are all perennials, mostly with the typical
Primrose flower and fragrance; but
PRIMULA malacoides and P. obconica
are treated as annuals. Nearly all are best
grown with plenty of shade, decayed
organic material and water. Misty hill
climates are ideal. The candelabra types,
P. helodoxa, P. japonica and P. bartleyi,
(to name a few) like conditions positively boggy. The Poison Primrose (P.
obconica) is frequently grown indoors,
though no other plant causes more
trouble to more people, the fine hairs
producing allergenic reactions on the
skin and eyes. The English and Polyanthus Primroses (P. vulgaris and P.
polyantha) have undergone astonishing
improvement in recent years: Pacific
Giant and Barnhaven Silver Dollar being
two notably fine strains.

788   PRIMULA helodoxa
PERENNIAL   3 ft
BURMA   SUMMER

789   PRIMULA japonica
CANDELABRA PRIMROSE
PERENNIAL   18 in
JAPAN   SUMMER

790   PRIMULA malacoides
FAIRY PRIMROSE
ANNUAL   10 in
CHINA   WINTER

791   PRIMULA obconica
POISON PRIMROSE
ANNUAL   12 in
CHINA   WINTER

792   PRIMULA X polyantha
POLYANTHUS PRIMROSE
PERENNIAL   10 in
HYBRID   SPRING

793   PRIMULA vulgaris
ENGLISH PRIMROSE
PERENNIAL   8 in
EUROPE   SPRING

794

795

PROSTANTHERA
LABIATAE

Short-lived but splashy flowering shrubs, Australian Mint Bushes are worth a place anywhere the soil is good and frost-free. The tiny mint-leafed foliage is strongly aromatic anytime, and the mauve trumpet flowers open in great masses each spring. PROSTANTHERAS tend to leggy growth; should be pruned to half-height after flowering. PROSTANTHERA ovalifolia is the most popular of 40 species, its colour holding better in filtered sun.

794   PROSTANTHERA ovalifolia
MINT BUSH
SHRUB   8 ft
NEW SOUTH WALES   SPRING

PROTEA
PROTEACEAE

South Africa's most famous flowering shrubs are not too difficult to grow once their needs are clearly understood. Acid, sandy soil is the first rule; perfect drainage the second (they are well grown on hillsides or terraced beds) full sun the third. They are slow-growers and short-lived but the beauty of the flowers makes every effort worthwhile. Proteas have almost endless variation of shape, size and colour; the name Protea itself recalling the old sea-god Proteus who was able to change shape at will. The flowers last well when cut and as they retain shape after fading are often saved for dried arrangements. Flower size is not necessarily related to shrub size. The startling King Protea (PROTEA cynaroides) produces ten-inch flowers on a three-foot bush and must be staked in case it overbalances.

795   PROTEA cynaroides
KING PROTEA
SHRUB   4 ft
SOUTH AFRICA   SPRING–SUMMER

242

796

797

796   PROTEA mellifera
CAPE HONEYFLOWER
CAPE HONEYSUCKLE
SHRUB   8 ft
SOUTH AFRICA   SUMMER

797   PROTEA patens
SHRUB   3 ft
SOUTH AFRICA   SPRING

PRUNUS

798

800

802

799

801

803

PRUNUS
ROSACEAE

A whole book would scarcely do justice to the hundreds of splendid PRUNUS for they include some of our best loved fruits (Almond, Apricot, Cherry, Peach and Nectarine) and almost all of the lovely flowering cultivars grouped loosely as 'Spring Blossom'! There is also the delightful dwarf PRUNUS glandulosa (Flowering Almond Cherry); the English Laurel (P. laurocerasus) and many other Laurels native to America, Europe and Asia; the ornamental Japanese Cherries and many many other shrubs and trees. All are deciduous and spring-flowering except the Laurels, which retain their leaves and flower in summer. Both deciduous and evergreen species bear fruits except for some sterile hybrids grown only for blossom. All PRUNUS species prefer a sunny position in cool winter climates, but will resist a great degree of summer heat. They are not too fussy as to soil. Ornamental species can be pruned by the natural cutting of blossom, but remember that if flowers of fruiting species are cut, there will be no fruit. Gardeners in fruit fly areas are wiser to stick to ornamental or very early fruiting varieties.

798   PRUNUS amygdalo-persica
FLOWERING PEACH
BLOSSOM TREE
TREE   15 ft
CHINA   SPRING–SUMMER

799   PRUNUS glandulosa 'Rosea'
FLOWERING ALMOND CHERRY
DWARF FLOWERING ALMOND
PINK BUSH CHERRY
SHRUB   4 ft
JAPAN   SPRING

800   PRUNUS laurocerasus
ENGLISH LAUREL
VERSAILLES LAUREL
CHERRY LAUREL
TREE   20 ft
SOUTHERN EUROPE   SUMMER

801   PRUNUS persica
PEACH
TREE   15 ft
CHINA   SPRING–SUMMER

802   PRUNUS persica 'Rubra'
FLOWERING PEACH
TREE   12 ft
CHINA   SPRING

803   PRUNUS X 'Pissardi'
ORNAMENTAL CHERRY PLUM
TREE   15 ft
CHINA   SPRING

244

804

806

807

805

804   PRUNUS serrulata
FLOWERING CHERRY
TREE   15 ft
JAPAN   SPRING

805   PRUNUS serrulata 'Mt Fuji'
JAPANESE FLOWERING CHERRY
TREE   15 ft
JAPAN   SPRING

806   PRUNUS subhirtella 'Pendula'
WEEPING CHERRY
SHRUB   10 ft
JAPAN   SPRING

PSEUDERANTHEMUM
ACANTHACEAE

Attractive in semi-shade, where its finely-veined leaves retain their delicate gold-green colouring, PSEUDERAN-THEMUM is a must for the tropical shrubbery or foliage display. During warm weather it produces dainty panicles of white flowers spotted with red-violet. These are attractive in the mass, but hardly worthwhile picking.

807   PSEUDERANTHEMUM
reticulatum
SHRUB   4 ft
POLYNESIA   SUMMER
TROPICAL

PSIDIUM

808

809

PSORALEA

810

PTERIS

811

PSIDIUM
MYRTACEAE

Guavas are such attractive trees they would deserve a place anywhere even if they did not bear fruit. Rich soil is necessary for good results, but they will do with less water and heat than most other tropicals, particularly PSIDIUM cattleianum which has a beautifully mottled trunk and glossy leaves with bronze new growth. Slightly acid cherry-red fruits follow the uninteresting white flowers in autumn—they are mostly used in jams and jellies. P. guajava loses its strongly-veined leaves in early spring and right away produces new ones of a delicate golden-pink. The apricot-size fruits have an unpleasant smell but are deliciously sweet to eat when ripe.

808   PSIDIUM cattleianum
CHERRY GUAVA
PURPLE GUAVA
STRAWBERRY GUAVA
TREE   15 ft
BRAZIL   AUTUMN

809   PSIDIUM guajava
GUAVA
PINEAPPLE GUAVA
TREE   15 ft
SOUTH AMERICA   LATE SUMMER

PSORALEA
LEGUMINOSAE

PSORALEAS are fast-growing shrubby members of the Pea family with heath-like leaves and blue, white or purple flowers. All of them do well in a light sandy soil, even on the poor side, and are fairly frost-tender. Grown easily from cuttings, the popular PSORALEA pinnata rapidly becomes a bare-trunked shrub which needs smaller plants in front to soften the leggy effect. Flowers are attractively shaded mauve and white.

810   PSORALEA pinnata
BLUE BUTTERFLY BUSH
SHRUB   8 ft
SOUTH AFRICA   SPRING—AUTUMN

PTERIS
POLYPODIACEAE

Graceful small ferns for the bush-house or open garden, the Brake Ferns are found in semi-tropical parts of every continent, needing only warmth and a sandy compost-rich soil to flourish and increase rapidly from seed spores. They are clearly identified by their wing-shaped fronds with softly rolled edges. Many have attractively variegated leaves —PTERIS biaurita 'Argyraea' is light green and silver.

811   PTERIS biaurita 'Argyraea'
SILVER FERN
VARIEGATED BRAKE FERN
FERN   15 in
TROPICS   ALL YEAR

PUNICA

812

813

PYRACANTHA

814

815

816

PUNICA
PUNICACEAE

Hot-climate shrubs that grow perfectly in the most alkaline or chalky soil, Pomegranates are raised more for decorative effect than their yield of fruit, and many named varieties are available. 'Flore Pleno' bears double blossom of vivid orange-red, has bright leaf colours in the autumn, and coppery new leaves in spring. There are also cream and red types, double or single; a two-foot dwarf variety 'Nana' with tiny flowers and inedible fruits. The fruiting varieties have single flowers and need dry summer heat to develop the fruit. They also need deeper and more regular watering than the purely decorative types.

812   PUNICA granatum
POMEGRANATE
SHRUB   10 ft
MIDDLE EAST   AUTUMN
SUBTROPICAL

813   PUNICA granatum 'Flore Pleno'
FLOWERING POMEGRANATE
SHRUB   8 ft
HYBRID   SUMMER
SUBTROPICAL

PYRACANTHA
ROSACEAE

A most useful genus of sturdy evergreen shrubs grown exclusively for their magnificent autumn berries. These of course colour better in the cooler districts, and fortunately poor soil and dry weather seem to improve the yield. Firethorns are dense spiny shrubs and train well as hedges, espaliers or even ground covers. The berries come in many colours, ripening from summer to winter according to variety. PYRACANTHA coccinea 'Lalandei' is the most brilliant red, P. rodgersiana 'Aurantiaca' the best orange-yellow, and flat-fruited P. angustifolia probably the most commonly grown. All have uninteresting white flowers in spring.

814   PYRACANTHA angustifolia
ORANGE FIRETHORN
SHRUB   10 ft
CHINA   AUTUMN

815   PYRACANTHA coccinea
 Lalandei'
SCARLET FIRETHORN
SHRUB   20 ft
SOUTHERN EUROPE   AUTUMN

816   PYRACANTHA rodgersiana
'Aurantiaca'
YELLOW FIRETHORN
SHRUB   12 ft
CHINA   AUTUMN

817

818

PYROSTEGIA
BIGNONIACEAE

Most brilliant of winter-flowering vines in hot climates, PYROSTEGIA bursts into a flaming sheet of colour at the first approach of the tropical dry season. But it also puts on a splendid show in warm sunny positions elsewhere. Any soil will do with regular summer water, and the Flame Vine uses tendrils to climb quickly over wall, pergola or other heavy supports.

817   PYROSTEGIA ignea
FLAME VINE
BIGNONIA
ORANGE FLOWERED STEPHANOTIS
VINE   20 ft
BRAZIL   WINTER

QUAMOCLIT
CONVOLVULACEAE

A fast-twining annual vine for warm weather shade, QUAMOCLIT grows quickly from seeds sown in late winter— but to be certain of germination, notch them and soak in warm water first. The vines need vertical support and produce banner-like flower spikes in the old Spanish colours of red and yellow. In mild-winter areas, QUAMOCLIT can be considered a perennial.

818   QUAMOCLIT lobata
MINA LOBATA
SPANISH FLAG
ANNUAL VINE   15 ft
MEXICO   SUMMER

819

820

QUERCUS
FAGACEAE

The distinctive Pin Oak is often used for street planting. It is most reliable; resistant to both frost and heat and remarkably free of diseases. Its most colourful period is late summer, when the glossy leaves turn a brilliant shade of red—but then the old dead leaves festoon the tree right through winter until forced off by new growth. American Oaks of merit include Red Oak (Q. rubra), Scarlet Oak (Q. coccinea) of the north and the Live Oak of the southeast (Q. virginiana).

819   QUERCUS palustris
PIN OAK
SPANISH OAK
TREE   50 ft
CENTRAL AMERICA   SUMMER

QUISQUALIS
COMBRETACEAE

A showy climbing shrub well worth growing in warmer climates, QUISQUALIS can be struck easily from heeled cuttings in sand under glass. Planted out in a rich soil, it climbs over heavy support or sprawls untidily; producing clusters of mixed red and pink flowers throughout the summer. QUISQUALIS likes a humid climate and should be watered regularly in hot weather.

820   QUISQUALIS indica
RANGOON CREEPER
CLIMBER   20 ft
ASIA–AFRICA   SUMMER
TROPICAL

R

821

822

823

824

RANUNCULUS
RANUNCULACEAE

Over 200 annuals and perennials from both northern and southern hemispheres, the RANUNCULI are represented in our gardens by two species only: RANUNCULUS repens (the charming old-fashioned Buttercup) which is inclined to become a pest in rich damp soil; and the more decorative R. asiaticus which has been grown and hybridized for centuries and is probably the biblical 'Lily of the Field'. Garden Ranunculi are planted in autumn from small irregularly shaped tubers. Deep, compost-rich soil is important, and regular watering essential. Ranunculi flower best in sunny open beds and are effective in mixed colours, which include red, yellow, orange, pink and white.

821   RANUNCULUS asiaticus
RANUNCULUS
TUBEROUS PERENNIAL   18 in
ASiA MINOR   SPRING

822   RANUNCULUS asiaticus
(Differing flower types)

RAPHIOLEPIS
ROSACEAE

Hardy evergreens for every climate, the Indian Hawthorns are really tough and grow from cuttings of half-ripened shoots. They are also inclined to scatter seed far and wide and seedlings can often be found in the vicinity. Sweet-scented RAPHIOLEPIS indica bears long sprays of delicate pale pink flowers followed by black berries—its leaves are slightly toothed . . . the more commonly seen Yeddo Hawthorn (R. umbellata) has leathery toothless leaves, red-centred white flowers in packed clusters and black berries. It flowers almost all year, and often holds both flowers and berries at the same time. Both species of RAPHIOLEPIS are particularly reliable in sandy seaside soil.

823   RAPHIOLEPIS indica
INDIAN HAWTHORN
SHRUB   4 ft
SOUTH CHINA   SPRING

824   RAPHIOLEPIS umbellata 'Ovato'
YEDDO HAWTHORN
SHRUB   8 ft
JAPAN—KOREA   SPRING

RAVENALA

825

REHMANNIA

826

REINWARDTIA

827

RAVENALA
MUSACEAE

A giant tree-like perennial, unsurpassed for dramatic tropical effect in warm climates, RAVENALA sends up tall woody trunks from which the leaves fall progressively, finally leaving great fans of Banana-like foliage high in the air. Spikes of greenish-white flowers appear in summer and large quantities of fresh drinkable water are stored in the leaf stalks—hence the popular name.

825 RAVENALA madagascariensis
TRAVELLER'S TREE
TREE 60 ft
MADAGASCAR SUMMER

REHMANNIA
SCROPHULARIACEAE

A graceful perennial that thrives in heavy shade, REHMANNIA spreads rapidly to form evergreen clumps in warm-winter climates, but is deciduous in cold. Rich soil and plenty of water are needed to produce the tall stems of handsome golden-throated flowers. These are pink, purple or cream according to variety and appear from spring right through to autumn. Grow from divisions.

826 REHMANNIA angulata
PERENNIAL 2½ ft
CHINA SPRING–AUTUMN

REINWARDTIA
LINACEAE

Coarse, untidy shrubby perennials that light up the winter days with brilliant golden flowers in great profusion. REINWARDTIAS are grown from cuttings or divisions in spring, do best in light soil in warm-winter districts only. They grow well in shade, but the flowers show up best in sun. REINWARDTIAS grow leggy and should be pinched back regularly to encourage branching.

827 REINWARDTIA trigyna
LINUM TRIGYNUM
YELLOW FLAX
SHRUB 3 ft
NORTH INDIA WINTER

RESEDA

828

RHAPIS

829

RHODODENDRON

830

RESEDA
RESEDACEAE

Only humble straggly little plants; nothing much to look at...but what a perfume! Grow them in rockery or patio pockets, or by favourite paths; but grow them massed to multiply the fragrance. Plant out in autumn or spring in lime-enriched soil, but keep out of full sun which scorches and fades the leaves and flowers.

828   RESEDA odorata
MIGNONETTE
LITTLE DARLING
ANNUAL   12 in
NORTH AFRICA   SUMMER

RHAPIS
PALMACEAE

Graceful dwarf species with Bamboo-like stems and brilliant green leaf fans, the Lady Palms are a great choice for courtyard planting and container work. They prefer shade, but will resist sun and even salt air. RHAPIS is also frost and drought-resistant, but looks much better with regular water and fertilizer. The yellow flowers are scarcely worth worrying about.

829   RHAPIS excelsa
LADY PALM
GROUND RATTAN CANE
PALM   4 ft
CHINA–JAPAN   ALL YEAR

RHODODENDRON
ERICACEAE

An enormously varied genus, ranging trom eighty-foot flowering trees to minute creeping ground covers—but the popular types are mostly large shrubs. All are of mountain origin and do best in woodsy conditions. This means semi-shade, acid soil rich in organic matter, plenty of moisture and quick drainage. At the same time RHODO-DENDRONS can stand a heavier soil than the Azalea types (see: AZALEA) and even alkaline soils can be made suitable with the addition of peatmoss and tanbark. Heavy feeding is beneficial, but wait till *after* flowering so the plant does not bolt to leaf.

830   RHODODENDRON X augustinii
'Blue Diamond'
SHRUB   3 ft
HYBRID   SPRING

831

833

835

832

834

831   RHODODENDRON X
'Cleopatra'
SHRUB   40 ft
HYBRID   LATE SPRING

832   RHODODENDRON X
'Countess of Haddington'
SHRUB   8 ft
HYBRID   SPRING

833   RHODODENDRON X
'Fragrantissimum'
WEEPING SHRUB   10 ft
HYBRID   SPRING

834   RHODODENDRON X
     'President Roosevelt'
SHRUB   12 ft
HYBRID   LATE SPRING

RHODOMYRTUS
MYRTACEAE

One of a small genus of tropical Asiatic shrubs, the Rose Myrtle is useful in the warm-climate garden or warm greenhouse, where its gay, hot pink Myrtle flowers appear in summer. Downy grey-green leaves and purple fruits help keep the shrub attractive all year, but it does require regular summer water and a mulch to keep the root system damp.

835   RHODOMYRTUS tomentosa
ROSE MYRTLE
SHRUB   8 ft
TROPICAL ASIA   SUMMER
TROPICAL

253

RHOEO

836

RIBES

837

RICINOCARPUS

838

RHOEO
COMMELINACEAE

Only one of its genus, the fascinating Boat Lily is a tough plant for indoors or out, where the glowing purple leaves make useful foliage contrast with lush green tropical plants. The tiny white flowers peep out of boat-shaped bracts which appear among the leaf bases— hence the great variety of popular names. RHOEO will stay healthy in very dim light and with the most casual of watering.

836   RHOEO discolor
MOSES IN A BASKET
MOSES IN THE BULRUSHES
MOSES IN THE CRADLE
MOSES IN A BOAT
ADAM AND EVE
BOAT LILY
OYSTER PLANT
PERENNIAL   15 in
MEXICO   ALL YEAR
TROPICAL, SUBTROPICAL

RIBES
SAXIFRAGACEAE

A deciduous shrub from western North America, RIBES sanguineum is closely related to R. sativum, the Currant of commerce. Spring flowers appear in drooping racemes, pink to deep red according to variety, and are quickly followed by felty maple-like leaves and blue-coloured berries. Best in a cooler climate, RIBES likes acid well-drained soil and plenty of moisture. The entire plant has a curious spicy fragrance.

837   RIBES sanguineum
FLOWERING CURRANT
SHRUB   6 ft
NORTH AMERICA   SPRING
HARDY

RICINOCARPUS
EURPHORBIACEAE

Charming shrubs from the eastern coast of Australia, the small genus RICINO-CARPUS is ideal for the smaller garden. Two species are commonly grown, the pink-flowered RICINOCARPUS bow-manii, and the white-flowered R. pini-folius (Wedding Bush). Both have soft needle leaves and masses of fragrant starry flowers in spring. It can only be established in acid sunny soil from a very small seedling.

838   RICINOCARPUS pinifolius
WEDDING BUSH
SHRUB   4 ft
EASTERN AUSTRALIA   SPRING

ROBINIA

839

ROMNEYA

840

RONDELETIA

841

ROBINIA
LEGUMINOSAE

The thorny ROBINIA is seen more often than planted, appearing spontaneously in the most unlikely places. This is presumably due to the attractions of its seeds to the bird population. Used in the country for street planting and stock shelter, it has been found almost indestructible, and in addition produces a fine crop of fragrant Wistaria-like flowers in spring. These are cream, sometimes with pink tonings.

839   ROBINIA pseudoacacia
FALSE ACACIA
BLACK LOCUST
TREE   40 ft
NORTH AMERICA   SPRING

ROMNEYA
PAPAVERACEAE

Crepy, nine-inch white Poppy flowers with a mass of golden stamens, ROM-NEYAS are wonderful in floral arrangements and last for days. Grow them from autumn divisions; the grey-green leaves and stems will appear in winter and gradually build up to 6 ft and more. ROMNEYAS like full sun, loose gravelly soil and not too much water, particularly at flowering time.

840   ROMNEYA coulteri
TREE POPPY
MATILIJA POPPY
PERENNIAL   6 ft
CALIFORNIA   SPRING

RONDELETIA
RUBIACEAE

Masses of gold-throated pink blossom in late winter and early spring identify lovely RONDELETIA, a splendid shrub for the mild frost-free area. Acid soil and semi-shade are helpful, and regular water and fertilizer are necessities. Prune to shape when young and remove faded flower trusses. The golden-green glossy leaves are always attractive—the flowers only lightly fragrant.

841   RONDELETIA amoena
SHRUB   4 ft
GUATEMALA   SPRING

842

844

846

843

845

847

ROSA
ROSACEAE

The best-loved flower in all the western world—though seen at its best only in areas with mildly alkaline soil, the Rose is staggering in variety of colour, form and scent. Over 125 wild species are known, and almost all of them have been used by hybridizers to produce the lovely blooms available to us today. An entire book could be written on cultural directions for varying climates—and your local nurseryman is the best adviser on varieties for where you live. Roses are planted in midwinter or after the last frost, and normally pruned at the same time except for winter-flowering types. Roses enjoy full sun, especially in the morning, and do best in a bed of their own, well away from marauding trees. They need regular feeding, deep watering and a good summer mulch to produce top quality blooms. While 9 out of 10 Rose plants bought today are of the Hybrid Tea or Floribunda types, many of the original species are coming back into fashion. They do not flower as continually as the modern hybrids, but have a charm all their own.

842   ROSA X bracteata 'Mermaid'
MERMAID ROSE
CLIMBER   40 ft
CHINA   ALL YEAR

843   ROSA banksiae
BANKSIA ROSE
LADY BANKS' ROSE
CLIMBER   20 ft
CHINA   SPRING

844   ROSA X floribunda 'Masquerade'
FLORIBUNDA ROSE
SHRUB   2½ ft
HYBRID   SPRING–AUTUMN

845   ROSA hugonis
GOLDEN ROSE OF CHINA
FATHER HUGO'S GOLDEN ROSE
SHRUB   10 ft
CHINA   SPRING

846   ROSA X 'Crimson Glory'
HYBRID TEA ROSE
SHRUB   to 8 ft
HYBRID   SPRING–AUTUMN

847   ROSA X 'Madame Meilland' ('Peace')
HYBRID TEA ROSE
SHRUB   8 ft
HYBRID   SPRING–AUTUMN

848

849

850

851

852

848   ROSA chinensis 'Minima'
FAIRY ROSE
SHRUB   10 in
HYBRID   ALL YEAR

849   ROSA X 'Milkmaid'
CLIMBING ROSE   15 ft
HYBRID   SPRING

850   ROSA rugosa
RAMANAS ROSE
SHRUB   2½ ft
JAPAN–KOREA   SPRING

851   ROSA X wichuraiana 'Lady Gay'
RAMBLER ROSE
CLIMBING SHRUB   60 ft
HYBRID   SUMMER

852   MIXED ROSES
SPRING
(Adelaide Botanic Gardens)

257

ROSMARINUS

853

ROTHMANNIA

854

RUDBECKIA

855

ROSMARINUS
LABIATAE

Hardy picturesque shrubs that put up with a great deal in the way of heat and poor soil. The glossy aromatic leaves are attractive and much used in cooking. Pale lavender flower spikes appear in winter, spring and autumn and bring bees from far and wide. Rosemary tends to woodiness and should be pruned regularly. It makes a splendid hedge, and its trailing variety ROSMARINUS pro-stratus is useful as a wall plant.

853   ROSMARINUS officinalis
ROSEMARY
SHRUB   6 ft
EUROPE–ASIA MINOR   SPRING

ROTHMANNIA
RUBIACEAE

Creamy white gardenia-scented bells; delicately spotted inside and felty brown outside . . . you are looking at ROTH-MANNIA, a tall graceful shrub once classed as a Gardenia but now moved to a genus of its own. The same conditions are required; moderate heat, acid soil and moisture, but ROTHMANNIA grows tall and slender, with quaintly marked waxy leaves and round nutty seed pods that persist right into winter.

854   ROTHMANNIA globosa
TREE GARDENIA
SHRUB   12 ft
SOUTH AFRICA   SPRING

RUDBECKIA
COMPOSITAE

All the way from the United States of America to the gardens of the world—that is the story of the glorious Gloriosa Daisy. Plant out in spring anywhere but particularly in groups among other summer perennials. RUDBECKIAS are not fussy provided they get full sun and plenty of water. The flowers are up to 7 in across in razzle-dazzle combinations of yellow, orange and mahogany—the raised centres purple-black. Most varieties are hybrids of RUDBECKIA hirta and self-seed regularly, but the spectacular 'Golden Glow' is a plant of a different species, R. laciniata—it does not seed but spreads rapidly from the roots.

855   RUDBECKIA hirta
BLACK EYED SUSAN
BIENNIAL   3 ft
UNITED STATES OF AMERICA
SUMMER

856

857

856 RUDBECKIA X hybrid
GLORIOSA DAISY
BIENNIAL 4 ft
UNITED STATES   SUMMER

RUELLIA
ACANTHACEAE

A tall-growing shrubby perennial for the warm-climate garden, RUELLIA macrantha demands rich soil, good drainage and plenty of water to produce tall stems of three-inch cyclamen and gold flowers. It can be flowered successfully in the greenhouse, but indoors or out needs a summer rest and cut back. Propagate from cuttings taken in late spring.

857   RUELLIA macrantha
PERENNIAL   6 ft
BRAZIL   WINTER—SPRING
SUBTROPICAL

858

859

RUSSELIA
SCROPHULARIACEAE

A tangled mess of leafless rush-like stems in cold weather, the hardy RUS-SELIA comes alive in summer—a glowing fountain of coral-scarlet flowers. RUSSELIA strikes from cuttings, grows easily, spreads rapidly and is at home in any sunny position with rich light soil. Most effective spilling over banks or walls, or with a dark background to highlight its vivid flowers.

858   RUSSELIA juncea
CORALBUSH
CORAL BLOW
CORAL PLANT
SHRUB   4 ft
MEXICO   SUMMER

SAINTPAULIA
GESNERIACEAE

Most stubborn and unpredictable of plants, African Violets have won enough hearts to make them America's most popular houseplant—and they are fast catching up in the southern hemisphere too. Propagate from leaf cuttings in small pots of a very moist compost. Give diffused morning light—temperature preferably not below 60°F. and plenty of humidity. From then on, you are on your own, but unless you have naturally green fingers you will probably need to buy a book on their likes and dislikes.

859   SAINTPAULIA ionantha
AFRICAN VIOLET
PERENNIAL   6 in
TROPICAL AFRICA   ALL YEAR

SALIX

860

861

SALVIA

862

863

SAMBUCUS

864

SALIX
SALICACEAE

Deciduous trees of particular value where drainage is a problem—Willows need and soak up water at an unbelievable rate. Thereby hangs the problem. If there is a drainpipe within yards, Willow roots will find a way into it, so they are best banished to boggy patches well away from domestic plumbing. All species will grow from large cuttings— even entire branches—just let them soak in a pond or large container until roots appear. The romantic Weeping Willow (SALIX babylonica) is probably most popular, with Pussy Willow of the silver and gold winter catkins a close second. Other worthwhile species are S. matsudana (the Corkscrew Willow) with curiously contorted branches, and the Dwarf Purple Osier (S. purpurea).

860   SALIX babylonica
WEEPING WILLOW
POET'S WILLOW
TREE   50 ft
CHINA   ALL YEAR

861   SALIX caprea
PUSSY WILLOW
GOAT WILLOW
SALLOW
TREE   20 ft
NORTH ASIA   WINTER

SALVIA
LABIATAE

Blue, purple and red Salvias are an enormous genus of over 500 species, valued for their colourful spikes of tubular flowers and their felty aromatic leaves at all times of the year. There are species for all seasons; annuals, perennials and shrubs, most of them extremely hardy, adaptable as to soil and enjoying full sun. SALVIA officinalis is the common Herb Sage of kitchen use—S. splendens, the vivid Bonfire Salvia much used for summer bedding. S. leucantha (the Mexican Bush Sage)—a shrub with flower spikes like imperial purple velvet—and the others are almost all blue-flowered, none of them much use for cutting. Indoors, the blossoms fall before they open.

862   SALVIA leucantha
MEXICAN BUSH SAGE
SHRUB   2½ ft
MEXICO   WINTER

863   SALVIA splendens
BONFIRE SALVIA
SCARLET SAGE
SHRUB   3 ft
BRAZIL   SUMMER

SAMBUCUS
CAPRIFOLIACEAE

Deciduous North American shrubs, the Elderberries are striking in the larger shrubbery, and when pruned regularly in winter can be used as a dense windbreak. They grow from heeled cuttings and do best in a damp rich soil in full sun. SAMBUCUS callicarpus has red poisonous berries, S. caerulea's are blue. S. canadensis is valued for great heads of snowy blossom and its variety 'Aurea' for the wonderful golden-green leaves and purple berries.

864   SAMBUCUS canadensis
ELDERBERRY
SHRUB   12 ft
CANADA–UNITED STATES OF
AMERICA   SPRING–AUTUMN

SANSEVIERIA

865

SANTOLINA

866

SARCOCHILUS

867

SANSEVIERIA
LILIACEAE

Common as houseplants, SANSEVIER-
IAS are really more effective massed in
the open garden in warm positions and
sheltered from the midday sun, which
fades the leaf colours. SANSEVIERIA
grows from creeping rhizomes like Flag
Iris and is valued for the attractively
variegated spiky leaves. The flowers are
uninteresting; greenish but quite fragrant.
Propagate from suckers or leaf cuttings.

865   SANSEVIERIA trifasciata
'Laurentii'
SNAKE PLANT
BOWSTRING HEMP
MOTHER IN LAW'S TONGUE
PERENNIAL   3 ft
WEST AFRICA   ALL YEAR

SANTOLINA
COMPOSITAE

Delicate silvery leaves like feather dusters
have brought SANTOLINA a special
place in the mixed border or rockery, and
it is usually clipped back into a neat
mound in early spring. But that is only
half its beauty—left untrimmed, it will
produce masses of yellow button flowers
in summer. SANTOLINA is hardy except
in frost, will grow any place where there
is sun and water.

866   SANTOLINA chamaecyparissus
LAVENDER COTTON
SHRUB   2 ft
MEDITERRANEAN   SUMMER

SARCOCHILUS
ORCHIDACEAE

Most beloved of Australia's native Orchids, SARCOCHILUS of the moist
coastal gullies can be established happily
on treefern slabs or sections of paperbark
trunk. But it does need regular water and
the cool, filtered sun conditions of the
bush-house to put on a good show. It
spreads over the host surface producing
clusters of four-inch sickle-shaped leaves
and racemes of strongly perfumed one-
inch flowers in spring.

867   SARCOCHILUS falcatus
ORANGE BLOSSOM ORCHID
EPIPHYTIC ORCHID   6 in
NEW SOUTH WALES–QUEENSLAND
SPRING

SASA

868

SAXIFRAGA

869

SCABIOSA

870

SASA (syn. ARUNDINARIA)
GRAMINEAE

Delicate sprays of green and white Bamboo leaves, spreading fast from underground stems, quickly cover shady damp places when you use SASA as a ground cover. Particularly effective for Japanese-type gardens it can become a pest when planted around shrubs and is best left on its own or prevented from spreading by sinking two-foot strips of galvanized iron around the edges of the planting.

868 SASA fortunei
(syn. ARUNDINARIA variegata)
DWARF BAMBOO
PERENNIAL   15 in
JAPAN   ALL YEAR

SAXIFRAGA
SAXIFRAGACEAE

A very large genus of charming dwarf perennials (more than 300 of them) SAXIFRAGAS are suited to cold alpine climates and rarely seen in the southern hemisphere. Exception is the ubiquitous Strawberry Geranium which is widely grown as a rock plant, houseplant and ground cover among acid-loving shrubs. Its delicate white-veined leaves spread rapidly from Strawberry-like runners and send up twelve-inch spikes of flesh-pink flowers in early spring.

869   SAXIFRAGA stolonifera
AARON'S BEARD
STRAWBERRY GERANIUM
ROVING SAILOR
MOTHER OF THOUSANDS
PERENNIAL   12 in
JAPAN   SPRING

SCABIOSA
DIPSACEAE

The spicy honey-scent of these charming flowers brings butterflies from miles around, and their slim straight stems make them a natural for summer and autumn arrangements. The annual species SCABIOSA atropurpurea is most common, in shades of pink, red, salmon, white and purple-black. Sow in spring or plant out in early summer; they will flower right through to winter if you snip faded flowers. Full sun and a little lime are their only special requirements.

870   SCABIOSA atropurpurea
MOURNFUL WIDOW
PINCUSHION FLOWER
EGYPTIAN ROSE
MOURNING BRIDE
SWEET SCABIOUS
ANNUAL   3 ft
SOUTHERN EUROPE   SUMMER

SCHEFFLERA

871

SCHINUS

872

SCHIZANTHUS

873

SCHEFFLERA
ARALIACEAE

Fast-growing tropical plants which are quite hardy in milder climates provided they are given good soil and regular water, the SCHEFFLERAS give a tropical air to courtyard plantings or driveways. SCHEFFLERA polybotrya, like most of the genus, has long-stalked leaves divided into leaflets, and clusters of tiny pinkish-green flowers in winter.

871   SCHEFFLERA polybotrya
SHRUB   8 ft
JAVA   WINTER

SCHINUS
ANACARDIACEAE

Naturalized in many areas of California and Australia, the Peppercorn Tree is, in fact, a South American import, and most useful for arid conditions. Heavy fissured bark; weeping Willow leaves; white flowers; pink peppercorns and a spicy aromatic smell from all parts make this a most useful tree for garden or street planting.

872   SCHINUS molle
CALIFORNIA PEPPER TREE
PEPPERCORN TREE
PEPPERINA
PERUVIAN MASTIC TREE
TREE   40 ft
SOUTH AMERICA   SUMMER

SCHIZANTHUS
SOLANACEAE

Delicate pastel pinks and mauves for winter and spring; SCHIZANTHUS are valued also for their fine fern-like leaves. They are seen in the open only in coastal regions for they are sensitive to frosts and hot winds. Elsewhere they are used indoors or in greenhouses with Cinerarias and Primulas. Wherever you grow them, they need rich, well-drained soil and flower better when fed lightly with bone meal.

873   SCHIZANTHUS pinnatus
POOR MAN'S ORCHID
BUTTERFLY FLOWER
ANNUAL   15 in
CHILE   WINTER–SPRING

264

SCHLUMBERGERA

874

SCILLA

875

876

877

SCHLUMBERGERA
CACTACEAE

The old-fashioned Easter cactus of northern countries, SCHLUMBERGERA does not seem to have attracted a popular name south of the Equator. A native of Brazil where it hangs epiphytically from trees, this Cactus requires rich porous soil with plenty of leafmould. Water and feed regularly, and shade in summer. The flat leaf joints sprout an abundance of red or pink flowers in midwinter.

874   SCHLUMBERGERA gaertneri
CHRISTMAS CACTUS
EASTER CACTUS
EPIPHYTIC CACTUS   2 ft
BRAZIL   WINTER

SCILLA
LILIACEAE

Quickly multiplying spring bulbs for filtered sunlight or even full shade, the prolific SCILLAS will grow in climates far warmer than Europe, provided the soil is right—that means rich, moist and preferably acid. The drooping English Bluebell (SCILLA nonscripta) has short, wide flowers, borne few to a stem in shades of blue, pink and white. Lovers of the English Garden have an emotional attachment to it, but for us in the southern hemisphere it is inferior to the striking Spanish Bluebell (S. campanulata). This bears tall flower spikes of a rich blue and spreads rapidly, both from bulbs and seeds.

875   SCILLA nonscripta
WOOD HYACINTH
ENGLISH BLUEBELL
SQUILL
HAREBELL
WILD HYACINTH
BULB   10 in
WESTERN EUROPE   SPRING

876   SCILLA campanulata
SPANISH BLUEBELL
ENDYMION
BULB   18 in
SPAIN   SPRING

877   SCILLA peruviana
CUBAN LILY
BULB   12 in
MEDITERRANEAN   SPRING

265

SEDUM

878

879

SENECIO

880

881

882

883

SEDUM
CRASSULACEAE

Hardy succulents from many lands, notable for their masses of brightly-coloured starry flowers in winter and spring. All SEDUMS grow quickly from cuttings and are used for ground cover work in rockeries and along driveways —but please not where you walk for they just crush into jelly. Grow them in any soil, no maintenance whatever is needed beyond a little water. Miniature SEDUM acre (the Goldmoss Sedum) is a popular ground cover in paved areas, needing no soil at all beyond what it collects; S. confusum is similar but larger and sprawls attractively over rock walls. S. rubrotinctum is a mass of juicy jelly bean leaves that turn bright red in full sun.

878   SEDUM confusum
YELLOW STONECROP
SUCCULENT   15 in
SPRING

879   SEDUM rubrotinctum
CHRISTMAS CHEER
JELLY BEANS
SUCCULENT   6 in
MEXICO   SPRING

SENECIO
COMPOSITAE

The enormous variety of Daisy-flowered plants called SENECIO make up far and away the largest genus in the vegetable kingdom—over 1,300 of them. The majority are splendid garden subjects; annuals, perennials, vines, shrubs and succulents, largely winter-flowering. The most popular include SENECIO cruentus (the Florist's Cineraria) now available in giant and dwarf types in a wide range of reds, blues and purples, and the golden-flowered Dusty Miller (S. cineraria) grown for its graceful silvery foliage. A good example of the large shrubby type is S. grandifolius with glossy eighteen-inch leaves and trusses of bright-gold daisy flowers in the cold weather. None are fussy about soil, but S. cruentus is best in semi-shade.

880   SENECIO amygdalifolius
PEACH-LEAF GROUNDSEL
SHRUB   5 ft
EASTERN AUSTRALIA   SPRING

881   SENECIO cineraria
DUSTY MILLER
SEA RAGWORT
SHRUB   2 ft
SOUTHERN EUROPE   SUMMER

882   SENECIO cruentus
CINERARIA
ANNUAL   2 ft
CANARY ISLANDS   WINTER

883   SENECIO grandifolius
BIGLEAF GROUNDSEL
SHRUB   15 ft
MEXICO   WINTER

SILENE

884

SINNINGIA

885

886

SOLANDRA

887

SILENE
CARYOPHYLLACEAE

Used mostly in the rock garden or low border, SILENES are easily grown in a light gritty soil. Most commonly seen SILENE maritima spreads its blue-grey leaves over about a square foot from the woody rootstocks and then produces loose clusters of many-petalled white flowers with an inflated balloon-like calyx. There are double white and pink varieties which can be grown as annuals or perennials.

884   SILENE maritima
SWEET WILLIAM CATCHFLY
CATCHFLY
SEA CAMPION
WITCHES' THIMBLE
PERENNIAL   6 in
MEDITERRANEAN   SUMMER

SINNINGIA
GESNERIACEAE

As the Cyclamen is to winter, so the velvety Gloxinia is to summer—most exciting of flowering indoor plants. A hothouse subject in Europe, in the southern hemisphere it is grown about the house or even in the garden in warm summer areas. Tubers are started in early spring in pots of sand, peat and humus, and should be watered lightly only until leaf growth appears. Water and fertilizer should then be increased through the flowering season—but should not be allowed to lodge on the leaves which may rot. Gloxinias are propagated from leaf cuttings which form new tubers when inserted in sandy soil. Flowers are in shades of purple, red, pink and white, many marbled or mottled.

885   SINNINGIA speciosa 'Arizona'
GLOXINIA
TUBER   10 in
BRAZIL   SUMMER

886   SINNINGIA speciosa
'Etoile de Feu'
GLOXINIA
TUBER   10 in
BRAZIL   SUMMER

SOLANDRA
SOLANACEAE

A sprawling rampant vine which needs solid support, the Cup of Gold grows rapidly from cuttings in damp soil and is particularly good near the sea where it resists salt spray. The enormous nine-inch flowers grow right through the warm weather and have a strong, rather unpleasant smell. One vine, well-placed and fertilized, can easily cover a carport in a single year.

887   SOLANDRA guttata
CUP OF GOLD
HAWAIIAN LILY
GOLDEN CUP
VINE   40 ft
MEXICO   SUMMER

267

888

890

891

889

SOLANUM
SOLANACEAE

A useful plant genus including the humble tomato, potato and eggplant, the SOLANUMS also boast many decorative species, particularly for warm-climate gardens. The showy Brazilian Potato Tree bears clusters of violet-blue Potato flowers on prickly stems among its beautiful glossy leaves. Its smaller relative, the Cow's Udder Plant, produces extraordinarily shaped fruit that makes one wonder at nature's power of mimicry. A spiny, untidy shrub, it is useful for tropical planting only. Prettiest of the genus are the Winter Cherries (SOLANUM capsicastrum) and S. pseudo-capsicum, with tiny white flowers and bright red berries that endear them to pot plant enthusiasts. They self-sow readily.

888   SOLANUM macranthum
POTATO TREE
TREE   15 ft
BRAZIL   SPRING

889   SOLANUM mammosum
COW'S UDDER PLANT
SHRUB   6 ft
CENTRAL AMERICA   AUTUMN

890   SOLANUM pseudo-capsicum
JERUSALEM CHERRY
WINTER CHERRY
SHRUB   2 ft
MADEIRA   WINTER

SOLIDAGO
COMPOSITAE

Goldenrod's tall waving stems crowned with clusters of minute purest-gold flowers announce the coming of autumn in the woods of their native North America and many other lands where this delightful plant has become naturalized. Its needs are few, but it grows so tall and spreads so fast that it quickly exhausts the soil unless regular water and manure are forthcoming. For the wild garden or back border.

891   SOLIDAGO canadensis
GOLDENROD
PERENNIAL   6 ft
NORTH AMERICA   AUTUMN

268

893

892

SOPHORA
LEGUMINOSAE

New Zealand's pride and joy (and national floral emblem); the gorgeously flowering Kowhai is most variable in size and form, and usually seen away from its native land as a rather tangled wiry shrub. But at its best it is a tall graceful tree which drops leaves just before the masses of golden blossom appear in spring. Kowhai is a rather fussy plant, doing best in well-drained soil of sheltered positions. It needs plenty of water; does not like a humid summer.

892   SOPHORA microphylla
KOWHAI
YELLOW KOWHAI
TREE   40 ft
NEW ZEALAND   SPRING

SOPHROLAELIACATTLEYA
ORCHIDACEAE

A splendid race of Orchids hybridized from the 3 natural species Cattleya, Laelia and Sophronitis the tongue-twisting SLC's are considered hardier than Cattleyas though requiring the same hothouse cultural treatment (See: CATTLEYA). The flowers are characterized by a finer texture and richer, deeper colourings. SLC 'Brandywine' is typical.

893   SOPHROLAELIACATTLEYA X
'Brandywine'
ORCHID   15 in
HYBRID   ALL YEAR

SORBUS

894

895

SPARAXIS

896

SPARTIUM

897

SORBUS
ROSACEAE

The colourful fruits of SORBUS trees were at one time used for both food and drink—but tastes have changed and these days they are grown for decoration only. The Mountain Ash (SORBUS aucuparia) comes into fruit first when the boughs droop under the weight of its orange-scarlet berries. It is propagated from seed or (more usually) cuttings to ensure quality of fruit and leaf colour. The larger Service Tree (S. domestica) is a finer plant altogether, producing magnificent autumn colourings and fruits the size of a small Plum. These are of course most popular with the feathered population.

894   SORBUS aucuparia
RANTY
ROWAN
MOUNTAIN ASH
TREE   25 ft
EUROPE–ASIA   AUTUMN

895   SORBUS domestica
SERVICE TREE
SERVICE BERRY
TREE   40 ft
EUROPE   AUTUMN

SPARAXIS
IRIDACEAE

Naturalizing like Freesias and Ixias, the vivid SPARAXIS is deservedly popular in warm-climate gardens, though its garish colours are a little much for subdued tastes. The flowers, generally in rust, orange, red and pink, are strikingly marked black and yellow and borne in an irregular group on wiry twisted stems. They prefer part-shade in light well-drained soil where they multiply rapidly from seed. The flowers are unfortunately inclined to close in dull weather, just when they would be most useful.

896   SPARAXIS tricolor
HARLEQUIN FLOWER
VELVET FLOWER
BULB   12 in
SOUTH AFRICA   SPRING

SPARTIUM
LEGUMINOSAE

The longtime favourite Spanish Broom stands out anywhere, with masses of canary-yellow Pea-flowers blooming throughout the late spring and early summer. Plant in full sun without worrying about the type of soil—it seems happy anywhere, even in coastal sand. But SPARTIUM will become untidy unless pruned back hard in early winter. The flowers appear on long rush-like stems, almost leafless, and are spicily fragrant.

897   SPARTIUM junceum
SPANISH BROOM
SHRUB   8 ft
MEDITERRANEAN   LATE SPRING

SPATHIPHYLLUM

898

SPATHODEA

899

900

SPIRAEA

901

902

SPATHIPHYLLUM
ARACEAE

Frequently mistaken in passing for Anthuriums, the SPATHIPHYLLUMS are in fact a much less delicate genus, capable of surviving great extremes of temperature short of actual frost. Always green or white in colouring, the flowers appear in summer and last up to several months on the plant. Avoid full sun because of fading and keep up the humidity during warm weather. Plant in early spring.

898   SPATHIPHYLLUM blandum
PERENNIAL   6 in–2 ft
SURINAM   SUMMER

SPATHODEA
BIGNONIACEAE

A sheltered position in warm climates only is recommended for this brilliant African—for both branches and leaf stalks are prone to wind damage. The flowers, which appear in large terminal clusters are individually 3 in or more in diameter, and look much better than they smell. The nearer the tree is to the Equator, the earlier it flowers, but in any case a young tree will seldom flower before 5 years.

899   SPATHODEA campanulata
WEST AFRICAN TULIP TREE
FOUNTAIN TREE
SORCERER'S WAND
FLAMBEAU TREE
BATON DU SORCIER
TREE   60 ft
WEST AFRICA   SUMMER

900   SPATHODEA campanulata
(close-up of flowers)

SPIRAEA
ROSACEAE

The hardy Garland Flowers (Spiraeas) are not particularly elegant or eye-catching for the most part of the year, but come into their own in early spring when they are almost smothered under the weight of long arching sprays of bloom, pink or white. All of them are hardy, though perhaps doing a little better in cold-winter climates. They grow in sun or shade, acid or even slightly alkaline soil. Heavy pruning is recommended after the flowers have faded, to encourage branching and prevent the shrubs becoming too leggy. The tiny individual flowers resemble miniature Roses, single or double according to variety. SPIREA japonica 'Anthony Waterer' is the popular cerise variety.

901   SPIRAEA cantoniensis
CHINESE SPIRAEA
SHRUB   5 ft
CHINA   SPRING

902   SPIRAEA prunifolia 'Plena'
BRIDAL WREATH
MAY
SHRUB   6 ft
KOREA   SPRING

SPREKELIA

903

STACHYS

904

STAPELIA

905

SPREKELIA
AMARYLLIDACEAE

Most often seen in formal flower arrangements, the Jacobean Lily is regal both in
colour and shape; somewhat resembling
a heraldic 'Fleur de Lis'. Surprisingly, in
view of its popular names, it is from
Mexico, not Europe. The bulbs grow
easily outdoors in pots, provided the soil
is light and rich with humus. Spring is
planting time, and the flowers appear
after the leaves, usually in midsummer.

903   SPREKELIA formosissima
JACOBEAN LILY
JACOB'S LILY
MALTESE CROSS
GOLD LILY
AZTEC LILY
BULB   12 in
MEXICO   SUMMER

STACHYS
LABIATAE

Furry grey tongue-shaped leaves in
dense clusters make an effective contrast
with green and other coloured foliage
when you plant STACHYS as a border
edging or ground cover. It is a high
altitude plant, but looks very messy
after frost and should be cut back in late
winter. Spikes of small purple flowers
appear in summer—but it is grown for
the leaves.

904   STACHYS lanata
LAMB'S EARS
LAMB'S TONGUES
PERENNIAL   12 in
CAUCASUS   SUMMER
HARDY

STAPELIA
ASCLEPIADACEAE

If it were not for the great beauty of their
truly remarkable flowers, STAPELIAS
would get short shrift from the plant
lover, for they smell faintly of *very* dead
meat. This is nature's way of attracting
flies which are their natural pollinators.
The plants are a leafless mass of velvety
four-sided branched stems from which
the flowers appear in clusters each
summer. Grow them in a very porous
mixture in pots or rock pockets and do
not water in winter.

905   STAPELIA gigantea
CARRION FLOWER
STARFISH FLOWER
SUCCULENT   9 in
TRANSVAAL   SUMMER
SUBTROPICAL

272

STENOCARPUS

906

STENOLOBIUM

907

STEPHANOTIS

908

STENOCARPUS
PROTEACEAE

Slow-growing, but worth waiting the 10 years or so it takes to flower, the magnificent Firewheel is an inhabitant of the damp coastal rain forests—though paradoxically tends to flower more heavily in cooler districts. The wheel-shaped flowers appear in the most irregular fashion—often right out of the trunk or larger branches—at any-time between Christmas and midwinter in the southern hemisphere. The glossy leaves too are fine for decoration.

906   STENOCARPUS sinuatus
FIREWHEEL TREE
WHEEL OF FIRE
QUEENSLAND WHEEL TREE
TREE   30 ft
EASTERN AUSTRALIA   AUTUMN

STENOLOBIUM
BIGNONIACEAE

Clustered bells of the most vivid yellow set off to perfection by a background of crepy green leaflets. That is what identi-fies the brilliant Yellow Elder. A useful though leggy shrub in areas with a very mild winter, it blooms throughout sum-mer and autumn, provided faded flower heads are pruned away. STENOLO-BIUM needs heat, water, rich soil and regular feeding to flower well and look its best.

907   STENOLOBIUM stans
TECOMA
YELLOW ELDER
YELLOW BELLS
YELLOW TRUMPET FLOWER
SHRUB   12 ft
WEST INDIES–CENTRAL AMERICA
SUMMER

STEPHANOTIS
ASCLEPIADACEAE

A delightful evergreen vine of moderate size, STEPHANOTIS is grown outdoors or in the bush-house everywhere—sometimes even in pots as a houseplant. The long-lasting flowers are used for bridal bouquets and have a hyacinth-like scent. Outdoors, plant with the roots in shade; it will twine its way up to the sun.

908   STEPHANOTIS floribunda
CLUSTERED WAXFLOWER
MADAGASCAR JASMINE
MADAGASCAR CHAPLET FLOWER
VINE   12 ft
MADAGASCAR   SUMMER

STERNBERGIA

909

STICHERUS

910

STOKESIA

911

STERNBERGIA
AMARYLLIDACEAE

Neither a Crocus, nor a Daffodil, this charming small bulb shines brilliantly in the autumn sunshine, and should be planted more often. It likes a dry, sun-drenched position in summer when it is dormant, and both flowers and leaves appear simultaneously with the autumn rains. Light, well-drained soil is needed, and STERNBERGIAS show up best in a paving pocket or at the edge of a bed.

909   STERNBERGIA lutea
AUTUMN DAFFODIL
AUTUMN CROCUS
BULB   9 in
MEDITERRANEAN   AUTUMN

STICHERUS
GLEICHENIACEAE

A hardy fern, much valued for arrange-ments, the STICHERUS is native to Australia and nearby islands. It is peren-nial, spreads by means of creeping stems and sends up wiry fan-shaped fronds all year round. It does not like full-shade or the fernery, preferring a sheltered position in filtered sun. Sandy soil and plenty of water complete the require-ments for successful cultivation.

910   STICHERUS lobatus
SPREADING FAN FERN
UMBRELLA FERN
CORAL FERN
PERENNIAL FERN   2 ft
AUSTRALIA   ALL YEAR

STOKESIA
COMPOSITAE

Rare and much sought after in European gardens, the beautiful azure-blue STO-KESIA grows like a weed in our southern climates—quickly spreading by under-ground stems into a dense clump. Plant it in the mixed border or large tubs and do not hesitate to pick the lovely four-inch Daisy flowers. They last well in water. Colours range from mauve through true blue to white.

911   STOKESIA laevis
STOKES' ASTER
BLUE THISTLE
PERENNIAL   18 in
NORTH AMERICA
SPRING—AUTUMN

912

913

STRELITZIA
MUSACEAE

Splendid in formal arrangements, wonderful feature plants for the open garden,
Strelitzias are cultivated world-wide.
Growing from a dense root mass which
is difficult to divide, they are amazingly
drought-resistant and yet do equally
well in moist tropical gardens. The
flowers are so unbelievably gorgeous
they remind one of a milliner's fantasy
or some exotic bird. Most commonly
seen STRELITZIA reginae has broad
leaves—its daintier cousin S. parvifolia
has almost invisible leaves atop tall
rush-like stems. The less colourful S. nicolai bears eighteen-inch purple and
white flowers among Banana-like leaves
—it is in fact often mistaken for a
Banana when not in flower. Strelitzias
are usually bought as advanced plants,
otherwise they take years to bloom.

912   STRELITZIA nicolai
BLUE STRELITZIA
WILD BANANA
PERENNIAL   15 ft
NATAL   SUMMER
SUBTROPICAL

913   STRELITZIA reginae
var. parvifolia
BIRD OF PARADISE
CRANE FLOWER
BIRD'S TONGUE FLOWER
PERENNIAL   4 ft
SOUTH AFRICA   ALL YEAR
SUBTROPICAL

275

914

915

STREPTOCARPUS
GESNERIACEAE

The delightful Cape Primroses are closely related both to Gloxinias and African Violets and have similar cultural requirements. Few of the original species are seen outside of specialist glasshouses: instead we have many improved hybrids in shades of mauve, magenta, rose and salmon. Cape Primroses flower in 12 months from seed and are useful indoor decorations.

914   STREPTOCARPUS X hybridus
CAPE PRIMROSE
PERENNIAL   10 in
AFRICA–BURMA   SUMMER

STREPTOSOLEN
SOLANACEAE

Useful in the frost-free garden, Apricot-flowered STREPTOSOLEN is a shrub that tries to be a climber. Easily raised from cuttings, it sprawls happily up banks and even walls with light support, especially when the water and drainage are generous. Flowers can be expected all year in a mild climate, but spring and summer are peak flowering seasons. Needs occasional thinning and pruning.

915   STREPTOSOLEN jamesonii
ORANGE BROWALLIA
SHRUB   6 ft
COLOMBIA   ALL YEAR

STROBILANTHES

916

STYPHELIA

917

SYMPHORICARPOS

918

STROBILANTHES
ACANTHACEAE

Iridescent violet-striped leaves are the main attraction of beautiful STROBI-LANTHES, a small tropical shrub of many uses in the warm-climate garden. It grows well from cuttings, and many gardeners propagate new plants yearly, for the leaf colour is best when young. A winter cutback is necessary in cold areas for the plant looks most forlorn. Violet flowers in hot climates only.

916   STROBILANTHES dyerianus
SHRUB   2 ft
BURMA–MALAYA   SUMMER
TROPICAL

STYPHELIA
EPACRIDACEAE

An attractive genus of flowering shrubs, closely related to the Australian native heaths (See:EPACRIS) but far more spectacular. All of them enjoy sandy acid soil conditions and filtered sun, and all have hanging clusters of long tubular flowers in a variety of colours. The best known are STYPHELIA adscendens (Golden Heath); S. triflora (Pink Five-corners); S. tubiflora (Red Fivecorners); S. viridus (Green Fivecorners).

917   STYPHELIA triflora
PINK FIVECORNERS
SHRUB   4 ft
NEW SOUTH WALES–QUEENSLAND
SPRING

SYMPHORICARPOS
CAPRIFOLIACEAE

Spreading fast from suckers, the curious SYMPHORICARPOS produces thin stems which bend almost double in winter under the weight of puffy white or pink-tinted berries. These are very useful for winter decoration. Snow-berries are deciduous, like rich acid soil, filtered sun and can be planted out from divisions in spring.

918   SYMPHORICARPOS albus
SNOWBERRY
SHRUB   4 ft
WESTERN NORTH AMERICA
WINTER
HARDY

SYRINGA

919

TABERNAEMONTANA

921

920

SYRINGA
OLEACEAE

Alkaline soil and a chilly winter are the keys to real success with Lilacs—but they can be flowered reasonably in warmer areas when given a light shade. Lilacs spread from suckers and flower best when a few of the older stems are cut out each year. Plant them in full sun but with the roots shaded if possible... their late spring flowering peaks vary by several weeks. The Persian Lilac (SYRINGA persica 'Laciniata') has finely divided leaves and pale lilac flowers; S. oblata has a graceful weeping habit with leaves colouring well in autumn. Most of the named varieties are hybrids of the Common Lilac (S. vulgaris). Their colour range includes white, pink, red, blue, mauve, purple and Primrose yellow —all have a unique, delicate fragrance.

919   SYRINGAX microphylla
ROUEN LILAC
CHINESE LILAC
SHRUB   12 ft
CHINA   SPRING

920   SYRINGA vulgaris
COMMON LILAC
SHRUB   20 ft
EUROPE   SPRING

TABERNAEMONTANA
APOCYNACEAE

The glossy leaves, deliciously fragrant white Periwinkle flowers, and white rubbery sap place TABERNAEMON-TANA in the botanical family APO-CYNACEAE. They need a semi-tropical climate or sheltered sunny spot to flourish, with a soil mixture of sand, loam and peat. Charming TABERNAE-MONTANA dichotoma bears orange-yellow fruit with a large depression, suggesting a partly eaten apple. The five-petalled flowers have spirally twisted petals.

921   TABERNAEMONTANA
dichotoma
SCENTLESS GARDENIA
FORBIDDEN FRUIT
EVE'S APPLE
PAGIANTHA
TAB FLOWER
SHRUB   6 ft
INDIA   SUMMER
SUBTROPICAL

TAGETES

TAMARIX

922

924

925

923

TAGETES
COMPOSITAE

If the scent of Marigolds is not to everyone's taste, we can all agree on the colours. Bold, brassy and wonderfully showy. In spite of their common names, all Marigolds hail from tropical Mexico, and are prone to frost damage: so they are usually planted out in early spring, giving better results when the soil is enriched with compost or a packaged plant food. African Marigolds and the miniature 'Minima' strain flower right through summer and well into autumn when the old flower heads are cut regularly. The smaller French types can be flowered through winter as well if planted very early. There are many named varieties, both in single and double types.

922   TAGETES erecta
AFRICAN MARIGOLD
AZTEC MARIGOLD
AMERICAN MARIGOLD
ANNUAL   3 ft
MEXICO   SUMMER

923   TAGETES X 'Minima'
DWARF MARIGOLD
ANNUAL   6 in
HYBRID   SUMMER

924   TAGETES patula
FRENCH MARIGOLD
ANNUAL   12 in
MEXICO   WINTER–SUMMER

TAMARIX
TAMARICACEAE

Hard to believe any plant as graceful and delicate as a Tamarisk could be so incredibly tough. The feathery masses of minute pink blossom move in the slightest breeze—yet the same trees thrive in howling coastal gales and salt-ridden soil that would kill most other plants. Grow them easily from cuttings and water regularly. Both spring and summer-flowering types are available.

925   TAMARIX parviflora
FLOWERING CYPRESS
SALT CEDAR
TAMARISK
TREE   12 ft
SOUTHERN EUROPE   SUMMER

TANACETUM

926

TAXODIUM

927

TELOPEA

928

TANACETUM
COMPOSITAE

Grown easily from seed or divisions, the common European Tansy is esteemed as highly for its golden button flowers as for its value as an aromatic herb. Not fussy as to soil provided sun and water are available, it is a useful tall plant for the back of the summer border. The variety 'Crispum' is a favourite food garnish.

926   TANACETUM vulgare
TANSY
BUTTONS
PERENNIAL   3 ft
EUROPE   SUMMER

TAXODIUM
PINACEAE

One of the few trees that can be relied on to thrive in a deep boggy spot, the American Swamp Cypress is the perfect choice by water, which it rapidly converts into delicate leaves of a brilliant green. As additional value, the leaves turn a glowing rust-red before falling in the autumn. The tree is completely white-ant proof, being the source of the oil used as white-ant repellent.

927   TAXODIUM distichum
SWAMP CYPRESS
BALD CYPRESS
TREE   60 ft
UNITED STATES OF AMERICA
SUMMER

TELOPEA
PROTEACEAE

State floral emblem of New South Wales, the gorgeous Waratah's great four-inch flowers can be seen at a distance in the coastal bushlands—and that is the meaning of both its botanical and aboriginal names...'Seen from Afar'. Not the easiest of plants to grow away from its own territory, it needs well-drained sandy soil enriched with acid humus—and a low phosphorus content in the soil.

928   TELOPEA speciosissima
WARATAH

929

930

929   TELOPEA speciosissima
WARATAH
SHRUB   8 ft
NEW SOUTH WALES   SPRING

TETRAPANAX
ARALIACEAE

A large shrub with magnificently shaped felty leaves, TETRAPANAX has won popularity as a hardy seaside plant, and grows easily in sandy soil. Useful for part shelter from the summer sun. It spreads from suckers, bears fluffy green flowers in autumn and the pith was once used to make paper in China. Lots of water needed.

930   TETRAPANAX papyriferus
RICE PAPER PLANT
CHINESE PAPER PLANT
ARALIA
SHRUB   12 ft
FORMOSA   SUMMER

TETRATHECA

931

THALICTRUM

932

THEVETIA

933

TETRATHECA
TREMANDRACEAE

Masses of showy pink bell-flowers on fine red stems typify charming TETRA-THECAS, miniature Australian shrubs that bring long-lasting splashes of spring colours to areas with light sandy soil. They enjoy sun or part-shade, and the same culture as South African heaths. Purple-flowered species are TETRA-THECA ciliata and T. pilosa. T. erici-folia is the more common pink-flowered type.

931   TETRATHECA ericifolia
BLACK EYED SUSAN
PINK EYES
FLOWER OF THE RANGES
SUB SHRUB   12 in
SOUTH EASTERN AUSTRALIA
SPRING

THALICTRUM
RANUNCULACEAE

Graceful airy perennials for the shady border, THALICTRUMS crown a mass of lacy columbine leaves with tall shivery stems of lavender and gold flowers. Plant their tuberous root masses in rich acid soil where the flower stems can hang over a shady path, or catch morning sunlight. THALICTRUM aquilegifolium has pink flowers, T. dipterocarpum lavender, and T. rugosa a soft gold.

932   THALICTRUM dipterocarpum
LAVENDER SHOWER
CHINESE MEADOW RUE
PERENNIAL   6 ft
CHINA   SUMMER

THEVETIA
APOCYNACEAE

A passing resemblance to Oleanders gives this attractive tree its name, though they are not related. They are, however, equally poisonous. A fast-grower given good drainage and ample water, THE-VETIA also does best in full sun. The flowers appear lightly at almost any time of the year, and together with the leaves quiver at the slightest suggestion of a breeze.

933   THEVETIA peruviana
YELLOW OLEANDER
BE-STILL TREE
TREE   12 ft
TROPICAL AMERICA   ALL YEAR

282

THRYALLIS

934

THRYPTOMENE

935

THUNBERGIA

936

937

THRYALLIS
MALPIGHIACEAE

The charming popular name of this plant is an understatement of the display given by a mature specimen in full flower. The red stems are literally weighed down by spikes of tiny golden star-flowers for weeks at a time. Individual flowers fall after a day, and the ground for yards around becomes vivid yellow. Success-ful in all but the coldest areas.

934   THRYALLIS glauca
RAIN OF GOLD
GALPHIMIA
SHRUB   5 ft
MEXICO   SUMMER

THRYPTOMENE
MYRTACEAE

A spicy Myrtle fragrance on winter days leads one quickly to Australia's delicate Heath Myrtles or THRYPTOMENES. Grow them anywhere the soil is well-drained and acid, preferably a little on the sandy side. Regular water and full sun-shine are necessities for all of the 20-odd species flowering in shades of white, pink and lavender. The flowers are cup-shaped and under a quarter of an inch across, the leaves tiny and heath-like. Both are borne on slender arching stems which make them just fine for cutting. THRYPTOMENE calycina is the hardiest white flowering type—T. saxicola the best pink.

935   THRYPTOMENE calycina
HEATH-MYRTLE
GRAMPIAN THRYPTOMENE
SHRUB   5 ft
VICTORIA   WINTER

THUNBERGIA
ACANTHACEAE

Gaily-flowered tropicals for the warm climate or sheltered sunny spot, THUN-BERGIAS come in many forms—peren-nial, shrubby or climbing. They grow in any soil, but prefer a light compost of sand, humus and decayed manure—and humidity helps immeasurably. Vining types are usually grown from seed—the shrubs from cuttings under glass. THUN-BERGIA alata (the orange-flowered Black Eyed Susan) is usually treated as an annual—T. grandiflora (the Sky Flower) is a more vigorous vine with pale blue trumpets. T. erecta, a useful shrub with yellow-throated purple flowers, thrives in mild coastal districts. Alto-gether more than 100 species are known.

936   THUNBERGIA alata
BLACK EYED SUSAN
ORANGE CLOCK VINE
GOLDEN GLORY VINE
ANNUAL VINE   6 ft
SOUTH AFRICA   ALL YEAR

937   THUNBERGIA erecta
SHRUB   6 ft
SOUTH AFRICA   SUMMER

TIBOUCHINA

TIGRIDIA

938

939

940

TIBOUCHINA
MELASTOMATACEAE

Gaudy South American shrubs for acid, well-drained soil, the Lasiandras (as they are commonly called) produce extra-ordinary colour effects at many times of the year. New growth is shaded with bronze and red, but quickly turns to a rich velvet green. Although the plants are basically evergreen, odd leaves turn scarlet or yellow in cold weather. The vivid purple flowers appear throughout summer and autumn but especially the latter. Lasiandras grow so leggy and brittle they are prone to wind damage, and should be pruned back after flowering and again in spring to promote a compact shape. Feed with acid shrub food and water well.

938   TIBOUCHINA granulosa
LASIANDRA
PRINCESS FLOWER
SHRUB   8 ft
SOUTH AMERICA   SUMMER

939   TIBOUCHINA semidecandra
(syn. urvilleana)
LASIANDRA
GLORY BUSH
SHRUB   10 ft
SOUTH BRAZIL   AUTUMN

TIGRIDIA
IRIDACEAE

Garish and gaudy, these dazzling members of the Iris family are most effective in a mass—because individual flowers last only a day. Spring-planted in sunny well-drained soil, they like plenty of water through the summer flowering period and multiply rapidly. TIGRIDIAS have been cross-bred to produce extraordinary colour combinations of vivid pink, yellow and purple, all with contrasting spots. Not recommended for cutting.

940   TIGRIDIA pavonia
JOCKEY'S CAP LILY
PEACOCK TIGER FLOWER
TIGER FLOWER
MEXICAN SHELLFLOWER
ONE DAY LILY
FLOWER OF TIGRIS
BULB   2½ ft
MEXICO   SUMMER

284

TILLANDSIA

941

TITHONIA

942

TILLANDSIA
BROMELIACEAE

Exotic members of the Pineapple family for semi-tropical gardens or greenhouse. All of them enjoy sun, regular sprinkling and a high summer temperature. Grow from suckers planted out in pots of acid sandy compost—the main exception being TILLANDSIA usneoides (Spanish Moss) which makes no roots, and merely hangs from tree branches. TILLAND-SIAS produce blue or violet flowers from a series of overlapping bracts.

941   TILLANDSIA cyanea
BROMELIAD   2½ ft
ECUADOR   AUTUMN

TITHONIA
COMPOSITAE

Surely the most vividly coloured of all daisies, brilliant TITHONIA produces orange-scarlet flowers continuously from midsummer to midwinter in warm-climate areas. Plant out in spring in full sun; it is both drought and heat-resistant. The flowers are useful for indoor work, but like Zinnias should be picked with care. The hollow stems are quite brittle.

942   TITHONIA rotundifolia
MEXICAN SUNFLOWER
ANNUAL   4 ft
MEXICO   SUMMER

TORENIA

943

TRACHELOSPERMUM

944

TRADESCANTIA

945

946

TORENIA
SCROPHULARIACEAE

Rather like small Gloxinias, the yellow-throated purple bells of TORENIA appear around the same time. Grow them in full sun in the open garden in any sort of soil you choose, but you will get better results if you enrich it with old manure. They are also useful plants for window boxes, and a white variety is available for contrast. Plant out in midsummer.

943   TORENIA fournieri
WISHBONE FLOWER
ANNUAL   12 in
INDOCHINA   SUMMER–AUTUMN

TRACHELOSPERMUM
APOCYNACEAE

Masses of starry white summer flowers scent the air for blocks around when you make a place for evergreen Star Jasmine. Though guaranteed to cover anything in time, it needs strong support from the beginning and a regular light trimming to prevent legginess. Make sure the roots are shaded in hot climates —the vine will quickly find its way into the sun.

944   TRACHELOSPERMUM
jasminoides
STAR JASMINE
RHYNCHOSPERMUM
SHRUBBY CLIMBER   20 ft
CHINA   SUMMER

TRADESCANTIA
COMMELINACEAE

Fast-growing foliage plants for green-house, home or open garden, the Wandering Jews quickly sprout roots on cuttings left in a glass of water. Plant them outdoors in moist shaded areas, or merely leave stems indoors in a container of water. Indoors, pinching encourages branching. Many attractively variegated varieties are sold of TRADES-CANTIA fluminensis. The Spiderwort (T. virginiana) is a different sort of plant. It grows quite tall, and each flower available in tones of blue, pink, mauve and white, lasts only a day.

945   TRADESCANTIA fluminensis
'Variegata'
WANDERING JEW
CREEPING JESUS
PERENNIAL TRAILER   12 in
SOUTH AMERICA   ALL YEAR

946   TRADESCANTIA virginiana
SPIDERWORT
ONE DAY FLOWER
SPIDER FLOWER
FLOWER OF A DAY
PERENNIAL   3 ft
EASTERN UNITED STATES OF
AMERICA   SPRING

TRICHINIUM

947

TRISTANIA

948

TRITONIA

949

TRICHINIUM
AMARANTHACEAE

A large group of Australian perennials and shrubs noted for fluffy pink or mauve flower spikes, the TRICHINIUMS are desert plants needing perfect drainage and water in any quantity during winter and early spring. Grow them in a compost of sandy loam and old manure. A position in full sun does best. TRICHINIUM rotundifolium is one of 50 species —the flower spikes are deliciously fragrant and useful for cutting.

947   TRICHINIUM rotundifolium
MULLA MULLA
WOOLLY BEARS
SHRUB   2½ ft
WESTERN AUSTRALIA   SPRING

TRISTANIA
MYRTACEAE

A useful group of trees from Australia, India and the Pacific islands, evergreen TRISTANIAS are hardy only in frost-free areas. They are useful small shade trees and have many attractive features: glossy laurel-like leaves summer flowers and brightly coloured shedding bark. TRISTANIA laurina is a popular street tree, producing masses of orange-yellow bloom in early summer.

948   TRISTANIA laurina
KANOOKA
WATER GUM
TREE   20 ft
EASTERN AUSTRALIA   SUMMER

TRITONIA
IRIDACEAE

Another look-alike related to Freesias and Ixias, the gaudy TRITONIAS flower chiefly in shades of orange, red and pink —the illustrated TRITONIA crocata being the most brilliant of 50-odd spring and summer-flowering species. The corms are planted from autumn any time to early summer in an open sunny position, and enjoy plenty of water until flowering. Good for cutting.

949   TRITONIA crocata
BLAZING STAR
FLAME FREESIA
MONTBRETIA
KALKOENTJIE
BULB   12 in
SOUTH AFRICA   SPRING—SUMMER

TROPAEOLUM

950

TULBAGHIA

951

TROPAEOLUM
TROPAEOLACEAE

Trailing annuals of great use for covering old stumps, fences and banks, Nasturtiums are easily started by scattering a few of the large seeds into loose soil anywhere. This is done in spring, except in warm climates where an autumn start gives a longer flowering period. Many colour varieties are available in cream, orange, red, mahogany and pink; single and semi-double. There are also dwarf non-trailing types for use in bedding. Young Nasturtium leaves and flowers have a spicy taste and are often used in summer salads. Water often but do not fertilize as this makes the plants run to leaf.

950   TROPAEOLUM majus
NASTURTIUM
INDIAN CRESS
TRAILING ANNUAL   6 ft
PERU   SPRING–AUTUMN

TULBAGHIA
LILIACEAE

TULBAGHIAS would make an ideal cut flower except for one thing—they smell distressingly like very strong garlic, especially when picked. They are therefore usually left in the garden, where a large clump will flower all summer long. Dainty in habit and of a delightful colour, they prefer rich damp conditions in filtered sun. They multiply rapidly.

951   TULBAGHIA violacea
SOCIETY GARLIC
SWEET GARLIC
BULB   18 in
SOUTH AFRICA   SUMMER

952

954

953

955

956

TULIPA
LILIACEAE

An entire book could be planned about Tulip varieties—and during the eighteenth century Tulipomania in Europe, many were. But for all that, these beautiful cold-climate bulbs are not common in the southern hemisphere except in limited highland areas with winter cold. Today's range of Tulip colours is nearly complete—white, red, yellow, purple, blue, green—they are all there; and if 'La Tulipe Noire' is not absolutely black, it is close to it. There are striped and speckled varieties: fringed and feathered types—species with one or many flowers to a stem. Massed under trees in spring, they are magnificent.

952   TULIPA (Massed planting of Mixed Species)

953   TULIPA X Cottage type
(COTTAGE TULIP)
BULB   30 in
ASIA MINOR   LATE SPRING

954   TULIPA X 'La Tulipe Noire'
(DARWIN TULIP)
BULB   3 in
ASIA MINOR   SPRING

955   TULIPA HYBRIDA
(BIZARRE AND LILY FLOWERED TULIPS)
BULB   2 ft
ASIA MINOR   SPRING

TWEEDIA
ASCLEPIADACEAE

Starry flowers of a delicate pale turquoise centred deeper blue and fading to pink. This colour effect belongs uniquely to the charming TWEEDIA which grows freely outdoors in mild summer climates. Strike cuttings in sand under glass, and plant out in rich well-drained soil in filtered sun. The greyish heart-shaped leaves are completely downy, and the plant will develop a trailing or twining habit if left unchecked.

956   TWEEDIA caerulea
SUB SHRUB   3 ft
ARGENTINA   SUMMER

957

ULEX
LEGUMINOSAE

An attractive flowering shrub for the garden—but a menace in the country; in some areas a proclaimed noxious weed. Gorse flowers best in overused soil; improve conditions and it bolts to leaf—or rather spines, for the true leaves are found only in very young plants, being replaced by green spines as the plant ages. Golden-flowered Gorse is admirably suited to clipping as a hedge.

957   ULEX europaeus
GORSE
FURZE
SHRUB   6 ft
EUROPE   SPRING

958

959

VALLOTA
AMARYLLIDACEAE

So long have these bulbs been grown around Scarborough in England it was once thought they were native to the district. Now we believe they were washed ashore in a Dutch shipwreck for they certainly grow wild at the Cape of Good Hope. VALLOTA flowers in summer—a vivid cluster of orange-scarlet above strap-like evergreen leaves. The bulbs need regular water and like most Amaryllids are planted with the neck at soil level.

958   VALLOTA speciosa
SCARBOROUGH LILY
GEORGE LILY
BULB   18 in
SOUTH AFRICA   SUMMER

VANDA
ORCHIDACEAE

Beautiful orchids for the glasshouse or sub-tropics, VANDAS grow erect, producing flowers at each leaf joint. Epiphytic, they are usually grown in large pots of tree fern fibre to provide anchorage for the aerial roots. High humidity is desirable and the temperature must not drop below 50°F. VANDAS need to be well staked before they grow really tall. The flowers usually include some shade of blue or mauve.

959   VANDA sanderiana
ORCHID   6 ft
PHILIPPINES   SUMMER

VERBENA

960

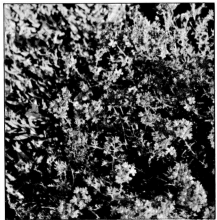

961

VERONICA

962

VERTICORDIA

963

VERBENA
VERBENACEAE

Two hundred and more species are recognized in this large family of perennials, most of them easy to grow, and suitable for warm, dry climates. The scarlet VERBENA peruviana is often seen as a ground cover in semi-tropical areas, V. rigida is used as a perennial rockery plant and V. hybrida is usually raised as a summer annual. Its many colours include red, pink, white, mauve and yellow; plain, striped or with a white eye. Most Verbenas have a pleasant spicy fragrance.

960   VERBENA hybrida
FLORIST'S VERBENA
ROSE VERVAIN
PERENNIAL   10 in
HYBRID   SUMMER

961   VERBENA rigida
VERVAIN
PERENNIAL   10 in
ARGENTINA   SUMMER
SUBTROPICAL

VERONICA
SCROPHULARIACEAE

A most varied genus of 250 plant species; perennials from the northern hemisphere, shrubs from the southern. Most of them bear loose spikes of blue or mauve flowers in warm weather. VERONICA derwentia is a native Australian shrubby variety, at home in cool rich acid soil. V. spicata the most commonly seen perennial, sending up summer flower spikes to 18 in—blue, mauve or pink according to variety.

962   VERONICA spicata
SPEEDWELL
PERENNIAL   18 in
EUROPE   SUMMER
HARDY

VERTICORDIA
MYRTACEAE

Not often seen outside their native Western Australia, VERTICORDIAS are a genus of 50-odd shrubs at home anywhere the soil is sandy and rich with leafmould. The feathery flowers appear in spring, absolutely massed. The colours include red, rose, white, yellow and brown, according to species. VERTICORDIA nitens is probably the most brilliant of a showy genus, bearing its flowers in dense plateaux —one for each year's growth.

963   VERTICORDIA nitens
JUNIPER MYRTLE
GOLDEN FEATHERFLOWER
YELLOW MORRISON
SHRUB   3 ft
WESTERN AUSTRALIA   SPRING

VIBURNUM

VINCA

964

966

967

965

VIBURNUM
CAPRIFOLIACEAE

Dare one class one genus of shrubs as the most beautiful and varied of all? It could only be said of the VIBURNUMS —120 species and many more named varieties; short, tall, evergreen or deciduous: many with brilliant autumn colouring and fruits that birds adore. The flowers, mostly white or delicate rose, are often as fragrant as Daphne or Hoya. Nearly all can be grown from cuttings and prefer a damp rich soil. VIBURNUM plicatum and V. tinus are evergreens. V. burkwoodii and V. carlesii deliciously fragrant deciduous types. Crepy-leafed V. opulus is in a class all its own with great clouds of greenish-white Hydrangea flowers in summer.

964   VIBURNUM burkwoodii
BURKWOOD'S VIBURNUM
SHRUB   5 ft
HYBRID   SPRING

965   VIBURNUM macrocephalum
CHINESE SNOWBALL TREE
SHRUB   10 ft
CHINA   SPRING

966   VIBURNUM plicatum
'Tomentosum'
JAPANESE SNOWBALL
JAPANESE VIBURNUM
SHRUB   6 ft
JAPAN   SPRING

VINCA
APOCYNACEAE

Fast-spreading perennials, often used for ground cover on banks or shady areas, Periwinkles come in a number of varieties flowering single or double in various shades of blue, white or purple. Plant out any time and give plenty of water— the trailing stems will send down roots wherever they reach, and then produce a mass of flowering shoots. The variegated leaf variety is particularly attractive.

967   VINCA major 'Variegata'
PERIWINKLE
CUTFINGER
PERENNIAL   TRAILING
EUROPE   SPRING

968

970

972

969

971

VIOLA
VIOLACEAE

Violas, Violets, Pansies—all are members of one genus, and the resemblance is easy to see in their cheeky face-like flowers. Most popularly grown types flower in winter and spring in deep rich alkaline soil. The annual Violas and Pansies enjoy full sun in mild areas, while perennial Violets need protection from afternoon sun and are best grown in tree-shade in really hot districts. All need plenty of water and provide colourful ground cover in late winter and early spring. VIOLAS are particularly effective in large tubs or containers where their trailing habit provides sheets of spring colour.

968 VIOLA cornuta
(as ground cover)
VIOLA
JOHNNY JUMP UP

969 VIOLA cornuta
VIOLA
ANNUAL 6 in
PYRENEES WINTER

970 VIOLA odorata 'Princess of Wales'
VIOLET
SWEET VIOLET
PERENNIAL 9 in
EUROPE–AFRICA–ASIA WINTER

971 VIOLA tricolor 'Hortensis'
HEARTSEASE
PANSY
PENSEE
ANNUAL 9 in
EUROPE WINTER–SPRING

VIRGILIA
LEGUMINOSAE

Fill in for slower growing trees with rampant, spring-flowering VIRGILIAS and they will reach man-height in a single season. They grow literally anywhere, without fuss. The foliage is fern-like and attractive—the flowers Pea-type, fragrant and borne heavily. So what is the catch? They become straggly in a year or two and only live about 10 years. As we said—strictly for quick cover.

672 VIRGILIA capensis
KEURBOOM
TREE 18 ft
SOUTH AFRICA SPRING

VITIS

973

974

VRIESIA

975

976

VITIS
VITACEAE

Two VITIS species, of similar appearance, are planted in southern hemisphere gardens. The first, VITIS coignetiae, a rampant Japanese plant, is grown for its incredible autumn colour display and can easily drape a large tree in a single season. The second, V. vinifera, is the fruiting Grape Vine, grown for its quick coverup effect in summer as well as the juicy fruit. But to get fruit quality you must choose the right variety for your climate, and spend time pruning, training and cultivating. In humid areas, Grape vines are subject to mildew, and must be dusted regularly with sulphur or Zineb.

973　VITIS coignetiae
GLORY VINE
ORNAMENTAL GRAPE
CLIMBER　90 ft
JAPAN　AUTUMN

974　VITIS coignetiae

VRIESIA
BROMELIACEAE

A hardy group of Bromeliads suitable for the open garden. The actual flowers are uninteresting, but are surrounded by colourful bracts, usually in red and yellow. These are particularly long lasting. VRIESIAS revel in a well-drained soil, rich in leafmould, for although not epiphytic, they are forest dwellers. Some VRIESIAS die after flowering once, but not until they have produced suckers for next season.

975　VRIESIA carinata
PAINT BRUSH
BROMELIAD　10 in
BRAZIL　WINTER

976　VRIESIA X Fl Belgian Hybrid
LOBSTER CLAW
BROMELIAD　18 in
HYBRID　AUTUMN

WATSONIA

977

979

978

WATSONIA
IRIDACEAE

Originally from South Africa, WATSO-
NIAS have become naturalized in Australia, and many other lands, where they
are often found by rivers or in the open
forest. They multiply and spread from
seed at an alarming rate. WATSONIAS
like full sun or part-shade in hot districts,
and are planted at different times of the
year according to species. WATSONIA
aletroides blooms in early spring, the
tubular orange flowers hanging from a
stem 2 ft or more in length. W. ardernei
flowers white to 3 ft and more, and is
often sold in a mixture with salmon-pink
W. meriana and mauve W. rosea which
grows tallest of all. Many other coloured
varieties exist, hybrids between the 3
species listed above.

977   WATSONIA aletroides
ORANGE BUGLE LILY
BULB   2 ft
SOUTH AFRICA   SPRING

978   WATSONIA ardernei
BUGLE LILY
BULB   3 ft
SOUTH AFRICA   SPRING

979   WATSONIA rosea
BULB   5 ft
SOUTH AFRICA   SPRING—SUMMER

WEIGELA

980

WISTARIA

981

983

982

984

WEIGELA
CAPRIFOLIACEAE

Masses of red, white and pink trumpet flowers bring leggy WEIGELAS to life for a short season in late spring, after which they are usually cut right back to prevent their becoming untidy. Their coarse crepy leaves burn badly in summer sun, so they should be planted in shade or filtered light. Leaves fall early without a colour display and the shrubs are bare for a long time. Rich acid soil and plenty of water bring out their best.

980   WEIGELA florida 'Variegata'
WEIGELIA
SHRUB   8 ft
JAPAN   LATE SPRING
HARDY

WISTARIA
LEGUMINOSAE

A small genus of twining climbers for temperate and frost-free areas, the Wistarias are extremely versatile. Train them as vines, fences, standard shrubs or even as pot plants, they burst themselves flowering in early spring each year. Seedlings take years to flower, so choose a grafted plant or cutting and give it good support. Wistarias like loamy acid soil and need water aplenty at flowering time to hold the blossom well. WISTARIA sinensis is the common single mauve species and flowers most heavily on bare wood, while the many varieties of W. floribunda often bloom after the leaves with racemes up to 4 ft long.

981   WISTARIA floribunda 'Alba'
WHITE JAPANESE WISTARIA
VINE   30 ft
JAPAN   SPRING

982   WISTARIA floribunda
macrobotrys 'Noda Fuji'
JAPANESE WISTARIA
VINE   30 ft
JAPAN   SPRING

983   WISTARIA sinensis
CHINESE WISTARIA
CHINESE KIDNEY BEAN
VINE   100 ft
CHINA   SPRING

984   WISTARIA sinensis
CHINESE WISTARIA
(close-up of blossom)

X

XANTHOCERAS

985

XANTHORRHOEA

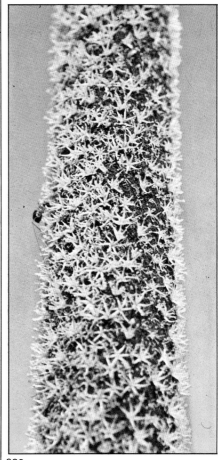

986

XANTHOCERAS
SAPINDACEAE

A spreading deciduous tree or woody shrub that flowers spectacularly in spring, when racemes of crinkly white blossom appear. The flowers have a Hyacinth fragrance, with yellow centres ageing to pink, and are followed by large black seeds. XANTHOCERAS is not particular about soil; but good drainage is important. The light green leaves remind one of the Mountain Ash.

985 XANTHOCERAS sorbifolium
YELLOW HORN
HYACINTH SHRUB
TREE   15 ft
CHINA   SPRING
HARDY

XANTHORRHOEA
LILIACEAE

Perhaps the most widely noticed summer plants in the Australian landscape, the Grass Trees or Blackboys have spread their influence to many other countries, where they are used as accent plants with Yuccas and succulents in dry sandy soil. The grassy leaf spikes, sometimes on a tall trunk, are striking any time of year, and come spring, spear-like flower stems shoot up, literally covered with thousands of honey-scented cream or white flowers.

986 XANTHORRHOEA hastilis
GRASS TREE
BLACKBOYS
GRASS SPEAR
SPEAR GRASS
GOONANGURRA
PERENNIAL   8 ft
NEW SOUTH WALES
SPRING—SUMMER

XYLOMELUM

987

YUCCA

988

XYLOMELUM
PROTEACEAE

Hardy Australian trees, the Woody Pears are grown more for their decorative, inedible fruits than the uninteresting brownish flowers. XYLOMELUM pyriforme is a slow-growing tree of about 15 ft, which bears 2 entirely different types of leaves—smooth and straight on the flowering branches, prickly on the barren ones. The grey-felty fruits are most decorative in spring.

987　XYLOMELUM pyriforme
WOODY PEAR
TREE　15 ft
AUSTRALIA　SPRING

YUCCA
LILIACEAE

The North American YUCCAS adapt splendidly to garden conditions but are in fact desert-dwellers—and so completely drought-resistant they are indispensable for low maintenance gardens in many modern buildings. Giant panicles of creamy bell-flowers are likely to appear any time during the warm weather, but the sharply pointed and serrated leaves are best kept away from paths.

988　YUCCA filamentosa
SPANISH BAYONET
ADAM'S NEEDLE
SILK GRASS
SPANISH DAGGER
PERENNIAL　6 ft
SOUTH EASTERN UNITED STATES
SPRING

989

991

990

ZANTEDESCHIA
ARACEAE

What's in a name? Fortunately, this family of bulbs can be remembered by their form and scent alone—for the name changes have been bewildering. First they were Arums, then Callas, then Richardias and now . . . would you believe ZANTEDESCHIAS? The White Arum Lily (ZANTEDESCHIA aethiopica) is a bog lover, revels in water and mud, flowers continuously. The Golden Calla (Z. elliottiana) has decorative silver-spotted leaves, yellow spathe and a spadix that develops into a spike of brilliant berry fruits. Dwarf Z. rehmannii (the Pink Calla) and its multi-coloured hybrids, grow less than 1 ft high with narrow spear-shaped leaves. All are wonderful for arrangements.

989　ZANTEDESCHIA aethiopica
ARUM LILY
LILY OF THE NILE
BULB　3 ft
SOUTH AFRICA　ALL YEAR

990　ZANTEDESCHIA elliottiana
CALLA LILY
GOLDEN CALLA
BULB　2 ft
TRANSVAAL　SUMMER

991　ZANTEDESCHIA rehmannii
PINK CALLA
BULB　10 in
NATAL　SUMMER

ZEA

ZEPHYRANTHES

992

993

995

994

ZEA
GRAMINEAE

Many ornamental varieties of the American Corn or Maize plant have been developed for garden use. Most are the work of Japanese hybridists and may be sown directly into the garden in spring. Some of them have leaves variegated in green, pink, yellow and white—in others, the variegations appear in the ears of corn themselves. These are picked, lacquered and used for autumn flower arrangements.

992   ZEA mays
CORN
INDIAN CORN
VARIEGATED CORN
ANNUAL   6 ft
UNITED STATES OF AMERICA
AUTUMN

ZEPHYRANTHES
AMARYLLIDACEAE

The last bulb genus in this book—but by no means the least. Easy to grow flowers for late summer and autumn, the Storm Lilies appear like magic after the first late summer rains, and in a warm climate are likely to bloom any time of year after a downpour. Useful in pots, rockeries or as border edgings, ZEPHYRANTHES can be planted any time—even moved for effect when in full flower. The white variety ZEPHYRANTHES candida in particular multiplies at an astounding rate from bulb offsets and seed. There are many coloured species and hybrids.

993   ZEPHYRANTHES candida
AUTUMN CROCUS
RAIN LILY
STORM LILY
WEST WIND FLOWER
BULB   10 in
ARGENTINA   SUMMER

994   ZEPHYRANTHES citrinus
GOLDEN STORM LILY
BULB   8 in
BRITISH GUIANA   AUTUMN

995   ZEPHYRANTHES grandiflora
PINK STORM LILY
BULB   12 in
GUATEMALA   SUMMER
SUBTROPICAL

996

997

998

ZINNIA
COMPOSITAE

Most popular garden forms of Zinnia are hybridized from ZINNIA elegans, discovered in Mexico in the eighteenth century. Brilliantly coloured members of the Daisy family, Zinnias are hot-weather plants, flowering outdoors through summer and autumn. Modern varieties include plain and striped colours; doubles and singles; cactus-flowered and crested types. There are also the miniature Thumbelina hybrids. Z. linearis is the only other species grown —it flowers from seed in 6 weeks.

996   ZINNIA elegans
ZINNIA
YOUTH AND AGE
ANNUAL   3 ft
MEXICO   SUMMER

997   ZINNIA X elegans 'Cactus Type'
CACTUS ZINNIA
ANNUAL   2½ ft
MEXICO   SUMMER

998   ZINNIA linearis
BORDER ZINNIA
ANNUAL   12 in
MEXICO   SUMMER

999

1000

ZYGOCACTUS
CACTACEAE

The curiously flowered Crab Cactus (ZY-
GOCACTUS truncatus), is most often
seen as a houseplant for winter decoration and is sometimes grafted onto the
tall trunk of other cactus species so that
the drooping stems and flowers can be
seen clearly. Many brilliantly coloured
named varieties exist. It is often called
Christmas Cactus in the northern hemisphere.

999   ZYGOCACTUS truncatus
CRAB CACTUS
CHRISTMAS CACTUS
EPIPHYTIC CACTUS   2 ft
BRAZIL   WINTER

ZYGOPETALUM
ORCHIDACEAE

Delightful orchids for large containers,
the ZYGOPETALUMS can be grown in
the open in most temperate climates,
and flower from autumn to spring. On
the sheltered patio or sunny terrace they
quickly make themselves known by an
effusion of delicious spicy perfume. The
flowers of popular ZYGOPETALUM
mackayii are delightfully coloured and
thrive in a pot mixture of Osmunda,
Sphagnum, tile chips and fibrous loam.
Water throughout the year.

1000   ZYGOPETALUM mackayii
ORCHID   30 in
SOUTH AMERICA
AUTUMN–SPRING

index common names

glossary

ACID
Soil deficient in lime.

AERIAL ROOT
A root appearing above soil level; used both for support and feeding.

AIR LAYERING
A method of propagation which stimulates new root growth from a plant *above* ground.

ALKALINE
Soil rich in lime.

ALLERGENIC
Said of a plant which produces rashes etc, on contact.

ANTHER
The pollen-bearing part of a stamen.

APHIDS
Minute sap-sucking insects which appear in masses, often on new shoots. Controlled by application of Derris Dust or Nicotine.

AQUATIC
A plant which grows naturally in water; sometimes floating, sometimes rooted in mud.

BIPINNATE
A compound leaf with branches of leaflets from its main axis. (See PINNATE).

BISEXUAL
A plant with flowers having both male and female reproductive parts; or a plant of one sex on which a branch of the opposite sex has been grafted.

BONE MEAL
A useful fertilizer rich in nitrogen and phosphate of lime.

BRACT
A modified leaf at the base of a flower, often the most colourful part.

BULBIL
A small bulb which appears at leaf joints, as in some Lilies.

CALCIFUGE
A lime-hating plant.

CALYX
The outer covering of a flower, consisting of sepals. Often decorative.

CARNIVOROUS
A plant capable of attracting live insects or animals and adapted for absorbing them directly as food.

CATKIN
A hanging spike of unisexual flowers.

COLD-HARDY
A plant not affected by frost.

CONIFER
A tree or shrub bearing cones such as pine, hemlock, spruce.

CORM
A bulb-like enlargement of the joint of root and stem. Planted like a bulb.

COROLLA
The entire circle of outer petals of a flower.

CULTIVAR
A plant variety produced by artificial means.

CULTIVATION
Specifically, breaking up the soil surface around a plant to admit air and water.

DECIDUOUS
A plant that sheds all leaves at the end of the growing season.

DERRIS DUST
A popular insecticide in powder form.

DISBUDDING
Removing side flower buds to concentrate growth in a single flower and enlarge it.

DIVISION
The method of propagating perennial plants by splitting the root system.

EPIPHYTE
A plant supporting itself without soil (growing on trees and shrubs) feeding generally from the chemicals in rain water and decaying plant tissue.

ESPALIER
A shrub, tree or vine trained formally in two dimensions only, generally against a wall.

FALL
A specialised hanging petal, as in Irises.

FAMILY
A group of related botanical genera.

FIBROUS ROOTED
Without any major or tap roots.

FLORET
A minute flower, dozens of which make up the centre of a daisy.

FLOWER
Bluntly, the specialised apparatus developed by a plant to enclose the sexual organs and attract insects and other pollinators needed for fertilization.

FOLIAGE PLANT
A plant grown for the decorative value of its leaves, rather than flowers.

FROND
The mature leaf stem of a fern.

FROST-TENDER
A fleshy plant which may be completely destroyed when the unprotected sap freezes.

FUNGICIDE
A chemical preparation for the destruction of minute funguses on decorative plants.

FUNGUS
A parasitic organism with no chlorophyll, and usually without leaves.

GENERIC NAME
A plant's first scientific name, indicating the genus to which it belongs.

GENUS
A group of closely related plant species.

GRAFTING
When a bud or shoot is severed from its parent plant and joined to a rooted section of another. Used for rapid multiplication of woody plants.

HABIT
The characteristic and most usual form of a plant which can be modified by training.

HALF HARDY
A plant which will resist a moderate degree of cold, in a sheltered position.

HEELED CUTTING
A cutting of new wood, still attached to portion of the hardened, previous year's growth.

HERB
(a) Any non-woody plant.
(b) a plant grown for flavoring purposes, etc.

HERBACEOUS PERENNIAL
A non-woody plant which dies back to the roots in winter, sending up new growth in spring.

HOTHOUSE
A glasshouse with artificial heating.

HUMUS
The rich debris resulting from the rotting of vegetables and other matter.

HYBRID
The result of cross-fertilization of different forms of parent plants.

INDIGENOUS
Native to a particular country or area.

INFLORESCENCE
The method of flower-bearing or grouping of flowers.

IRON CHELATES
An organic compound used to prevent iron deficiency in plants.

JUVENILE
The second leaves to appear from seed— sometimes varying a lot from the leaves of an adult plant.

LANCEOLATE
A spear-shaped shoot.

LATERAL
A shoot arising from the stem any distance from the terminal.

LAYERING
Pinning a branch down to ground to produce roots.
LEAF CUTTING
A method of propagating many tropical plants from portions of their leaves.
LEAFLET
A leaf-shaped segment of a compound leaf.
LEGUME
A plant which produces pea-type seeds in a pod, or the seeds of such a plant.
LIGNOTUBER
A swelling at the base of a trunk which contains nourishment for the renewal of growth after destruction of the main plant. Found in many Australian Eucalypts.
LOAM
A friable soil containing topsoil, sand, clay and silt particles.
MALATHION
An effective but foul-smelling insecticide.
MICROCLIMATE
A purely local combination of climatic conditions.
MILDEW
A whitish minute fungus which disfigures roses and other plants. Spray with Bordeaux mixture.
MULCH
A soil covering to conserve moisture or prevent root damage by heat or frost. May be of organic matter, pebbles or even plastic.
NATURAL CROSS
A hybrid which has occurred naturally between two distinct, but usually related plant species.
NATURALIZED
Specifically said of bulbs planted in casual groups in lawns and shrubberies, where they are left to multiply year after year.
NEEDLE
A specialized elongated leaf, in conifers.
OFFSET
A small outside division from a mature plant.
ORGANIC
Composed of live or formerly living tissue.
PALMATE
Leaflets arranged like a fan.
PANICLE
A branching cluster of flowers.
PEATMOSS
An organic material used particularly in potting composts: very acid and water-retaining.
PENDANT
Describing a hanging flower cluster.
PERENNIAL
A plant lasting more or less permanently and usually of soft rather than woody growth.
PERGOLA
An ornamental garden shelter, often used as a support for climbing plants.
PERIANTH
The combined calyx and corolla of a flower.
PETAL
One decorative unit or segment of the corolla.
pH BALANCE
The degree of acidity or alkalinity in soil.
PINCH BACK
To prune soft leading shoots with the finger nails to encourage branching.
PINNATE
Like a feather, specifically a leaf with leaflets arranged on both sides of a centre stalk.
PIP
(a) The seed of a fruit.
(b) A dormant terminal tip of the hizome of certain plants (e.g., lily-of-the-valley).
PISTIL
The prominent female organ of a flower.

POLLINATION
The placing of pollen on the stigma of a flower, and the first stage of fertilization. In nature performed by honey-seeking insects.
PROCUMBENT
A plant which trails without rooting at intervals.
PROPAGATE
To reproduce a plant by means of cuttings or divisions. This is to ensure it comes absolutely true to type, which a seedling might not.
PSEUDOBULB
The thickened bulbous stem formed by some orchids for the storage of nutrient.
RACEME
A stem with flowers along its length. The individual flowers with pedicels on stems.
REFLEXED
Petals bent backwards from the flower's centre.
RHIZOME
A rootlike underground stem which produces buds of new growth at intervals.
ROOT CUTTING
A method of propagating Wistarias and other plants from small sections of root.
RUNNER
A trailing stem which takes root at intervals.
SCALE
A segment of lily bulb which may be detached for propagation.
SCION
The bud or shoot which is grafted onto the stock of another plant.
SEPAL
The individual segment of a calyx.
SERRATED
Having saw-toothed edges.
SHOOT
An immature combination of leaf and stem.
SHRUB
A woody plant, without the single trunk of a tree.
SPADIX
A fleshy spike of minute flowers – characteristic of the ARUM family.
SPATHE
The sheath or bract which encloses a spadix.
SPECIES
The basic or minor unit in plant naming.
SPECIFIC NAME
A plant's second name.
SPIKE
A series of flowers on a single stem with the flowers individually steamless (sessile).
SPORE
The reproductive cell of a plant.
SPORT
A plant variety resulting from natural mutation.
STAMEN
The male or pollen-bearing sexual organs of a flower.
STANDARD
(a) The upright petals of many flowers.
(b) A shrubby plant specially grafted onto a tall treelike trunk.
STERILE
A plant incapable of reproduction by seed. Generally a hybrid.
STIGMA
The female part of a flower which receives the pollen, and connects to the ovaries.
STOCK
The parent plant onto which the scion of another is grafted.
STOLON
A shoot which bends to the ground and forms roots and growth as a complete new plant.

SUB-TROPICAL
A plant native to areas outside the true tropics, but not able to survive cold winters.
SUCCULENT
A plant with fleshy leaves and/or stems acting as reservoirs against drought and evaporation.
SUCKER
A shoot which appears from an underground root.
TEMPERATE
A mild coastal climate.
TENDRIL
The threadlike curling end of a leaf or stem which enables many climbing plants to take hold.
TERRESTRIAL
Plants which grow on the earth's surface such as orchids and bromolieds in contrast to tree-dwelling or ephiplytic varieties.
THRIP
A sap-sucking insect, colonies of which rapidly disfigure leaves.
TIP CUTTING
A cutting of new growth used for the propagation of carnation and perennial daisy plants particularly.
TROPICAL
A plant native to the warm climates between the tropics of Capricorn and Cancer, needing a wet summer and a dry warm winter.
TUBER
A thickened underground stem for storage of food.
TWINER
A plant which climbs by winding around itself or other plants.
UMBEL
A group of flowers growing from a common point on a stem.
VARIEGATED
A condition of many plants where the natural green of leaves is broken by other colours. Usually the result of a virus infection.
VARIETAL NAME
A plant's third scientific name.
VARIETY
A recognizably different member of a plant species capable of propagation.
WINDBREAK
A specialised planting (generally of trees or shrubs) to protect smaller and more delicate plants.
XEROPHYTE
A plant adapted to growing in dry regions.
ZINEB
A popular fungicide powder for treating fungus infections.